A. J. A

A. J. A.
Symons

HIS LIFE AND SPECULATIONS

JULIAN SYMONS

Oxford   New York
OXFORD UNIVERSITY PRESS
1986

Oxford University Press, Walton Street, Oxford OX2 6DP

Oxford New York Toronto
Delhi Bombay Calcutta Madras Karachi
Kuala Lumpur Singapore Hong Kong Tokyo
Nairobi Dar es Salaam Cape Town
Melbourne Auckland

and associated companies in
Beirut Berlin Ibadan Nicosia

Oxford is a trade mark of Oxford University Press

First published 1950 by Eyre & Spottiswoode Ltd.
First issued, with Julian Symons's Afterword, as an
Oxford University Press paperback 1986

British Library Cataloguing in Publication Data

Symons, Julian
A. J. A. Symons: his life and speculations.
1. Symons, A. J. A.—Biography 2. Authors,
English—20th century—Biography
I. Title
828'.91209   PR6037.Y43Z
ISBN 0–19–281916–X

Library of Congress Cataloging in Publication Data

Symons, Julian, 1912–
A. J. A. Symons, his life and speculations.

1. Symons, A. J. A. (Alphonse James Albert),
1900–1941. 2. Bibliographers—Great Britain—
Biography. I. Title.
Z1004.S9S9 1986   010'.92'4 [B]   85–29658
ISBN 0–19–281916–X (pbk.)

Printed in Great Britain by
Richard Clay (The Chaucer Press) Ltd.
Bungay, Suffolk

ACKNOWLEDGEMENTS

Besides my general debt to many friends and acquaintances of my brother, who have provided helpful suggestions, corrections and criticism, I owe the following specific acknowledgements of gratitude for assistance in shaping this book:

To the executors of the late James Agate for permission to print notes written by him to my brother; to Mr. Ian Black for the use of his interesting, but as yet unpublished, reminiscences; to Mr. Sidney Davis for his recollections of twenty-five years ago; to Captain Harold Fisher, M.C., for permission to print notes from his diary, and letters written by him to my brother; to Mr. Desmond Flower for the loan of letters; to Miss Christina Foyle, Mr. Gilbert Foyle and Mr. William Foyle for the light they cast upon my brother's association with them; to Dr. Philip Gosse, for letters and recollections; to Messrs. Harrap & Sons for their permission to use material from James Agate's *Ego* 4; to Mr. H. V. Marrot for some instructive conversation; to Mrs. Doris Langley Moore for the loan of letters; to Mrs. F. G. Nutt for her generous assistance, given to an enterprise which she did not fully approve; to M. André Simon for a memorable meal, and a peep into the early history of the Wine and Food Society; to Mr. Oliver Simon for an evening of reminiscence; to the late Percy Smith for his amiable answers to my persistent enquiries; to the late Edward Wadsworth for the loan of letters; and to the executors of the late Dr. G. C. Williamson for their permission to print extracts from letters written by him to my brother.

I have also made use, in various places, of the recollections of my brother written by Mr. Desmond Flower, Mr. Vyvyan Holland, Sir Shane Leslie, Mrs. Doris Langley Moore, Mr. Percy Muir and M. André Simon.

I must thank my mother, my sister and my brothers, for their help in filling many of the gaps in my own knowledge of my brother's life; and finally my wife, whose suggestions and encouragement have helped me to write this book.

JULIAN SYMONS.

CONTENTS

LIST OF ILLUSTRATIONS

"There is a free one" many say, but err.
He is not that returning conqueror,
Nor ever the poles' circumnavigator.

But poised between shocking falls on razor-edge
Has taught himself this balancing subterfuge
Of the accosting profile, the erect carriage.

The song, the varied action of the blood
Would drown the warning from the iron wood
Would cancel the inertia of the buried:

Travelling by daylight on from house to house
The longest way to the intrinsic peace,
With love's fidelity and with love's weakness.

W. H. AUDEN.

To say nothing but good of the dead is a pious convention which has reduced biography to the level of memorial
sculpture. I had no wish to add to the number of literary
tombstones reciting in favourable phrases the virtues of
their subjects.

A. J. A. SYMONS.

CHAPTER I

A ROOM IN PALL MALL

———————————

ONE day in the last month of 1922 a young man named Vyvyan Holland was walking along Pall Mall. It was his habit to walk along the street staring firmly at the ground; but when about to turn from Pall Mall East into Lower Regent Street, he departed from this custom so far as to look up at the first floor windows on the opposite side of the road. He saw there, written upon a large signboard, and also painted across two windows, the words THE FIRST EDITION CLUB.

The sign made an appeal to one who collected first editions, and had long regretted that no authoritative body existed, which would elucidate their subtleties for the neophyte. Holland crossed the street, entered the building, and walked upstairs. A door was opened; and framed within it he saw, not the elderly, untidy and possibly bearded figure of his expectation, but a very tall, thin young man, wearing a lavender-coloured suit of an advanced cut.

Rather dubiously, the visitor entered a room lined with books; a large paper-littered desk bulked prominently in the central space. What were the objects of the Club? Holland enquired, and the tall young man became enthusiastic. The First Edition Club, he said, was an experiment, or an adventure; nothing like it had ever existed in England. And yet it was plain that both the amateur and the more specialized book-collector had great need of a central organization which would promote bibliographical interests of all kinds; which would hold exhibitions of books and manuscripts for the pleasure of the enlightened, and the instruction of the ignorant; would encourage the general standard of book production by the beauty of its own publications; would establish a bibliographical library, and arrange lectures and discussions; would, not least, give advice on the market prices of books, and arrange for the representation of members at auction sales. . . .

All this, or something very like it, the lean young man told his slightly bewildered visitor, talking in a rich, deep voice, with brown eyes flashing brightly behind thick horn-rimmed spectacles. His own name, he said, was Symons—A. J. A. Symons, and he was both Secretary and Director of the Club. Perhaps the visitor still hesitated; for the Secretary produced, like a trump card, a pearl-grey book which he invited Holland to examine. He explained that this pearl-grey book, with its pleasant inset label which read *Bibliographical Catalogue of the First Loan Exhibition* 1922 *First Edition Club London*, was the first of the many books to be published by the Club. The edition was limited to 500 copies, and the book would undoubtedly become rare. The price was two guineas, which was very little (perhaps the visitor regarded the slimness of the book, and its paper boards, doubtfully) for a book certain to become valuable in a short time; to members of the Club, however, the price was *one* guinea. The subscription to the First Edition Club—the young man continued relentlessly—was also two guineas, but to purchasers of the book this also was reduced to *one* guinea. The visitor was conquered. "A quarter of an hour later", Holland wrote, in an account of the interview which he set down nearly twenty years later, "I had become a member of the First Edition Club and went away firmly clutching a copy of the *Bibliographical Catalogue*, and nursing a feeling of having in some way got the better of the First Edition Club."

Holland's acquaintance with the enthusiastic young man who sat at the big paper-littered desk ripened slowly; but, like others who climbed that flight of stairs, he retained a firm impression of a strong and surprising personality— a personality surprising, particularly, in an atmosphere breathed most easily by those who have found a refuge from the dangerous highways of life in the remoter culs-de-sac of literature. The First Edition Club, at the time of Holland's visit, had been in existence for a few months, and those who had, in that time, become interested in the Club and its Secretary (or, as was not unusual, in the Club through the personality of its Secretary) were aware that there was something unusual about both.

It was clear, from the fact that the Club was housed in one room, that its resources were modest; less clear was the exact position of the Secretary. He was frequently the only person in the Club, and he gave the impression, without making any positive statement, that he was its originator and sole functionary; but upon occasion he would introduce to visitors a thin and nervous man named Max Judge, and would refer to Judge as the Club's proprietor. Max Judge, although still a young man, was obviously some years older than his companion; and he displayed, together with an ardent bibliophilic enthusiasm, a shy brusqueness which contrasted oddly with the Secretary's self-assurance. Those who pressed for further information, and asked how the Club proposed to implement the ideas expressed in its book of rules and objects, might be told frankly that the Club rested at present on uncommonly slender pedestals. Its basis was the Secretary's own conviction that there must surely be sufficient book collectors in England to support a Club which professed such worthy aims; and Mr. Judge, who shared the Secretary's views, although he expressed them less eloquently, was temporarily the Club's financier. If the enquirer was a person of some position, or literary consequence (like J. A. Waley Cohen, authority on Thackeray, or Sir William Garth, K.C., well-known book collector), he would be invited to serve on the Club's Advisory Committee. It was through the generous help of certain members of this Committee that after six gestatory months, during which the Club was able to offer its members (who numbered less than fifty) little more than convenient items of information about current book sales, the first exhibition was held and the *Bibliographical Catalogue*, which had been so proudly shown to Holland, published. The exhibition showed examples of work by a varied and curious collection of artists and writers: J. D. Beresford and G. K. Chesterton, Norman Douglas and H. G. Wells, Percy Smith and Hugh Thomson, among others. The exhibits were, in fact, simply the items that members of the Club were able to lend; and, since the Club's one room in Pall Mall was obviously incapable of housing an exhibition, the books were shown in a house at Sussex Square, Bayswater, "kindly lent by Mrs. Leonard Cohen". Press representatives were invited to see the exhibition, but few came, and fewer noticed it. The printing of the Catalogue was given to a young man returned to England from the Far East, who had been an early visitor to the room in Pall Mall: Oliver Simon, who had then quite recently begun his career with the Curwen Press.

Those members of the Club who came into frequent

contact with the Secretary became increasingly aware that his was a mysterious, as well as a remarkable, personality. He revealed an interest in literature which was much greater, and of a different and more creative kind, than is common among book collectors; he could, and at small provocation would, recite long poems by Edgar Allan Poe; he professed a great admiration for Poe, for Algernon Blackwood, for the artists, poets and prose-writers of the Nineties, and in general for all artists who dealt romantically with macabre themes. Not less surprising than the depths of the young man's knowledge was the extensive area of his literary ignorance. It was said of George Moore that he had never read a book, but gathered his artistic opinions, and patched out his aesthetic creed, with gossip gleaned from Parisian cafés: the statement had, to be sure, an element of exaggeration, but it conveyed a useful half-truth about the scrappy nature of Moore's knowledge. This young man, like George Moore, gathered what was useful from the conversation of others with greater learning, but less percipience, than himself; but he was plainly not a scholar, although his eager advocacy of certain chosen writers, and deep knowledge of their works, gave at times an impression of scholarship. His professions of faith were made with an ardent ingenuousness that delighted even those of his hearers who did not share his view of the merits of Poe, Blackwood and Aubrey Beardsley: for most of the members of the First Edition Club were much older than the Secretary— who admitted that when the Club was founded he was in his twenty-first year—and few things give more delight to the middle-aged man who possesses artistic sensibility but lacks power to express it, than creative enthusiasm in the young. Moreover, the voice in which his often heretical opinions were expressed was a fine one, rich and yet clear, deep without harshness; and his physical appearance was pleasing, once an initial, sometimes disagreeable, impression of foppishness had been overcome. He was nearly three inches over six feet in height, and of a strikingly erect carriage; his hair grew thick and black above a low forehead, his nose was large, straight and impressive, the lips thin, the chin determined. It was a strong face, but an agreeable one; and when he laughed, as he did frequently, the solid lines broke up into a nutcracker effect that was almost boyish.

The interests of this curious bibliophile, as he soon revealed, were not confined within the world of books. He might remark casually that in spite of his youth he had been a partner for some time in a firm of auctioneers; he might admit to a knowledge of furs and antique furniture which exceeded that of an amateur, while it was less than that of an expert; he might elaborate with eloquent words and excited gestures upon the fascination exerted on logical minds by games of chance, and the way in which probabilities might be estimated to make success virtually certain. There was no sport, he might suggest, in which these probabilities could be more nicely weighed than in horse racing. It was an illusion of the ignorant that one who backed horses was sure, in the long run, to lose money; it would be truer to say that—as had been shown by the successful careers of many professional backers— anyone who backed horses with due regard for the ineluctable laws of chance, was certain to *make* money. There were many systems of play which were foolproof, if they were adhered to unflinchingly; and ruined gamblers should blame, not luck, but their own errant human nature. He might, in a burst of confidence, add that he had himself, not long ago, held an interest in a racing stable; but he would be even more reluctant to give details of the

exact nature of this interest than he was to tell those who
became friendly with him any one of his three Christian
names. The first of them, he admitted to a few friends, was
Alphonse: but he would accompany this admission with a
request that his interlocutor, if desirous of expressing
a degree of friendship, would use the first two of his
three initials and call him simply A.J.

The young man spent his days in the room at Pall Mall;
at night he went home to sleep in a solid mid-Victorian
house at Clapham. The house was named Mount Lebanon,
and not infrequently the young man was the sole occupant
of its twenty rooms.

CHAPTER II

MOUNT LEBANON

W HEN I was six years old my family moved from Number Eighty-two to the Big House. Number Eighty-two was 82, Lavender Hill, Battersea; the Big House was a box-like double-fronted house of grey brick in Cedars Road, Clapham. The houses were less than half a mile apart, but there was a wide social distance between them. Number Eighty-two had only a tiny back garden, and the front door opened on to the bustling main road of Lavender Hill; street stalls were a minute's walk away. The garden of the Big House was a hundred yards long, and a semi-circular gravel drive led up to the front door. My father named the house "Mount Lebanon", a little too appropriately, because of its association with cedar trees. The twenty rooms in "Mount Lebanon" included a billiard room with a full size billiard-table; but it was not, my eldest brother Alphonse would say regretfully, a mansion, for it had only one staircase.

One of these twenty large rooms was set aside as a playground, and there, a shy, ugly child with a heavy head and thin legs, "imprisoned in the tower of a stammer", I played intricate and elaborate games with toy soldiers and bricks and railway engines. At that time I was anxious to be a tramcar conductor; but my wishes changed from month to month, and were conditioned largely by the gifts that came to me from the auction rooms in Moorgate which

8

my father owned. Two gifts that pleased me particularly were the tram conductor's outfit and a Red Indian suiting, which had as accessories a number of headdresses varied in style and colour, and two or three fine fur-covered shields. I was lonely in my games, for the life of my three elder brothers, my sister and myself, moved within a narrow family circle, and my father and mother positively discouraged us from asking our friends to visit our, as we regarded it, palatial home.

My loneliness looks pitiable in retrospect, but was not without its compensations at the time; chief among them was the power of arbitrary decision in all the games I played. This power was exercised particularly in the military campaigns undertaken with some 300 lead soldiers and several imitation 75 mm. guns which came to me from that treasure-house of delights, the Moorgate Auction Rooms. These campaigns would be accompanied by a continual quiet muttering: "Rupert", I would murmur, "now attempts to turn the flank of the Ironsides, but Cromwell foresees his move and brings up reserves". I did not much welcome the interruption of my games that came with the entrance of Alphonse, who was born twelve years before me, and my other brothers Stanley and Maurice, who were respectively one and three years younger than Alphonse. They would ask on what principle my battles were conducted and decided, a question to which I could give no satisfactory reply; they would then briskly organize the game on a logical basis, and in the scientific military encounter that followed I played an insignificant part. One year my brothers gave me as a birthday present a model of a three-inch howitzer gun, which fired a steel shell that created great havoc among toy soldiers and wooden fortifications. The howitzer was an ingenious toy, but it was so much more

9

powerful than my 75 mm. guns, and so much more complicated, that I was a little frightened of it, and never took it out of its box when I played by myself.

It was not only my battles with toy soldiers that were disturbed by my brothers' incursion. They also organized for me the tangle of railway lines, engines, carriages, stations and buffers of which I was the nominal owner. They made an intricate order out of my genial chaos, constructed great inclines up which trains pulled, or failed to pull, with maximum effort, their load of trucks, and arranged hair-breadth escapes for engines crossing the same points from different directions, instead of the tumultuous catastrophes that I favoured. A network of railway lines, level crossings, tunnels and stations covered the whole playroom, in the middle of which Alphonse, tall, thin and excitable, presided. In the strange sheltered lives that we led at this time, he ruled over all such joint brotherly games.

It is true that he had no taste for any kind of sport which involved co-operative effort, so that he regarded without approval Maurice's interest in football and cricket; but within the boundaries of "Mount Lebanon" he was the mentor of his sister and younger brothers. Some would have called his amusements childish, for in his late teens he did not despise the sailing of model yachts and the flying of model aeroplanes on Clapham Common; and, as I have already suggested, he was prepared to participate in my battles with toy soldiers, which he wished to conduct on the lines of H. G. Wells's *Little Wars*. But his real delight was in other, more serious and complicated games —card games, word games and spelling games—of his own invention, which I sometimes played but at this time did not fully understand. I do not know that I can at all adequately convey the character or the charm of those weekday evenings and quiet Sunday afternoons spent in the cloistered air of "Mount Lebanon". Part of the charm was in the seriousness with which we played, part in the family feeling that linked us. In a room nearby my father and mother would, in an appropriate Victorian way, be taking a nap after a solid near-Victorian meal of soup, turkey and ham and roast potatoes (the turkey drawn and cooked by my father's own hands), and a good boiled pudding. In such surroundings Alphonse presided, with an air of faint impatience, over a family circle that contained my two other brothers, my sister Edith, and myself. It was within this narrow family circle that the best of our games were tried out and perfected.

We must have played some dozens of games within the four walls of "Mount Lebanon"—games of all sorts, home made and commercial, complex and simple, intellectual paper games and riotous balloon fights, a very good card game called "The Last Card Trick", which I have never seen played outside our family and the object of which is simply *not* to take the last trick, and a most formidable game called "Stock Exchange" which deserves a word to itself, because it indicates the fascination that gambling, and the processes by which money changes hands, always held for my brother. "Stock Exchange" was a game for three, four or five players, who were supposed to be stock dealers. Six, eight or ten slips of paper (the number varying with the number of players) were then given the names of such companies as Daimler, Courtaulds, G.E.C., Chrysler, whose stocks were supposed to stand at par at the start of the game. Cards were dealt out face downwards, a red card representing an increase in share value from one to ten points, a black card a corresponding decrease. Each player looked at two of the cards, remaining ignorant of the rest, and players took it in turn to quote prices at which they would buy and sell. More cards were

A. J. A. Symons

dealt out and as the game developed, with each player having a partial knowledge of the stocks' situation, rapid fluctuations of price occurred. At last, after six or eight cards had been dealt round, settling day came, and those dealers who had sold stock at 95 which closed at 120 suffered enormous fictitious losses. This game, both in the amount of paper work necessary and in the concentrated attention it required, was perhaps the most difficult we played. Our greatest creation, however, and the one that gave us most pleasure, was the Race Game.

The Race Game needs no more apparatus than a piece of cartridge-paper or cardboard, some metal racehorses, and a pack of cards. The cartridge-paper is marked so that a race may contain up to 120 moves; the cards are turned up and horses moved along accordingly, an ace counting one, court cards ten and other cards face value. The first horse past the post is the winner. It is as simple as that: but from that keystone we constructed a most elaborate structure.

Each of us had a certain number of owners, trainers, jockeys and horses, and each owner started with a certain amount of "money". It was a rule that all owners, trainers, jockeys and horses must be named after existing Turf celebrities, although this rule was infringed by Alphonse, one of whose prominent owners (he frequently, in the game, rode his own horses) was Mr. Alphonse James Albert Symons. When a horse won a race it received ten start in the next race; if it won three races in succession it received thirty start, and if in addition there was a jockey on it who had already ridden five winners the start would be thirty-five. A placed horse received a start of five for each place, and only the last three races counted in a horse's record, so that a horse with the record 111220 would start on ten. A horse that had run six races was said to be six years old, and all horses went to stud at the age of ten. A great deal of betting went on before races, each player acting both as backer and as bookmaker, and making bets on behalf of his owners; it happened not infrequently that an owner went broke and that the stable was sold up, a proceeding that caused some excitement—a three year old with the record 111 was a valuable animal. Programmes were arranged in advance, and reports of races were written by Alphonse after each meeting (see page 14). These reports contained very often libellous and insulting remarks about other owners and jockeys. At the end of the season a list of leading owners, trainers and jockeys was published: apart from this list the game had no winner, no losers and no end. Like all of our games it was played not for money, but for love.

Akin, at least in my mind, to these games, were Alphonse's poetry recitations in the ground floor front room. The blinds would be pulled down if it were daylight, or if it were evening the lights turned out, and he would recite one of the many longish poems that he knew by heart. He recited "The Raven", "The Bells" and "The Sphinx", and I can remember clearly the dark room, with furniture and faces faintly visible and the tall figure with his back to the fire speaking with dramatic emphasis as he reached the poem's climax:

> Keeping time, time, time,
>   As he knells, knells, knells
> In a happy Runic rhyme,
>   To the rolling of the bells—
> Of the bells, bells, bells—
>   To the tolling of the bells,
> Of the bells, bells, bells, bells—
>   Bells, bells, bells—
> To the moaning and the groaning of the bells.

13

A. J. A. Symons

In reading "The Bells", he told us, it was most important that emphasis should be placed upon the fifth "bells"; and he demonstrated, "Of the bells, bells, bells, bells, *bells*, bells, bells", to his and our complete satisfaction. Alphonse communicated to all of us his literary discoveries; they were accepted on trust as being authentic and (by me at least) irrefutable. He had at that time a violent and uncontrolled, though generous, temper, and I viewed him with a mixture of awe and admiration which was increased by his employment of a technique of ambiguity through which he would place a cloud of mystery round the simplest event. My mother and my brothers already told stories of him which seemed apocryphal, even if they were true: of how he often came home from school with bootlaces undone and a bloody nose after fighting for no discoverable reason; how once at Number Eighty-two he had gathered the family round a curious steam engine with a dial reading up to a hundred, and warned them very seriously that when the dial reached ninety they should drop to the floor or go outside the room—and how the dial in fact had reached the number four; how my mother had given him five shillings a week to buy translations of Theophile Gautier; how, when he went into the army at the age of eighteen, he had been put in temporary charge of a sickbay, and had read stories to the occupants while they polished his buttons. He was already, in a small way, a legend.

These were the days of family prosperity. My father was a short, fair, thoughtless, generous and irascible man with a vandyke beard. He was a remarkable character, and had himself some legendary characteristics. We knew little of his early life, but were led to infer that in his youth he had studied at Heidelberg University. Perhaps it was

KING SOL FAILS.

VICTORY FOR VERCIOROVA AGAIN.

VELVET GLOVE BEATEN.

No. 63. PRINCES PLATE OF £900. 5 fur. A.A.

'122	VERCIOROVA	SIR E. HULTON	(M)	ARCHIBALD	1
302	SWINDLE	MR. KENNEDY	(Q)	CARSLAKE	2
101	VELVET GLOVE	MR. DIXON	(A)	DONOGHUE	3
011	King Sol	Mr. Walsh		T.Morgan	0
030	Knight of Manister	Mr. Ingram		P.Jones	0
300	Valerian	Col. Oddie		Piggott	0
000	Yokel	Mr. Howard		Elliott	0

2 lengths: same. Winner trained TAYLOR..MANTON.

7/4 Velvet Glove. 2/1 VERCIOROVA.9/4 King Sol.
7/1 Swindle. 10/1 Knight of Manister, Yokel.
100/7 others.

Velvet Glove was not gambled on by the followers
of Donoghue or of Lines, and was only nominally
favourite. Indeed, there was no great betting,
Swindle receiving as much attention as any.
The kidding tactics of Archibald were responsible
for the result. Verciorova was almost left at the
post, and after Velvet Glove and King Sol shot to
the front, was nowhere noticeable. Towards the
finish all the leaders weakened, and Archibald
came bowling up, to win quite easily. King Sol
rolled badly, and was not able to keep up the
pace, finishing about fifth. Swindle ran very
well in Carslakes' strong hands, at one time
seeming a winner.
The easy defeat of King Sol says little for
Golden Corn and Swansea China, who were miles
behind him recently, but Verciorova paid a
compliment to Pondoland, who beat him easily
recently. Early in the season Verciorova won
from Symons and other useful animals.

there that he acquired the habit of quoting from the Old Testament and Plato in moments of stress, but he found elsewhere his considerable ability as a cook, and the flair for the purchase of clothing and furniture that mended our family's penurious fortunes and earned him a small fortune quickly during the 1914-18 war, when he purchased the Moorgate Auction Rooms, and conducted auction sales with a great deal of verve and enjoyment. He found elsewhere also the heady optimism that prompted him in these days not merely to purchase "Mount Lebanon", which might be called a good solid investment, not merely to fill the thirty-six foot long drawing-room with Buhl furniture, which might be regarded as a personal foible, but also to buy four race-horses. My father always loved to gamble and to attend race meetings, and I think the purchase of these four horses, which were named a little oddly Buenasuerte, En Avanti Savoia, Hay Vee and Pavlos, was the crowning event of his life. It was certainly the turning-point of his fortunes; for his knowledge of horses was not equal to his knowledge of furniture, and Buenasuerte and the others ate up a large part of his small fortune in the two years during which my mother's name appeared as a racehorse owner in *Ruff's Guide*. We children had little part in the dazzling delights of horse racing that gave so much pleasure to my father: but it is obvious that the magic names of our horses had something to do with the fervour with which we (I do not include myself—but I watched with a fervour almost equal to that of the players) played the Race Game at this time. There were those magnificent animals cantering daily over the Wiltshire downs, and occasionally running in races; and here were we, immured within a London suburb. The Race Game was a very obvious escape mechanism by which we also could become

at once owners, trainers, jockeys, backers and book-
makers, and participate vicariously in the activities of that
romantic world.

In the early days of 1919, my father had little thought
of possible setbacks to prosperity. He entertained on
Sunday mornings our local doctor, an amiable man and
fluent talker, who shared my father's love of gambling
and intended, besides, to stand for Parliament as a Liberal
at the next election; sometimes other acquaintances of
my father would call, men who had in mind simple but
foolproof schemes for making a lot of money quickly,
and needed only my father's financial approval. Champagne was drunk among the Buhl furniture in the drawing-
room (which was never used except on Sundays), stories
exchanged of large sums of money won and lost, but
mostly won, at race meetings: and Alphonse was thought
to be of an age to share in the champagne, and listen
to the conversation. Among my father's other Victorian
ideas was the firmly-held belief that the family is the
natural basis of a community: and in pursuit of this idea
he intended that the management of the Moorgate
Auction Rooms should pass eventually from his shoulders
to those of Alphonse. A great deal of Alphonse's time,
therefore, was spent at the Auction Rooms, among roll-
top desks, books, clothing, and antique furniture. His was
the moving hand in one of my father's most notable
transactions of this time, the purchase from Canada of a
large number of secondhand typewriters, which were sold
at an enormous profit; and indeed, in Alphonse's telling
of the story, my father's part diminished and even disappeared, the whole affair becoming, in a retrospect not
altogether accurate, a tribute to Alphonse's financial
genius. On another occasion my father, who had a desire

to own a hotel almost equal to his desire to own race-horses (and both of these desires were gratified), sent Alphonse to look at and report on a hotel in France. My brother did not know French: but that did not prevent him from buying the hotel, and paying a deposit on it. The deposit was irrevocably lost, and the incident buried, although it was not forgotten.

On Sunday afternoons we often walked among the faded splendours of that part of London which is misnamed Clapham Park. Alphonse had a malacca cane, of which he was very proud (he had, also, two monocles at this time, but I do not know that he ever wore either of them out of doors): and, swinging this cane gaily, he would conduct his three younger brothers down the wide sweeps of King's Avenue and Clarence Road, pausing occasionally to regard the massive, decaying Victorian houses with an almost proprietorial affection, and instructing our ignorance with regard to particular points of architectural detail. In these walks I followed my brothers rather like a small dog, stopping when they stopped, looking at the houses they looked at, and being rewarded finally with a Milk Tray chocolate from a bag bought by one or other of them on the walk.

Such was the pattern of our lives for two years after the war. Alphonse was adaptable and intelligent, and in spite of his youth he assumed a considerable authority at the Moorgate Auction Rooms: but sometimes this assumption of authority was sharply checked. He bought, in my father's name, and brought home, a fine edition of the works of Oscar Wilde: but my father, scandalized by the introduction into the family home of the writings of this perverse and immoral figure, refused positively to pay for the books. They had to be returned to the vendor personally by his son; the occasion, and the humiliation, were not without subsequent effect.

In 1921 our brief prosperity ended, never to return. The racehorses had been disastrously costly, and had been accompanied by rash and unprofitable speculations at the Auction Rooms: and our manner of living was suddenly and drastically altered. The racehorses, the Buhl furniture, the billiard table and the Moorgate Auction Rooms were sold, and my father turned from auctioneering to the keeping of a hotel at Brighton where he superintended the cooking personally, from the hotel to a bookmaking business, and from that back to the management of an auction room. But he had lost the touch that made his fortune, and none of these ventures met with the success that his optimism forecast for them. He remained volatile, excitable, generous and optimistic until his death in 1929; he leaves with me the memory of a great family man, with a Victorian severity in sexual matters, and an intense love of gambling. He had nothing more tangible than this love of gambling to bequeath to his sons, but to his widow he left "Mount Lebanon", which had been kept throughout the setbacks of his last years. "Mount Lebanon" no longer housed Buhl furniture and two maids, but it was a good substantial Victorian house.

Such was the declining curve of my father's fortune in his last decade. But at the time of which I wrote in my first chapter he had just started, with all the gaiety and confidence in the world, upon his ownership of the small private hotel on the front at Brighton which would, he thought, repair his ravaged fortunes. Edith and I accompanied our parents, Stanley journeyed up and down between London and Brighton every day; only Maurice and Alphonse stayed in London. My father was now quite unable to provide Alphonse with financial backing; and even if he had been able to do so, I doubt if he would have thought such backing prudent, in his son's own interest. It was fortunate for Alphonse, therefore, that just before our family emigrated to Brighton, he received an offer of employment from Max Judge, a man he had met through the Moorgate Auction Rooms. The offer carried with it the salary of £4 a week; and this was the sole financial support of the Secretary and Director of the First Edition Club at the time when he received visitors at the room in Pall Mall by day, and returned to sleep, at weekends, alone in what had been, very recently, our family residence

CHAPTER III

BACKGROUND OF A YOUNG MAN

F EW things are more fascinating to the biographer than the way in which certain figures in his story obstinately refuse to assume the features of life. People knew of them, met them, talked with them; and yet their names raise hardly a ripple in the pool of memory. My brother's first benefactor, Max Judge, has remained, for me, one of these indeterminate figures. I have talked with many people who were friendly with my brother in his youth, and have a vivid remembrance of him: but the name of his partner, echoing down a quarter of a century of insecurity and war, evokes only the vaguest recollections. He was a background figure, dimly recalled as somewhat stiff in conversation, with a manner slightly unprepossessing, and lacking altogether my brother's rich enthusiasm. It is certainly known, however, that he was the son of the well-known architect Sir Mark Judge, and that at the time my brother met him Max Judge desultorily pursued his father's occupation in an office employing one draughtsman.

He was, it would seem, a man (and there are many such) who, while incapable of originating enthusiasm himself, was easily fired by the enthusiasm of others; and he was impressed at once by my brother's verbal demonstration of the profits to be made by selling books and antique furniture. The young auctioneer (as he sometimes represented himself to be, with a minor infraction of truth) thought that he had gained much valuable knowledge at the Moorgate Auction Rooms, and that the connections he had established with booksellers could be turned to good account. All that was needed, he believed, to make that knowledge monetarily fruitful was a little capital. Judge was able to provide the capital: and the two friends (for their relation was certainly that of friends rather than that of employer and wage-earner) entered business as booksellers and dealers in antique furniture. One room in Judge's offices was painted with red walls and a black ceiling; books ranged the walls; and the venture was launched under the name of "The Collector's Room".

It was not a success: and although the reasons for its failure cannot be exactly dissected, it may be surmized that my brother's knowledge and experience was not, after all, equal to that of many of the people with whom he was dealing. He was an amateur, and the path of an amateur antique-dealer is not likely to be a smooth one. The heavy losses incurred in a few months of trading were, however, retrieved, and much more than retrieved, by a curious *coup*. My brother later invested the story with an aura of romance which took it into the realm of fantasy: it was, none the less, based firmly on fact.

The premises which Judge occupied in Lower Regent Street had been taken on lease. During the war this lease, together with those of the adjoining properties, had lapsed, and it was the intention of Cox's Bank to erect a new building on the site. The Building Restrictions Act, however, made it necessary to postpone their plan of demolition, and construction of the new Bank building; and all the tenants received, and Judge among others accepted, an offer to extend their leases until the end of the war. After the 1918 armistice Judge, with the other tenants, received notice to vacate the premises; but this notice remained in his case unanswered. Demolition of the building began, but still his offices remained occupied, although the ascent to them had become an uneasy operation. A solicitor's letter was sent to the over-faithful tenant, but that too was ignored; it was succeeded by a summons to a meeting at the Bank's offices. By my brother's account he, on Judge's behalf, attended this meeting, and, when asked why he had not vacated the premises, said that he liked them and proposed, at present, to continue in occupation. When told that he would be evicted he pointed out that the lease ran until the end of the war; and the Bank's solicitor realized the legal trap into which he had fallen. The war did not end until an Act of Parliament had been passed to confirm that all hostilities had ceased, and until that time it would not be possible to evict the tenant. In the meantime the demolition of the building was being held up; and the Bank finally agreed to pay a sum in compensation. The amount fluctuated with every account of the story which my brother told in later years; it was, I believe, in the neighbourhood of £3,000.

My brother acted in this affair on behalf of Max Judge and not, directly, for his own profit; but its successful issue must, I think, have provided him with the Indian motor cycle on which he careered uncertainly up and down the roads of Clapham and the Brighton front ("Do you think this is a race-track?" a policeman asked him, and it is very likely that he did); this investment was soon exchanged for a set of the Bombay Edition of Kipling's works, and the set of Kipling's works for a more tractable motor cycle. The success of this *coup* must also have made Judge listen attentively to my brother's new suggestion that, since the sale of fine books and antiques had proved unprofitable, they should become professional backers of horses. It may seem difficult to believe that anybody could, in cold blood, be convinced by the logic of the argument which I have already outlined: but in youth blood is not cold, possibilities seem magically probable, and it hardly seems that the frequently-invoked law of averages can fail, in the end, to bring fortune to the courageous. Besides, my brother must, I am sure, have reminded Judge that they were playing with their winnings; and one of the principles from which he never swerved was, that it is foolish to let capital lie idle in a bank when it can be put to profitable use.

No record remains of their brief career as professional backers, except that my brother adhered to a faith, not altogether rational, in the likely success of the horses ridden by G. Duller, a successful jockey over hurdles (he is now a trainer) who had comparatively few mounts; the partners backed Duller's mounts regularly, and on one occasion brought off a successful double. But this win did not balance their losses, and *Ruff's Guide* proved as untrustworthy for my brother as it had been, a year or two earlier, for my father. He was unable, as so many others have been, to gauge successfully the laws of chance. The period of the partners' attendance at race meetings and of their close attention to the form of horses, the reputation of trainers, and the state of the going, was bright but brief, and also costly; and the last profits of the *coup* must have been used by the amiable Judge for providing the furnishings of the First Edition Club in its home at 17, Pall Mall East. Here my brother was to be employed fully as Club Secretary, and when, because of the decline of his business, Judge was faced with the need either to dispense with the services of his draughtsman or to sever his business relation with my brother, he decided to let the draughtsman go.

Background of a Young Man

The First Edition Club, in its inception, had another object, apart from those which my brother eloquently described to visitors; its founders intended to use it also for the purchase and sale of fine books. During the Club's first year of life they did so, and the roughly-kept cash account of the workings for this year shows that the sale of books was much the most profitable feature of the Club's transactions. The members, at the end of a year, still numbered only sixty, and there was no sign that they would ever reach three figures, for the Club was hampered by lack of money from holding exhibitions or fulfilling most of its other stated objectives. It seemed plain that the First Edition Club, although it might be an engaging toy, was not a business proposition; and Judge proposed to abandon it. He raised no demur when my brother said that he considered the Club a potential asset, and proposed to carry on its activities; probably he considered this as a characteristically grandiloquent gesture on the part of his young friend. Judge willingly made over his rights in the First Edition Club, and in an agreement made on the 4th of May, 1923, between the "Retiring Partner" (Max Judge) and the "Continuing Partner" (my brother) it was recorded that "Whereas the Club has shown no profits . . . and there are liabilities at the date of these presents owing by the Retiring Partner amounting to about £200", their partnership should be dissolved, the Retiring Partner should have no further liabilities and "The Retiring Partner hereby confirms and declares that the scheme and title of the First Edition Club originated with and belongs to the Continuing Partner".

With the signing of this agreement Max Judge faded out of my brother's life; and, fading, leaves in my mind a number of questions which full knowledge might resolve quite dully. Yet there must surely have been something remarkable in the character of a man who lent himself so readily to such odd ideas, and a strong spirit of introverted romanticism must have moved behind that stiff and unimpressive mask. Were Judge alive to-day he might make clear much that is ambiguous, both in my brother's life and in his own relation to it: but he died tragically no more than five years after the dissolving of their partnership.

My brother had now, in ordinary commercial terms, lost his job; but he was the sole owner of a Club, although he had no visible means of maintaining it—and he was not yet twenty-three years old! It must have seemed to him that he had taken a long step on the road to fortune, and to fame.

"A.J."—we may now call him by the name which, at this time, he had firmly adopted, borrowing it, as on one occasion he admitted, from the Raffles stories—"A.J.", said one of his friends reflectively after his death, "was above all someone who had his way to make in the world." He was. From an early age he longed ardently for a fame which should be both social and literary: and he resolutely endeavoured throughout his life to put aside all relationships that did not lead him to this desired end. He was not, at last, successful: he was too generous, and too amiable, and too deeply interested in many things, ever to be confined within the narrow career of a "self-made man" in its ordinary terms. It is necessary to cast back a year or two to see the extent, and something of the cause, of this determination to achieve a position of importance in the world.

English society in 1919 (when my brother was demobilized from the Artists' Rifles) offered many and varied opportunities to an ambitious young man, who was prepared to pursue one course single-mindedly. My brother's eloquence might have led him to lay the foundation of a political career; his histrionic ability might have moved him to become an actor; his urge towards literature might have been translated into journalism: and A.J. was not deterred from these occupations, I am sure, by any doubt of his ability to succeed in them. But these obviously open ways did not offer the prospect of quick social success that he wanted, and, more or less, they excluded the possibility of literary achievement. His model, or one of his models, was Disraeli, who had achieved fame as a wit, a writer, and a negligently flamboyant personality; and it was with all of these Disraelian characteristics in mind that he bought and read books on etiquette, considered his appearance in a monocle, wore a lavender-coloured suit, and spent hours in practising calligraphy, copying page after page from the *Dictionary of National Biography* until he had achieved a tiny, crabbed, but beautiful Gothic script. My father deprecated these essays in penmanship, saying that the single essential of handwriting was that it should be easily read.

Within our family enclave A.J. was an arbiter, and a creator: but he itched with the consciousness of unrealized ability, and the desire to see that ability recognized by others. He cultivated the acquaintance of the amiable doctor who was a prospective Parliamentary candidate, and one day solemnly told us that the doctor had invited him to dine at the Authors' Club; which seemed, certainly, a great step taken towards becoming an author. Their friendship was based partly, perhaps, on the Sunday morning champagne, but chiefly, I think, upon the doctor's genuine liking for this inventive, self-confident and voluble young man. Their friendship received a slight check when one day my brother accompanied the doctor

A. J. A. Symons

on his round, and was so much affected by the sight of an injury that he fainted; so that the doctor, on his next visit, was told that although his patient was better, that was "No thanks to him and his fainting friends". More important to A.J. was his meeting, when he was in his late teens, with Captain Harold Fisher, a man also recently demobilized from the army, and then in his early thirties. Fisher was a brisk, vigorous and in appearance noticeably military figure, who played rather consciously the part of Philistine to my brother's equally consciously-played aesthete; but his brusque manner and forthright air concealed an oddly romantic mind, and a wide knowledge of literature. Their friendship became firm when my brother discovered with delight that this curious military man shared his own passion for debate, and also his love of invented games.

The first tangible fruit of this new friendship was the formation of the Outspoken Debating Society, in which the moving agents were Fisher, my brother, and two young solicitors named Sidney and Percy Davis. The Outspoken Debating Society met sometimes at Fisher's house in Balham, sometimes at the Davis's near Wandsworth Common, and more rarely at "Mount Lebanon". Visitors were welcomed and the amiable doctor, my father, and my brother Stanley, attended one or two meetings. Fisher's diaries, preserved with an obviously characteristic care for order, record the subjects of discussion:

Jan. 13, 1921.   At the Davis's. Psychological value of religious ceremonial.
Feb. 18, 1921.   Symons, the Davis's and Leslie Kinworthy for the evening. Discussion: the qualities that make poetry readable.
Feb. 24, 1921.   At Davis's. Discussion on the qualities which make for immortality in literature.

Background of a Young Man

Mar. 10, 1921.   At Davis's. Discussion: Psychology of the
                 Crowd.
Mar. 21, 1921.   Symons at my place till midnight.

The procedure of the Outspoken Debating Society was
unusual. There was at first an opener and opposer, and
everyone was expected to speak. Later, however, one
member was selected at each meeting to act as Master; it
was his duty to introduce the subject, the opener and the
opposer, and finally to summarize the views expressed,
and put the motion to the vote. A.J. found that the rôle
of Master suited him particularly well. It gave him an
opportunity, which he found congenial, for weaving his
own views into the thread of a presumedly impartial
discussion, and at the Outspoken Debating Society he
enjoyed himself in sharpening the sword of empirical
argument which he later used very effectively.

Fisher was impressed by the extent of his young friend's
reading which, in poetry at least, already exceeded his
own. At Fisher's home they competed in reciting "The
Bells", and, encouraged by his companion's eager attention, Fisher told strange stories of adventures and adventurers which struck sparks off A.J.'s ready imagination;
among them was the story of Emin Pasha, which remained
for several years in my brother's mind. The final link in
their friendship was A.J.'s enthusiastic acceptance of a
game which had been nurtured a long time in Fisher's
mind, but required an inverted romanticism about warfare
equal to his own to bring it to happy birth: the War Game.

I cannot speak of the War Game with knowledge,
because I have never played it or seen it played: but there
can be no doubt that in the seriousness with which it was
regarded by its protagonists, in the number and complica-
tion of its rules, and above all in the time it took to play,
it was a game to end all games. It was played upon

a one-inch Ordnance Map, with pieces specially constructed to represent infantry, cavalry, and artillery; a session of four or five hours was likely to result only in the pushing back of one section of a line a mile or two; and as sessions were held weekly, a campaign was usually not concluded for some months. The preliminary explanations were not conducted quickly, as can be seen from Fisher's diary:

Oct. 20, 1921.	For the first time explained to Symons my general ideas for a strategic war game.
Oct. 31, 1921.	Further explanations to Symons of my new game with demonstrations on 1″ Ordnance Map of elementary rules.
Nov. 2, 1921.	Continuation of discussions and explanations of my War Game at the Davis's.
Nov. 4, 1921.	First practice game of new War Game with Symons on the Swinton-Cirencester Street.
Nov. 8, 1921.	Second practice game with Symons.
Nov. 19, 1921.	Symons and I commenced the most considerable campaign at the new War Game we have yet played, starting at 3.30 p.m. and playing until 9 p.m., with a short interval for tea.
Nov. 29, 1921.	First campaign of War Game on full scale commences. 1st Cavalry Division and 2nd Infantry Divisions on each side involved.

For a year the War Game occupied a good deal of my brother's time, and his characteristic passion for verisimilitude in games (which he was delighted to find that Fisher shared) is well expressed by the typed reports of Campaigns which accompanied the War Game, as well as the Race Game. These home-made and elaborate inventions were for him battles of wit in which rules were strictly adhered to: but it was more than a pleasure, it was almost a duty, to take advantage of any loophole in the rules. "The War Game", Fisher told me, "was constructed so as to respond to the rules of strategy and since the principles of strategy are similar to the principles of life, the few players the game had derived a great deal of benefit from it. The arrangement on which we worked in the beginning was that I devised the rules and A.J. spent his time trying to circumvent them—at which, as you can imagine, he was very good."

The influence of Fisher on my brother's youthful mind helped to discipline his frequently wild enthusiasm, and the equally wild desire for experiment that prompted him in childhood to push his finger between the gear wheels of a mangle and to climb along banister rails so that he dangled over a high stairwell, from which he had to be rescued. Fisher also instructed him in the need to order his thoughts logically, and encouraged in him, perhaps unwittingly, a Carlylean admiration of what A.J. later called "the destiny-defying power" of the strong man which "must always delight our dramatic sense". To Fisher, also, my brother revealed the doubts and anxieties that lay behind his self-confidence, feelings that were perhaps revealed to only one other person in his life: the girl he was to marry, Victoria Emily, or as she called herself Gladys, Weeks.

When A.J. met Gladys Weeks he was still in the Officers' Training Corps of the Artists' Rifles; and he must at once have been attracted by a social ease which he was conscious of lacking, and by a mind that was as romantic as his own. He saw her more and more frequently after his discharge from the army; they went for long country walks, and he confided to her his social

A. J. A. Symons

and literary hopes and aspirations. He was desolate when
he did not hear from her, and wrote in his crabbed Gothic
hand: "Perhaps I have offended you, perhaps you have
re-read my letters and no longer like them. . . . I have not
heard from you for a week, and I have sent three tele-
grams and a letter. On Tuesday I waited two hours for
you in the rain, yesterday one hour only in grey weather,
grey reflected in my mind." He recounted to her his
triumphs and occasional failures at the Debating Society,
his unsuccessful attempts to write a fable in Poe's manner
about a man "living, yet uncertain whether my existence
is that of a corporate being or that of a disembodied soul",
a man who had purchased a curious clock which instead of
telling the hours signified instead such abstractions as
Fame, Love—and Death. "As usual", he wrote to her,
"my story is eluding me. . . . This will never do; I shall
remain an auctioneer all my life."

Gladys Weeks was convinced, as the young man was
himself, of his talent: but when he proposed that they
should get married she wanted to know something of his
background. She was able to support herself very comfortably, by her skill as a dress designer: would she have to
support her husband as well? To her, as to the other people
he wished to impress, A.J. made only vague references to
himself as an auctioneer, and to his share in the conduct of a racing stable: but to her, as to others, it
was plain that he had very little money. At last he
wrote to her words that he probably did not care to
say:

All last night, and for hours this morning, I have thought
of what I should write to you. I have long felt, despite
your confidence, that you did not fully understand me:
ignorant of my past life, you could not: but I never imagined there was so great a need for explanation and reassur-

ance, that you were so far from knowing me, or I from you.

You probably do not know that Dickens' early life was spent in a blacking factory, where the disgraceful toil, the soul destroying system, left an impression on him so deep that for years afterwards he could not bear to think or talk of it, and his wife found out only by accident. I have always chosen to keep quite unrevealed and secret my own skeleton, though I have often hinted that I have one. I have. . . .

At an incredibly early age (14) I left school and left home, and a drudgery by no means as extreme as that Dickens endured, but still dreadful to memory, began. (It meant labour from 8 to 8). All I will say of it is that it lasted three years, during which time I went home only for week ends, that I learned a great deal, that I was utterly lonely. All that I know, I taught myself. At school, such as it was, I certainly surprised my masters, and those three years of apprenticeship were for me years of solitary study among people who, though they had started level with me, could not take from me the consciousness of attainments and abilities infinitely superior. (During this space I gained my knowledge of furs. This is the only hint I will give you.)

About that time, I first became imbued with the idea that I could write, and that I could build and shape my life as an architect plans a house, selecting and rejecting the material to hand. I cannot convey to you the resolve and determination with which I held the idea of joining an O.T.C. and for the first time, mixing with people who, by the chance of fortune and education, were on the plane to which I had, by my own efforts, raised myself. You know that I was successful—but more successful than you know, for though I came into contact with men and boys who were clever and learned, no one of them could dwarf my inner consciousness of myself as their equal—their superior. This was felt by others, and I was quickly a recognized force and influence. . . .

Then I met you. From that point you know: but you will never know how much *you* have taught me. Still I hold my idea of building my life as an architect plans a house; and I have taken you as a corner stone. I built it again, if you like, with your love as a foundation. I count on you now as I count on myself. . . .

The letter is remarkable as evidence showing the tough-
ness and the sensitiveness, the passion and the pride, of
this young man of twenty-one. Its revelations are not,
after all, remarkable: what is remarkable is the depth of
the humiliation he felt during his three years' apprenticeship to a firm of fur dealers. My parents were far from
realizing his grudge against the condition of life into which
he had been born, and his determination to escape from
it; they saw, and noted with some distress of mind, only
its outward manifestations in fights over imagined slights
and insults, and his return home one day in tears because
of a superior's sarcastic reflections on the apprentice's
inability to spell a long and unusual word. The scar that
these years left on my brother's character remained
sensitive almost throughout his life: and this, together with
the strange enclosure of our family life and our brief
glimpse of prosperity, was the conscious force that drove
him to concealment of the past, except where it could be
romanticized; to an interest in bibliophily which, since
it is generally a pursuit of the well-to-do, might lead to
interesting social contacts; to an individuality of dress
that was at times startling. He had, as his friend said, a way
to make in the world; or, as he said himself, he was
building and shaping his life as an architect plans a house.

CHAPTER IV

THE DILATORY BIBLIOGRAPHER

A MONG the friends made by A.J. while the First Edition Club lived through its first precarious year under the patronage of Max Judge, were the booksellers William and Gilbert Foyle. These two brothers had already achieved an extraordinary business success. They had begun in the nineties of the last century by selling textbooks which they kept in the kitchen of their Shoreditch home, and then, while still in their teens, had opened, and traded successfully from, a small shop in Peckham. A prime factor in their success was the speedy service they gave by examining each morning's orders on their arrival, and parcelling at once all volumes in stock. These volumes were taken by William Foyle, on his bicycle, to the City Office in which he worked during the day; he obtained the remaining books for orders after office hours, and sent them off on the same day. The brothers worked every evening, and at weekends; and in those halcyon days of individual enterprise their enthusiasm brought a quick reward. They moved from the suburb of Peckham into central London; they extended their business to include general literature, as well as textbooks; within a few years the business expanded enormously, until Foyle's became the largest bookshop in the world.

William and Gilbert Foyle built their business by a mixture of caution and expansiveness, combined with an unvarying industry. In the early twenties expansiveness was in the ascendant, and they were prepared for the kind of experiments that afterwards flowered in the Book Clubs and Literary Luncheons, the Art Gallery and Lending Libraries, that are now associated with their name. They had recently opened a Rare Book Department; and it was perhaps for this reason that they were peculiarly receptive to the ideas that my brother expounded to them when he came in to buy and sell first editions. He talked of the Club of which he was Director, Secretary, and moving spirit; and he cannot have failed to represent to them the advantages of prestige, and eventually of income, that would come from association with a Club so obviously destined to fill a gap in English literary life. Perhaps the brothers saw in the ambitious, eloquent, and apparently single-minded young man, a figure who reminded them, with a difference, of their own youth; perhaps they were simply ripe for literary adventure. In July 1923, two months after Judge had resigned his interest in the First Edition Club, A.J. entered a partnership agreement with William and Gilbert Foyle by which the brothers became part owners of the Club and, in effect, its financiers. Profits were to be shared, A.J. was to devote his full time to the Club's business, and was to receive the familiar sum of £4 per week. It was agreed that the Foyles' partnership in the Club should not be made public, and they were officially known simply as the Club's "Trade Agents".

The room in Pall Mall was, of course, no longer available. It was replaced for a short time by premises in Great Russell Street, but these were soon discarded in favour of the former Vestry Hall of the Church of St. George, Bloomsbury, at number 6, Little Russell Street. This rather curious home for a bibliographical Club never failed to arouse a certain not altogether justified risibility

The Dilatory Bibliographer

among the more irreverent members. The Vestry Hall
had a large and fine Exhibition Room with a beautiful
circular bay window, and another room, used as an
office, which housed some large quartos and folios (probably supplied by the Foyles) in impressive bookcases.
The rent of the Hall was remarkably low, but it had the
demerit of a certain ecclesiastical dinginess which hung
around the whole building; the visitor walked through
iron gates into a large courtyard where children played
and scribbled facetiae upon the neighbouring church
wall and there, hidden in the church's shadow, he found
the Club entrance.

Ensconced in this neglected Bloomsbury eyrie, a few
yards from the British Museum on one side and New
Oxford Street on the other, the Secretary and Director
sent out one of those manifestos in pamphlet form about
his own activities which he issued at intervals throughout
his life to a generally unheeding world. The First Edition
Club, he said:

> Exists to-day as the nucleus of an organization which will
> eventually exercise a far-reaching and beneficial influence on
> the whole art of book collecting. It will extend encourage-
> ment to the tyro, give support and authority to the great
> body of collectors, and lend authority to the expert. Its influ-
> ence, extended by lectures and addresses, will raise the art of
> book collecting from the position of a barely tolerated foible
> to that of a highly specialized artistic pursuit, recognized by
> all interested in our literature and art as worthy, not only for
> its own sake, but also as playing an important part in the
> maintenance of our literary standards, and the production of
> books worthy of a cultured community.

The manifesto's tone was admirable: but it could be
justified in practice only through a large increase of
membership, which A.J. expected to obtain through

publications and exhibitions. The Club's second publication was *A Reply to Z*, an essay written by Hazlitt in answer to an attack by an anonymous critic (in fact, Christopher North), with an Introduction by Charles Whibley; the third was a Bibliography of the works of W. B. Yeats, compiled by A.J., and the fourth *Sixty-three Unpublished Designs* by Claud Lovat Fraser. The presentation of the Yeats Bibliography was undistinguished, but *A Reply to Z* had a charming title page and pleasantly thin hand-made paper, and the Lovat Fraser book (which was introduced by Holbrook Jackson) was an amusing eccentricity printed on Ingres paper, specially dyed yellow by hand.

It is extraordinary that my brother, whose knowledge of book production must, when he started the First Edition Club, have been negligible (the Catalogue published in 1922 shows clearly the work of an inexpert hand), should have acquired in two years sufficient knowledge to supervise the production of these admirable books, and that he should have attained sufficient pure bibliographical knowledge to compile the little book on Yeats. But he was exceedingly adaptable, amazingly observant of things that interested him, capable of gathering as much knowledge in a week as others garner in a year; and he speedily turned knowledge gained from others to his own uses, refining on it and improving it as he had refined on and improved the games we played at home. He had a dazzlingly ingenious and dramatic mind, and a natural good taste; and his eloquence developed daily. These qualities served him well.

Publications and exhibitions were helpful: more helpful still to the Club was the dinner given early in 1924 in the Exhibition Room. The sixty members present included A.J., my brother Stanley, and Gladys Weeks; old friends like Mrs. Leonard Cohen and Max Judge; a sprinkling of figures well-known in the narrow world of bibliography or the wider world of publishing, like Sir Israel Gollancz and Ambrose Heal, John and Allen Lane, Bernard Newdigate and Sir Philip Sassoon, H. Gordon Selfridge and Ralph Straus. The menu of this first dinner remains, and the names of the speakers; and one guest remembers that the toast of the Club was proposed by Sir Israel Gollancz in a speech remarkable rather for length than for wit. A.J.'s reply was brief, but it was not delivered before consultation with Sir William Garth, at this time the Club's Elder Statesman. Certain phrases Garth particularly approved: "We are devotees of a leisurely hobby in a very hurried age", and "The Club has no past, only a long beginning, of which this is the culminating point". Half a dozen newspaper men were seated at one end of the table, by the bay window; and this time they reported the occasion fully. Several of the Club members, moved perhaps by the newspaper reports, felt that they had attended a historic function, and began to regard the First Edition Club, for the first time, as an institution that might possibly be permanent. American book collectors heard of the Club, and some joined it. The membership doubled itself quickly, and continued to increase; when the partnership had been in existence for twelve months, A.J. was able to tell his partners that the Club had more than 200 members. This time saw, also, an important change in his private life; early in 1924 he was married to Gladys Weeks at Marylebone Register Office. William Foyle was one of the witnesses, and my father was the other; after the ceremony Foyle said to my father, smilingly, "You have a wonderful boy".

My brother had excited a spirit of adventure in the

brothers Foyle in more ways than one. They had agreed, perhaps to their own surprise, that it would be delightful to own a yacht, and their partnership with A.J. extended from the Club to joint ownership of a small seven-ton ketch named the *Griffin*. On this recently purchased yacht, which was stationed at Maldon on the River Blackwater, my brother and his wife proposed to spend their honeymoon; and, that company might not be lacking, they invited a number of friends and relations to spend a day or two sailing with them. A.J. had no experience of handling a yacht, but he had bought a book on sailing and was confident that he would not find himself in difficulties.

Experience showed his companions on the yacht (although I doubt if it showed him) that his confidence was misplaced; indeed, by one friend's account, the yacht itself was poorly made and badly found, with old sails, clumsy fittings and amateurish paintwork, and was so difficult to handle in rough weather that when A.J. had it taken from Brightlingsea to Burnham-on-Crouch by two experienced sailors they lost the dinghy and nearly got wrecked. The honeymoon yachting was a series of misadventures for almost all the visitors: those that concerned William and Gilbert Foyle when they came down for a weekend are typical. William Foyle was, at this time, considerably run down in health, and was so nervous that he found difficulty in walking across a bridge. A weekend on the yacht, A.J. suggested, would certainly do him good.

They set out from Maldon with a favouring wind, and sailed gaily and easily down the river. The day was fine and warm, and A.J. may well have been able to carry out his conception of ideal yachting, which was to hoist the sails, tie up the sheets, lean back on cushions, smoke cigarettes, and talk. The favouring wind, however,

carried them onward to the sea and when they attempted
to return they found it impossible to do so. They decided
to hug the coast as nearly as possible and make for the
river but a combination of bad weather and ignorance
prevented them from making much headway. They were
out in the North Sea for two days in the *Griffin*, which
had no sleeping accommodation; and they had only
potato crisps to eat. At last the wind dropped and slowly
and painfully they limped to the mouth of the Blackwater
and tacked their way up it, becoming considerably
involved with other boats on their way. On the way up
the river, also, a sudden gybe caused the boom to swing
over and knock William Foyle almost senseless into the
hold; as he lay prostrate the yacht gybed again and he
heard the voice of his young friend shouting cheerfully but
a little late, "'Ware boom."

On their return from the honeymoon the couple lived in
a flat at Upper Gloucester Place, near Baker Street, where
Gladys gave full play to her decorative skill, and dedicated
herself whole-heartedly to the cause of her husband's
social and literary advancement. He was charming, but
not altogether easy to live with, now, and at a later time.
He exacted, or presupposed, a high standard of character
and culture in his wife, he expected her to possess the skill
and tact as a hostess which would assist his designs, and he
was extravagantly careless with money. To the other side
he was never less than an exceedingly entertaining companion; he was delicately thoughtful in many ways in
which most, or almost all, people are careless; and he paid
his wife the intellectual compliment of assuming that she
wished to move on his own plane of thought, and the
emotional compliment of never doubting that her ambitions marched with his own. Sometimes, in those early
days, he would come home in the evening and read to

her a story by Algernon Blackwood, or Poe, or Ambrose
Bierce; or he would tell her of the accession of new
members to the Club, and the visit of inspection paid by
Margot Asquith; or, if she reproached him with paying
her less attention than in the days before their marriage,
she would find a poem, or a small present, awaiting her as
a reminder that he was not forgetful. Often he came back
to work on an enormous book that he was compiling, a
book that was to be a landmark in bibliography, called
tentatively *A Select Bibliography and History of the Books
of the Nineties, with Notes on their Authors*. This book was
to trace, for the benefit of book collectors, the history of
the works of many forgotten figures, from Francis
Adams to Theodore Wratislaw, and of the whole movement associated with the *Yellow Book* and the *Savoy*; it was
to embody new theories and set a new standard in bibliographical research. A.J. persuaded the Foyles of the
importance of this adventure into past literary history;
they helped him with information from their vast stock
of books, and backed the project with money. Very soon
he was writing letters to publishers to enquire the number
of copies they had printed of some distantly-published and
long-remaindered book of poems; he wrote letters also
to authors, and entered into lengthy correspondence with
Laurence Housman, and into a correspondence that soon
became friendship with Lord Alfred Douglas. He went to
Ebury Street to see George Moore and discussed with him
the dates, occasions and revisions of his early works.
Moore was much flattered, like most of the other writers
my brother approached, by this move towards a lifetime
canonization; he entered with gusto into the bibliographical game, and signed a number of first editions of
his books for A.J., including a copy of his early *Pagan
Poems*, which he had disowned and tried to destroy. In

return the ageing novelist asked for help in the opening pages of a story he was writing: "I need a few lines giving the names of the books" to be shown by a great collector to some visitors. "I think he would choose, for the sake of the ladies, first editions of Shelley and Keats and writers of that period. He mentions Landor, and I wish you could supply me with a dozen names and a few accidental remarks that he might make, perhaps." This help must have been given gladly, and with a sense on the young man's part of the honour that was done him; for George Moore had joined his select literary pantheon of great writers.

This great book, then, was firmly in progress: but still the bibliographer found time to see his friends. He expected that his wife should display a degree of enthusiasm for the elaborate games that he had invented, or adapted; and here again Gladys did not fail him. There were evenings spent in sessions of the War Game played with Fisher, and one night a week was given to the Race Game. The newly-married couple also played roulette and contract bridge: the first on a table, and with a wheel, that A.J. had bought, the second in their own home and at the houses of friends. A.J. invested the undoubted skill with which he played these, and other, games of chance with a thicker than customary cloak of mystery. He worked out a number of systems at roulette, and played them, but he was never eager, as are so many players of systems, to instruct the tyro by explanation; nor was he ever a firm adherent of any standard bridge convention, preferring when possible to play with the same partner and baffle opponents by using a convention of his own. At roulette he backed several chances on each individual throw, and made hedging bets in case he was wrong on his first choices; after a series of small losses he would

increase his major bets until he was successful. Some of
his friends said, although not to his face, that he played
games too keenly, and with the sole purpose of winning
money, and he lent colour to this by boasting on occasion
that he made an income out of bridge; but in this (as was
frequently the case) he did himself less than justice, for he
commonly showed as great an absorption in a game of
roulette played with his family, when no more was at
stake than the temporary exchange of the pretty mother-
of-pearl counters that he collected, as when he was playing
for stakes that were beyond his modest means. Games
that contained the elements of chance and skill in proportions not too unequally balanced exercised extraordinary fascination over him, and indeed the mere
sequence and logic of numbers interested and mentally
intoxicated him. He did not despise such a game as Beat
Your Neighbour, with its speedy fluctuations of fortune,
its deadly knaves and apparently innocuous aces; and I
have known him to become absorbed in the sequence of
winning cuts to be obtained from a pack of cards.

So, happily, passed the early days of marriage: but as
the days turned into months Gladys became aware that
her husband was not progressing beyond a certain point,
literary or social; nor was his income increasing. The
Club's membership stayed at a little over 200, in spite
of the appearance of one or two more publications, of
which *Ten Tales* by Ambrose Bierce, with an Introduction by A.J. may be noted; and A.J. showed no sign of
attempting any creative literary work. They moved in
a different, and more expensive, social circle, but A.J.
dazzled his new friends, as he had his old, by his skill in
argument, his amazing memory, and his dramatic
imagination. One friend was astonished by his ability to
read a piece of prose once, and then repeat it almost

verbatim, another retained the memory of a lunch at which, from the moment of his arrival, A.J. began to tell a dramatic tale which he had recently read of a plot against the life of James I, and maintained it for an hour and a half with unquenched vivacity in phrases that, had a secretary been there to record them, might with little alteration have been given the dignity of print. Such triumphs alternated with occasions when his sense of social insecurity gained the upper hand, and he would consider himself insulted because his host had served an inferior, or at least a different, wine from one that had been promised; but even triumphs are not an adequate substitute for a balance at the bank. An advance obtained on the Nineties Bibliography was quickly swallowed up, and Gladys urged her husband to give himself more to creative writing; but this he was unwilling, or unable, to do.

His attendance at the Debating Society where he had first sharpened his claws was less and less frequent; but his friendship with Harold Fisher remained. It was a relation in some respects equivocal on his side, for Fisher must have seemed at times a little uncomfortably like a ghost from the past, a brisk ghost who knew too many secrets. Fisher had introduced him to the works of many writers, had punctured many enthusiasms with kindly ridicule; and from others A.J. was prepared to accept neither ridicule nor hints that they had anything to teach him. Yet Fisher was an influence not lightly nor easily discarded; in his presence A.J. felt uncomfortably youthful again. "Hardly ever, when we meet, do I say the things that my mind most wishes to utter. The consciousness that you have watched my mind waking from juvenility to (shall we say?) its present immaturity, and that to you I am what I was yesterday, while to myself I am what I shall be to-morrow, these are inhibiting conditions",

A. J. A. Symons

he wrote. When other friends criticized the Nineties poets
A.J. was content to defend them verbally: but when
Fisher did so he found it necessary to write long letters in
reply, to copy out poems by Dowson and extracts from
Pater, in order to try to convince "the Philistine articulate". When the critical-creative task of writing the
biographies of the Nineties authors that were to be a vital
part of his book seemed too complex and disturbing, it was
to Fisher that A.J. turned for help, asking him to write a
brief biography of John Addington Symonds which "will
be infinitely instructive for me. I find my task very difficult; and if you endure the same agony in miniature, your
introspective mind will make discoveries for my guid-
ance". The relationship between them, an unwilling one
on A.J.'s side, was that of master and pupil; and criticism
from Fisher of the worth of A.J.'s bibliographical researches, and of his failure to produce any original writing,
moved my brother to indignation. Perhaps Fisher meant
to stir his friend to activity; if so, he was certainly successful, for the post brought him a long letter:

My dear Harold,
Something must be done. I saw that, dimly, some months
ago, when the first faint sounds of your crusade came up the
wind. And now that the pale pennons of the hostile force are
actually visible from my windows, I must perforce defend
myself, though with something of the hesitation that an
intelligent, humanitarian Saracen might have felt when men-
aced (and amused) by the Children's Crusade (if, for the
purpose of analogy, we may suppose that ineffectual, pathetic
attempt ever to have been a menace to anything save itself).
Or, to change the metaphor, I see you as Don Quixote,
battering at my gates with a wooden sword; and from sheer
inability to bear the noise and nuisance, I must gird on my
armour to do unwilling battle. It is not my fault that, like
your illustrious fore-runner the Don, you seem faintly
ridiculous.

The Dilatory Bibliographer

Let me remind you of your earlier missions. In the dim
dawn of our friendship, you set yourself to save my soul
from sophistry, the influence of "an Irish actor sent to prison
for lese-majeste" and the subtle dangers of dilettantism. Those
ministrations were not without value and effect. It was the
crusade of Godfrey de Buillon (I forget the spelling of his
name). Time passed, and it became clear (even to you, though
for long you maintained a pleasant uncertainty) that, from
those dangers, my soul (or self), positively did not need
saving any more. But the true Crusader is never long without
a shrine to save, and presently you were fighting an entirely
imaginary evil, one which gave you the pleasure of many
private reveries on my strange lack of something (moral
strength to decline valuable gifts, one gathered) and of indulging (have you forgotten?) in many sermons; sermons
that (so delightfully unreal were they, so utterly did they
convey your conviction of superior moral sense) one could
even enjoy, though undue repetition sometimes made them
tiresome. It was the Crusade of Richard Coeur-de-lion.

And when, some months ago, you told me (and my wife)
that I was "insufferable", and that my gifts as a writer could
never equal yours, I feared that yet another attempt was
being made (or prepared) to save my poor, my all unworthy
soul. Not that I object to the thing being saved; I rather like
it, but you make it so inconvenient, and, when the Crusade
is at its height, my pleasure in your company is temporarily
diminished. Between Crusades you are charming. I saw last
night (I have seen for weeks) that the flood is at the full. Not
only am I without power to write, but I have a hole (instead
of a bump) of originality; in the matter of direct derivation,
I pile Pelion on Ossa—nay, Moore on Wilde, and both (per-
chance) on Poe; my much reading has given me many
quotations but few personal thoughts; and not only have I
no critical canon, but I am even and ever at the mercy of the
winds that blow, deny my masters for that others jeer them,
and shine, if at all, fitfully and again, and only in the presence
of the Justified Ones of Wednesday. Thus Ser Harold (or
should I say, Childe Harold?) strong in his conviction (as are
Crusaders always) of intellectual power and originality,
force of literary expression, and fitness to right this intoler-

able wrong. Sadly (but sternly) I am prompted to produce an original work of art. It has been your amusement for years so to prompt me, secure in the possession of an unfinished and (theoretically) indubitable masterpiece. It is the last, it is the Children's Crusade!

My dear Harold, what is a happy Infidel to do when the solemn armies of Christendom set out to save him? While your forces were distant, were slowly taking up position, they could be apprehended as a spectacle; but all things, even the Parcels Post, arrive in the end, and your motley crew is at my gates. Useless to retort upon you with the frankness that yourself exacts, for long experience has shown me that such retorts but make you angry or incredulous. A conviction of the divine Rightness of Fisher is not easily shaken. What *can* I do (since I do not want to fight) but plead? Therefore, please, Harold, take your ridiculous regiments away! Let us meet in amity, and do not further threaten the towers of my self-respect.

Sincerely yours,

A.J.

Bibliography: To save you the researches that I am sure you will wish to undertake, let me say that the whole of the first page is taken from Beerbohm; all the second, from Beerbohm, Wilde and Moore; all the third and fourth from Shakespeare, Sismondi and Kant; the conclusion from Goethe or F. Anstey.

The tone is friendly, but menacing; the "original work of art" was a stiff little four-line epigram. The letter brought a rhymed reply from Fisher covering eight pages, written in forms parodying various well-known poems, and bubbling with a good humour at which it was impossible to take offence, joined to a plainness of speech which A.J. cannot have found other than infuriating:

> Oh you! Whom Vanity's light bark conveys
> On fame's mad voyage by the wind of praise,
> With what a shifting gale your course you ply,
> For ever sunk too low or borne too high!

48

The Dilatory Bibliographer

When Fisher suggested that my brother should guess which lines he had written, and which were quotations (the four lines above are from Pope), A.J. made two wrong guesses. "He never showed any curiosity after that", Fisher remarked, "as to which were mine and which were quoted, and I never told him." It is doubtful if the ironic piece that the terrifyingly facile Fisher sent to the ardent aesthete a month or two later pleased my brother much more:

To A.J.
(with apologies to R.K.)

When the last bibliography's written, and the last little
    memoir is done,
When the last section's gone to the printers, and at last you've
    a place in the sun,
You will rest, and faith—you will need it, lay the 'Nineties
    aside for a while,
From Olympus look down on your servant, delighted to
    bask in your smile.

And those that were hard shall be easy, and those that were
    difficult, plain,
When you've reckoned up all that was Beardsley and
    declined to include Barry Pain,
And Harland, John Davidson, Dowson, caviare to the
    general, all,
Shall be household words to a public which at present scarce
    knows them at all.

And only the 'Nineties shall flourish, and only the 'Nineties
    remain,
Of all the Victorian greatness that sometimes, I've thought,
    was your bane,
And you shall be King in that Kingdom, a monarch revered
    near and far,
For your horoscope surely proclaims it, you were born
    'neath a Bodleian star.

A. J. A. Symons

The *Nineties Bibliography* had taken on for A.J. something of the aspect that the famous "Key to All Mythologies" assumed for Mr. Casaubon in George Eliot's *Middlemarch*, although he resembled in no other respect that muted figure whose blood was "all semicolons and parentheses": the book was at once delightful to him as evidence of his own knowledge and industry, and painful because he shared some of his friends' doubts about its intrinsic worth. He became absorbed in the minutiae of his task, and in an introduction heavy with bibliographical learning discussed such questions as the propriety of regularizing the title-page inscription by printing it in small, even capitals instead of attempting to maintain the original proportions between lower case, capitals and italics; of recording the actual size of a page instead of using such ambiguous terms as "quarto" and "octavo", and of stating the number of copies originally printed of each book, a task which "has involved research extending over the whole world"; and he departed from strict bibliographical practice by saying that he thought it useful to possess *any* edition of a book, whether the first or the third, which contained new material in the way of a preface, a fresh article or a new story. At the end of his Introduction he justified, in words that express his own dubiety, his choice of occupation:

> It may seem, to one glancing through these pages crowded with detail, that to treat so minutely a decade which after all is but an interesting backwater in the stream of literature is an effort disproportioned to any possible result, evidence of an ignorance of proportion and wrong sense of values. The compiler is well aware how limited in interest and range the period of his affections was, as he is aware that it produced works which will last longer than its detractors, and a legend which will last as long as those works: and he would reply with Pater that "nothing which has ever interested living

men and women can wholly lose its vitality—no language they have spoken, no oracle beside which they have hushed their voices, no dream which has once been entertained by actual human minds, nothing about which they have ever been passionate, or expended time and zeal". The accumulation of facts, if the facts are essential ones, has a permanent usefulness. It may be that this book will become the first in a series of comprehensive records, a volume in what would be, at least, the best *documented* history of any literature yet undertaken.

The Introduction, then, was written; and though the biographies proved less tractable, the eager author ordered proofs and revised proofs, and then page proofs, of much of the bibliographical material. Vast dummies of the books were ordered and, unlike Mr. Casaubon, A.J. had at least the satisfaction of seeing much of his work in type: but as the costs of the book mounted the compiler's zeal diminished. He left it alone altogether for some months while he played bridge, worked out new systems at roulette, strove to make his calligraphy less cramped, and dined out more and more often. His relations with the Foyles became less intimate, although he took Gilbert Foyle to Ascot; perhaps they were becoming alarmed by the extent of their involvement in this literary adventure. He supervised the production for the First Edition Club of *Letters to Conrad*, a charming little piece of preciosity. Letters from Henry James, H. G. Wells, John Galsworthy, James Gibbons Huneker, and other friends of Conrad, were wrapped in a differently-coloured paper for each correspondent, and the whole was enclosed in a decorative slip cover. *Letters to Conrad*, like most of the Club's publications of this time, has appreciated considerably in value in recent years.

When A.J. turned back to his Bibliography from the pleasures of dining and playing bridge, and from the care of the Club which, although it was backed by the Foyles, he regarded as his own property, he found himself confronted by new snippets of knowledge which called for incorporation; he saw certain grounds for dissatisfaction in his own system of classification; and, so far from finding it easier to write the biographies left uncompleted, he became unhappy about those he had already written. The galley proofs were filed elaborately on his shelves in big snap-spring folders; and they stayed there for years, long after the type had been distributed, a *memento mori* of a task unachieved, a curiosity of unpublished literature. He began the book in 1925, with the expectation of finishing it that year; but although the passing years found it uncompleted, he did not regard it as unduly delayed. When, after three years, William Foyle wrote to him and suggested, not unreasonably, that publication of the book would be a great asset to A.J., and that if he was not prepared to finish it the Foyles could find someone else to complete the task, my brother was indignant. "It would take another person, supposing there were one competent to do it, much longer by years than it will me to finish the book", he observed, and continued with a hauteur which in the circumstances was slightly comic, "In view of your pressure, however, I have now reluctantly decided to complete the book as quickly as possible, and to do so by cutting down the scale of the biographies. I think I can do so in some ways without harming the work." But although the scale of the biographies may have been cut down, the book was not completed, and two years later he wrote to another friend interested in it that "My New Year resolution" (for 1930) "was to complete the Bibliography, and during January I have worked (and am working) steadily away at it." When, however, this friend expressed his eagerness to see the complete manuscript he was rebuffed, like William Foyle, in almost mystical terms.

Dear ——,

You mistook my meaning slightly. I am working steadily on the completion of the manuscript, but I can hold out little hope of its completion in "a month or two". All I can be certain about is my continued application to a task the end of which is still not within forecast.

Yours sincerely,
A. J. A. Symons.

CHAPTER V

BROTHER SPECULATOR

By the time he had reached his middle twenties my brother had fulfilled, in some degree, several of his early ambitions. He was the part-owner of a Club, and of a yacht; he was known, if not as an author, as an expert on literary matters; his social horizon was widening every day. But he aspired, also, to the membership of Clubs; not only because membership of a good Club seemed to him socially desirable, but because he found greater pleasure in the kind of social intercourse that a Club of carefully selected members can provide, than in almost any other activity. He did not, I think, greatly enjoy the company of most women, for he demanded in his companions a kind of intelligence which few women possess, and a seriousness which many women positively dislike. He had a great appreciation of humour, but no liking for the inconsequent frivolity which, for those who enjoy the company of women, is one of their chief charms. When he liked women he treated them as intellectual equals, frequently perhaps with the consciousness that he was paying them a compliment; and generally they enjoyed his elaborate courtesy, while retaining a feeling that there was some depth in his nature that remained untouched in relation to them. In a wholly male company he had no uneasy doubt that his pretensions might appear ridiculous, no fear that he might be thought less impressive than comic; and he did not hesitate to appear, where men were gathered together, as refulgent as possible.

These things made him by choice a clubman, and a member and founder of Societies. Sometimes in conversation he would recall wistfully the glories of the Clubs of the eighteenth century, when the members and not the surroundings made the Club, and when the nine assembled members of the Literary Club included Edmund Burke, Oliver Goldsmith, Dr. Johnson and Sir Joshua Reynolds. Whatever illusion he may have cherished about the free intellectual air of Clubs of the present day must have been broken when, after giving dinner at one famous Club to Lord Alfred Douglas and two other guests he was called before the Committee and reprimanded for bringing into the Club a man who had been in prison. "If I cannot dine here with a major living British poet I shall resign", he said: and did so. This, his first major venture into Clubland, was unsuccessful, but he soon made another which was more successful, and which had a considerable influence on his later life.

One of the early, and most enthusiastic, members of the First Edition Club was Dr. G. C. Williamson, a Doctor of Literature, a Fellow of many societies, a holder of the rosette of the Legion of Honour, a Justice of the Peace. Dr. Williamson had been for years a collector of books and pictures, although he was not a wealthy man; he had begun his career as an author by writing newspaper articles on archaeological matters local to the district of Guildford where he was born, and lived, and continued it by producing many such publications as the *Life of John Russell, R.A.*, *Guildford in the Olden Time*, and a catalogue of the Pierpont Morgan Collection of Miniatures in four volumes. Throughout his life Williamson had been interested in the arts, and admired those who practised them; both the First Edition Club, and its youthful and romantic Secretary, made a strong appeal to him. He had given already many proofs of his interest in the Club, by introducing prospective members; now he showed his interest in my brother personally by proposing A.J. as a member of a select and distinguished dining Club named Ye Sette of Odd Volumes.

The rules and general proceedings of Ye Sette of Odd Volumes provide an excellent illustration of British upper-class culture at play; the spectacle may be found entertaining or distressing according to the viewer's taste, but it had very little in common with the Literary Club of Johnson and Reynolds.

The Rules of the Sette, for example, begin: "The Sette of Odd Volumes shall consist of twenty-one, this being the number of volumes of the Variorum Shakespeare of 1821". This whimsical tone is maintained in some of the other rules, such as the one which provides that "Each Odd Volume on his admission ... shall pay Three Odd Pounds and Three Odd Shillings. For the official Badge he shall pay Ten and a Half Odd Shillings"; or Rule XVI which provides that "There shall be no Rule XVI"; or Rule XVIII, "No Odd Volume shall talk *unasked* on any subject he understands." The singing of "The Lay of the Odd Volumes" with its repeated chorus line: "We are Odd, very Odd! You may take it—we are Odd!" preceded every dinner, and showed the members of the Sette proclaiming in themselves at play a quality which few would have welcomed in application to the affairs of their everyday life. Every Odd Volume was expected to assume a title symbolical of his occupation or inclination, and was known by this denomination at meetings of the Sette. Thus Williamson was Brother Horologer, Ralph Straus Brother Scribbler, and Vyvyan Holland (the young man who, it will be recalled, had

Brother Speculator

looked up some years before and seen the words *First Edition Club* on a board in Pall Mall) Brother Idler; the name that A.J. chose for himself on his election was Brother Speculator. Twelve years later, when he had been asked to serve a year's term as His Oddshippe, my brother gave in his balanced prose reasons for selecting a name which expresses fittingly his attitude to life, both inside and outside the dining club in which he used it:

> When I had the honour of being elected to the Sette twelve years ago, I chose the title of Speculator, not because I am unduly addicted to the sharp excitement of the gambler's thrill, nor because I have devized two invulnerable systems at roulette, nor because I once had a share in a racing stable, nor because there was a time when I played bridge every day; it was because I realized very clearly that even for those whose wagers are neither ante-post nor starting-price but non-existent, even for those who neither gain nor lose, because they never stake, even for those who cross no t's, no cheques and no rubicons, life remains, in Stevenson's phrase, "a bazaar of dangerous and smiling chances". We are engaged, willy-nilly, in the risk of existence, and set in a gamble we cannot evade. To call oneself a speculator is merely to recognize the limiting circumstance of life, to realize that we are all speculators; it is to count and measure our chances.

At the time of my brother's election to the Sette the members and associate members included some of the most important legal lights and literary luminaries in England; although there was a considerable proportion of members whose merits were more plainly social than intellectual. Every new Odd Volume was expected, soon after his admission to "make a literary, scientific, or artistic communication to the Sette". These addresses were printed in a limited edition, and distributed to the Sette and their friends. Such an occasion moved A.J. to unusual

creative effort. He read a paper on one of his favourite
Nineties writers, Frederick William Rolfe, better known
as Baron Corvo, but (at that time) hardly known at all.
The paper, which was in effect a short biography, was
exceedingly well received by the Sette, and a little later
was reprinted in *Life and Letters*, when Desmond McCarthy
was editor of that magazine. In the following year A.J.
read an address on Emin Pasha, and later one on Edgar
Allan Poe; both of these pieces were reprinted, that on
Emin Pasha as a separate booklet, and the address on Poe
again in *Life and Letters*.

These addresses impressed the brethren: they were not
less impressed by the feline assurance of the newcomer,
by his knowledge of books, by the mystery with which he
deliberately surrounded himself, and by the studied grace

*These three signatures provide a good example
of A.J.'s talent in amateur forgery. The* Daily
Sketch *published them and invited its readers
to pick out the forgery, which is actually the
central signature. Those above and below it
are in the hand of the* Daily Sketch *reporter.*

Brother Speculator

of his calligraphy. It was at the Sette of Odd Volumes
that he first exploited his talent for forgery, offering to
forge the name of his friend Maurice Healy, K.C. on a
cheque, which he would then present at Healy's bank.
The forgery was executed, presented, and paid without
question; the wager cost Healy a bottle of champagne.
On another occasion, when G. D. Roberts was reading a
paper on the Old Bailey, A.J. took as guests Sidney Davis,
who had been a friend of his Debating Society days, and
his brother Percy Davis. Both were now partners in the
firm of Bulcraig and Davis, and in introducing them A.J.
said that he arrived accompanied by two solicitors. Later
in the evening he copied several names on the menu,
including that of Lord Chief Justice Hewart, one of the
guests. In a speech on behalf of the visitors, Hewart said,
with perhaps too near an approach to earnestness, that
he had seen that evening the handiwork of an Odd Volume
who had told them that he was accompanied by two
solicitors. In that hotel, and on that occasion, he had
admired it: but he assured the Odd Volume that if he
were called upon to pass judgment in another place
upon such handiwork, that Odd Volume would need
more than two solicitors to save him from being
confined in a not too well furnished hotel for quite a long
time.

The paths by which men discover themselves are
curious; the Sette of Odd Volumes permitted my brother
to move out of the social half-world in which through
sheer uncertainty he had scented frequently a hostility
in others which existed only in his imagination, into
the full light of upper class society. There was no doubt of
the social standing of his fellow Odd Volumes, nor of
their appreciation of his talents; the elaborate jokes and

mock-insults in which the Sette indulged were very much to his taste; and if there was at first something strange to him in this intoxicating social air, he soon became accustomed to its headiness. His friendship with Dr. Williamson was firmly cemented through the Sette, and so was that with Vyvyan Holland; he met there also André Simon, with whom, some years later, he was to start the Wine and Food Society.

Almost all of his new friends found something mysterious about his antecedents, his surprising knowledge and his dandyism, combined as they were with an equally surprising ignorance, and no very visible means of support. A few found this combination objectionable. Osbert Burdett, for instance, was grateful for the help my brother gave him with his book *The Beardsley Period*, and charmed to find so much knowledge of the Nineties in one so young. When he mentioned the name of A. J. A. Symons to one of his friends however, he found that his pleasure in A.J.'s society was not universal. The friend's view is worth repeating because it was, with some variations, the view of others:

> His impression of you (Burdett wrote to A. J.) was that you were so much accustomed to regard people as clay to be shapen to a vessel of your own design that he does not believe you would ever give a frank and candid opinion of any work that you thought had been written by anyone you had met or foresaw the possibility of meeting.

Often this impression was intensified in visitors to the First Edition Club by a nebulous feeling that they were in the presence of a literary adventurer, whose suggestions should be examined with some care; my brother's exquisite suits, extravagant shirts and ties and pointed hand-made shoes did nothing to dispel this feeling, which was sometimes increased by the sight of a calligraphy too beautiful (it was thought) to be quite respectable. He must have lived precariously, although for him enjoyably, during these years, when his only fixed income was the £200 a year he received as Director of the Club. He summed up what may have been his principal means of support neatly, in the first three lines of a triolet:

> When Mr. Symons buys a book
> He buys it cheap, or not at all.
> He sells it, and the price is tall.

He never permitted the Club to be used as a means of dealing in books, and book dealers were not eligible as members: but, like the famous Thomas J. Wise, he indulged his own nose for the private purchase of books likely to be readily saleable at a profit. He added many books to his own growing library ("Not a day passes", he told a friend grandiloquently, "without at least two books being added to my collection"); he sold many at a large profit. Few details of this background activity remain, and their detailed recounting would be tedious. He concealed his bookselling activities as much as possible because although there is nothing reprehensible, by the ordinary standards of commercial morality, in buying books cheap and selling them dear, such an occupation did not fit nicely into the pattern of social appearance which he had set for himself. In the position that he wished to occupy, concealment of his bookselling activities, of his business relations with the Foyles, and of his personal history and background, became inevitable.

This was the reverse side of a medal which shone very brightly on its other face. He was accepted by most people

as a fascinating, delightful and mysterious figure in literary
London; and there was nothing false in this conception.
Something of the attraction his enthusiasm and youth
aroused in the staid hearts of the older Club members may
be seen in a letter sent to him by Dr. Williamson (then in
his late sixties) at the end of 1926. The "Gulliver" referred
to was a definitive edition of *Gulliver's Travels*, a very
handsome and ambitious piece of book production edited
by Harold Williams, a leading Swiftian scholar, and
published by the Club.

> Dear man (or rather, boy) of mystery
> Fancy only being a quarter of a century old and possessed
> of the book knowledge you have! When you attain to the
> age of this decrepid old writer you will be a veritable
> encyclopaedia of information on typography, calligraphy,
> cartography and all other kindred subjects! What a joy to
> be only five and twenty!! How I wish that it was possible to
> run over part of life again in all the vigour and spirit of youth.
> All possible congratulations on Gulliver which according to
> promise *is* on my table for Christmas Day and a jolly fine
> book it is. . . . I am going to read it with delight and chuckle
> with pleasure at being Chairman of a Club that can produce
> so fine a book thanks to the energy and skill of a Director
> who has accumulated—goodness knows how or whence—
> such stores of typographic ability in so short a space of
> years.

The feeling expressed thus enthusiastically by Williamson was felt, in varying degrees, by the many people
who liked him. It is difficult to analyse his unconventional
charm. Part of it came from the flattering attention he
gave to all companions whose interests ranged with his
own, and the helpful enthusiasm he showed for their
ideas; part from the contradictions and eccentricities of
his nature—those who knew him as a dandy were at first

incredulous of his tales about sailing a yacht or playing bridge almost professionally, and then delighted when the tales were discovered to be true; part from his bubbling good nature. He helped many people, as he helped Burdett with *The Beardsley Period*, and Moore with details for his novel; and he did so much less from hope of reward than from a desire to make some achieved work, whether his own or another's, as nearly perfect as possible. Christina Foyle, William Foyle's daughter, has told me of the charming gravity with which he would become a life member of the short-lived Societies which she and her brother formed in their schooldays; and he did this because he was delighted by the enterprise shown in the pursuit of any unusual objective among the sobrieties of a generally commonplace world. He interested himself in other peoples' hobbies and, if they were constructive or ornamental, went out of his way to give them information or assistance; few things pleased him more than the chance to introduce to an expert a man who might be useful to him.

He had made great progress in these middle twenties; but he had greater plans, plans which, if they came to reality, would widen the horizon of the First Edition Club, and round off his own social success. One day in 1926 he apologized for breaking an engagement with Fisher, and said in his note of apology, perhaps with a recollection of his architectural metaphor of the past: "In furtherance of my plans, I'm just off to stay with the Hon. Oliver Brett, the keystone of an arch."

CHAPTER VI

THE FIRST EDITION CLUB LIMITED

THE plan that my brother had in mind was the incorporation of the Club as a Limited Company, which would raise money through the issue of Debentures to be taken up by its wealthy supporters. He would retain the controlling interest himself, sever the partnership with the Foyles (who had for some time realized, and regretted, the unprofitable nature of their investment) and enlarge the membership by holding exhibitions every month, and by offering the facilities for eating, drinking, and leisurely reading available in other, and more famous, London clubs. Such a programme clearly could not be carried out in the Vestry Hall of 6, Little Russell Street, and he therefore envisaged also removal to a new home, more fitting to the Club's authority and wide scope. With a suitable house, and with adequate backing, the First Edition Club would be, at last, a financial success.

Does the idea of such a limited company seem merely chimerical? It was, nevertheless, realized, and the new home was found. My brother may have understood at the time (it is very plain in retrospect) that the trade conditions of the later twenties were, for the first time since the war, favourable to such a scheme. The General Strike had been defeated, and a Conservative Government seemed firmly in power; there was a small trade boom, and several of the First Edition Club's backers, whose capital was invested in stocks, felt happier about the national situation than they had done for years. It happened also that at this time, largely through the tireless activity of Doctor Williamson, supplemented by the effect of A.J.'s personality, the Club attracted the interest of a few comparatively wealthy book-collectors who were prepared to give it, at least temporarily, the kind of financial and social backing whch it had hitherto lacked. Chief among them were the Honourable Oliver Brett, afterwards Lord Esher, who was to be "the keystone of an arch", and Lord Vaux of Harrowden.

The negotiations were protracted, but at last the First Edition Club Limited held its first meeting, in the Vestry Hall. Lord Vaux was appointed Chairman of the Board; the other directors were Brett, Williamson, A.J. and Albert Ehrman, owner of what my brother called "the best collection of blind stamped bindings (covering the period between the invention of printing and the mid-sixteenth century) in this country". By the terms of agreement the limited company purchased the First Edition Club, paying for it £750 in cash, and a considerable number of Debentures. The Foyles received as their share a sum in Debentures equivalent to the amount of money they had put into the Club. Perhaps they did not view this altogether favourably, although A.J. wrote to them grandly: "You have Debentures covering every penny you have advanced". It is true that these Debentures had little value until the Club's financial success was achieved: none the less, A.J. regarded himself as the Foyles' benefactor, since, at least on paper, he had made good their loss. My brother was also allotted, under the agreement, 1,489 out of the Company's 1,500 fully paid and issued shares.

Before these details were finally agreed, however, the

directors looked for a suitable new Clubhouse: and their eyes (or those of the Secretary) fixed on the beautiful early eighteenth century house in Great Russell Street that had been the home of Topham Beauclerk, that aristocratic and dissipated conversational wit who once got Doctor Johnson out of bed at three o'clock in the morning to "have a frisk". The Secretary was a happy man in these days. He was able to spend money freely, for the first time in his life, without feeling disturbed by the prospect of an early and ominous reckoning, and nothing could have pleased him more than the prospect of finding for the Club's home a house of great architectural beauty and historical interest. His fine Italian hand is visible in the production of an elaborate and expensive booklet, "Proposals for the enlargement of the First Edition Club", which was circulated to all members. In this booklet a full page is lovingly given to a reproduction of the bronze memorial tablet set up by the Duke of Bedford in commemoration of Topham Beauclerk's occupancy of the house; the beautiful main staircase, surmounted by a painted ceiling, is dwelt on, and the panelling of hall and dining room, exhibition and coffee rooms. On the ground floor was the Director's office ("suitable for use as reception room for official dinners"), on the first floor the exhibition and coffee rooms, on the second writing rooms, a card room, libraries, and on the third "accommodation for the Resident Director"—that was A.J. There was even a flat roof suitable for conversion into a roof garden. The Club's future was lyrically described in the booklet: "Innumerable avenues of development are possible. . . . Book-collectors will find a bibliographical library open at hours when the British Museum and other libraries are closed. . . . Matters of book-collecting and literary interest will be debated in the pages of a quarterly periodical, issued free to members. A special type will be cut for the Club's finest productions. Publishing projects will be on a larger and more ambitious scale".

The booklet was sent out, the enthusiasm of members aroused, and then—the whole affair collapsed. Whether, at a late stage, the other Directors became alarmed by the expense in which they would be involved—the purchase price of the house alone was £24,000, and the total expenditure would have been £40,000 (which was all to be covered by the issue of interest-bearing Debentures); whether the vendors decided that this new Company was of too speculative a nature; or whether the two sides were simply unable to agree on terms of purchase: the transaction, after weeks of negotiation, came to an unfruitful end. This was a setback; but, after the first disappointment, A.J. agreed that the purchase of this house might have placed a strain on the Club's resources. Very soon his enthusiasm had been transferred to an almost equally desirable new home, also near the British Museum: Number 17, Bedford Square. The negotiations for the purchase, not of the freehold, but of the lease, of this property were carried through successfully, and it became the Club's home. The cost was to be covered by the issue of £15,000 (instead of £40,000) worth of debentures.

If Number 17, Bedford Square, lacked a little of the distinction of the lost house in Great Russell Street, it had beautiful Adam ceilings and fireplaces. The ground floor was in part arranged already as a dining room, and folding doors in black and gold lacquer (brought by a former owner, it was said, from an Italian palace), separated the dining room and lounge. Large windows opened from the lounge on to an Italian garden paved with pure white marble, and a great marble staircase led up from this garden to the exhibition room in which the showcases had been designed by one of the Club's most enthusiastic members, Ambrose Heal. Accommodation for the Resident Director had not been forgotten; he was installed in a flat on the second floor. In May 1928 ex-King Manoel of Portugal, himself the owner of a famous library of Portuguese books, opened the new premises. The opening was accompanied by an exhibition of books printed by English private presses, including a complete collection of Morris's work for the Kelmscott Press, and specimens of the Doves, Eragny, Ashendene, Gregynog, Nonesuch, Golden Cockerel and other presses. Sir Frederick Kenyon, Keeper of the Printed Books at the British Museum, complimented the Club on its new home, and congratulated it upon past achievements and A.J. made some remarks on the departure of rare books to America (which was at that time receiving much attention in the press) into which he introduced, typically, a reference to his favourite subject of racehorses. We should, he said, envy rather than deprecate those who want to buy fine things and are prepared to make sacrifices to obtain them; it was nonsense to say that the Americans had all the money, while English people paid more money for racehorses than any other nation in the world. We, apparently, wanted bloodstock; the Americans wanted books. This rather simple view was greeted with applause.

Some of the many newspaper reports of the formal opening referred to the rapid progress of the Club "started six years before in a single room in Pall Mall": and the achievement was indeed a remarkable one which had conjured out of a hand-to-mouth and uncapitalized existence six exhibitions and eleven publications. How much more might be accomplished now that a Limited Company had been organized, and a firm financial basis found! When the Club moved to Bedford Square it seemed to my brother that his future life was securely established: but, more than this, he felt the glow of fulfilled ambition in the creation of a *Club*—not a mere converted Vestry Hall, however fine, but a Club where wit and wealth might be gathered together on equal terms, as he fondly imagined they had been in Johnson's day 150 years before. Fondly: for the gap between Johnson and the aristocratic *littérateurs* of his time was a wide one, and acknowledgement of the merits of the "Great Cham" of literature was not at all the same thing, for Horace Walpole or Lord Chesterfield, as frequenting his society. The ideal my brother sought was not, in England, possible of achievement, and as his friend Sir Shane Leslie says:

> He moved like a messenger of the Gods, a Hermes of letters, chiefly in the underworld of the writing and bookselling community. If that underworld had not been so limited in England he would have found scope to make money, collections and friends on a larger and sufficient scale. In Paris, Rome, Vienna, such a life could have been lived: and he would have established himself as a character and moved from salon to salon. But England—London— knows no salons where all manner of literary lions and adventurers can meet under the wand of some presiding blue-stockinged lady.

But at this time my brother saw none of the perils in his way. Satisfied that he had arranged satisfactorily his social and financial position, he turned aside to justify the reputation he had gained among men of letters, through the power of his conversation. With a certain conscious elegance and dilettantism he began to substitute works for words.

In 1928 The Fleuron published in an edition limited to 300 copies, and printed in an elegant type called Lutetia,

then used for the first time in England, the story of Emin
Pasha which Harold Fisher had told my brother several
years earlier, and with which A.J. had dazzled the Sette
of Odd Volumes. My brother's interest in African exploration remained remarkably constant throughout his
life: and, as he never selected a subject which had not some
bearing on the contradictions and complications which he
divined, at first dimly and in the end with uncomfortable
clarity, in his own nature, it is tempting to speculate on
the features in Emin's story which especially attracted him.
The nature of this reticent and publicity-hating man, who
ruled African natives by conciliation, and who embodied
many negative and passive virtues which ended in unwillingness to resist his own murder, was apparently far
from my brother's dreams of influence and power: but the
romantic transformation of a penniless doctor into His
Excellency Emin Bey (a name which had been simply
taken from his predecessor in place of his own name of
Eduard Schnitzer) must have affected him strongly, and
the very unworldliness of Emin appealed to the part of his
own nature which desired an isolated life given to literature, a life which he knew he would never lead. But
beyond all this he was fascinated by the mere physical
details of African exploration, as other imaginations are
excited by drink, and others still by colour. He immersed
himself in the details of poisoned skewers concealed by
leaves, gigantic, grave-like elephant pits and the forest
"choked with undergrowth, steaming with malaria, and
dark as London on a foggy day". He could not resist
sending to his friend Vincent Marrot a few typical details
that had been omitted from his study:

Dear Vincent,
    Here is a sentence that will go in future editions of Emin.
I mislaid it when arranging the first.

The First Edition Club Limited

"They saw the Kigelia, whose pulp cures wounds; the tall tamarind and golden detaria; long thorned mimosas and sharp edged grasses; red passion flowers and lemon-yellow grass-lilies; thistles six feet high, and fan-shaped ferns."

Rather fine?

Yours, A.J.

Emin is an admirable essay, full of epigrammatic phrases ("We often say that extremes meet when we mean that mediocrities encounter") and dazzling half-truths ("There are but two methods of government: conciliation and coercion; though there are as many methods of mis-government as there are active political parties"). Those "future editions" airily referred to never appeared in my brother's lifetime: but a well-merited reprint has been published recently.

Later in the year he produced, not an instalment of his famous *Bibliography of the Nineties*, but an *Anthology of Nineties Verse*. The book was produced by Elkin Mathews and Marrot, the firm in which Vincent Marrot was then a director. In appearance and shape it resembled the *Yellow Book;* it flaunted a Beardsley drawing on the yellow board cover, and another on the title page. This An-thology, which contained characteristic work by John Barlas, Michael Field, Eugene Lee-Hamilton, Vincent O'Sullivan and Victor Plarr, as well as other better-remembered writers of the period, might command more readers to-day than it did twenty years ago. Certainly the stream of epigrams in my brother's introduction ("There are fashions in verses as in vintages"; "What is written may perish; but it cannot be destroyed") would be noticed now, and so would his conclusion, written with the architectural delights of Bedford Square in mind, that "In writing, as in architecture, there are many styles; and our admiration of St. Paul's or Shakespeare need not blind us to the more elaborate if lesser beauties of an Adam ceiling or the poems here collected." But at that time the book was dismissed rather briskly by most critics, and the anthologist's reward was not a large one. He wrote also, for the amusement of his friends, *An Episode in the Life of the Queen of Sheba*, a rather laborious joke which is mentioned here only because it was his single experiment in fiction.

He expressed an intention at this time of producing, at last, a book—a book telling the stories of nine strange careers. Corvo and Emin, two of them, were already written; he wrote, and read to the Odd Volumes, two more dealing with the curious story of the preacher Edward Irving, and with the unhappy life of Edgar Allan Poe. In a talk he gave to the To-morrow Club at Cambridge he remarked casually that "It can hardly be denied that Poe possessed a mind as original as Leonardo da Vinci's". His article in *Life and Letters* (adapted, like all of these pieces, from his Odd Volume address) made less extravagant claims, but showed clearly the attraction and interest held for him by this macabre figure who "would with equal enthusiasm explain or expound the laws of music, mathematics, literature, cryptography, conchology or chance," whose handwriting was "innocently beautiful", who was despised because of his birth, and who was moved to the bouts of drinking that caused his death (in my brother's view) by some inflexible sexual inhibition derived from childhood.

He was diverted from these studies (he planned, but never wrote, an article on Jimmy White, the gambler and racehorse-owner who committed suicide) by glimpses of a publishing scheme that was, as he wrote to an interested firm, "of vast magnitude". His idea was a brilliant one and anticipated, in some points, both the Book Clubs of

the thirties and the new editions of the classics which are
selling so well to-day. No English publisher, he suggested,
had systematically taken advantage of modern methods
of book production. He proposed to do so by publishing
editions de luxe, of a kind put out by semi-private presses,
well printed and typographically attractive, and bound in
half leather with patterned cloth sides, at a cost of half a
guinea a volume or less. To-day there seems nothing
revolutionary about this idea, because two or three
courageous publishers have carried it through successfully:
but in the late twenties, as he rightly said, the only current
standard editions of classics were almost all unpleasing,
and physically out of date. The scheme was approved, at
least in theory, by Methuen, and *The Gateway Standard
Editions* edited by E. V. Lucas and A. J. A. Symons passed
the stage of argument about suitable titles, and reached that
of specimen page-proofs: and then, alas, for reasons now
unfathomable, was dissipated. Did my brother make
unreasonable demands for his idea, and his editorial
services? "Naturally", he wrote to Lucas, "I want as much
as I can reasonably get", and he suggested a royalty of sixpence to him on a volume published at half a guinea. Or
was the speculation too risky? The idea, anyway, was
reduced from its grandiose conception to a mere inexpensive library of "Gateway Editions", and A.J. had
nothing to do with its final form.

His association with Methuen was at this time a close
one: for he had signed a contract with them, upon remarkably favourable terms, to write a new, and definitive,
biography of Oscar Wilde. Wilde, like Poe, was a writer
of whose ideas he was admirably fitted, through the long
study that some give to the prophecies of fortune-tellers
and others to Biblical predictions, to make an exegesis.
Long rows of Wilde's works, in different editions, to-

gether with biographies and memoirs from many hands, lined one of his bookcases; and two or three years earlier he had given expert evidence for the defence in a case brought against Christopher Millard by a lady named Mrs. Chan Toon, and expressed his belief that a short play called *For Love of the King* put out under Wilde's name was certainly not his work. Much material for this biography was already in his hands: now he began to gather more, expressing confidently his view that the book would be finished within a year.

6
Little Russell Street,
Bloomsbury,
W.C

Holborn
8626

from A J A Symons

CHAPTER VII

THE INGENIOUS FINANCIER

———————————

THE First Edition Club was, in outward appearance,
a success; the modest Vestry Hall of Little Russell
Street was forgotten. Downstairs at 17, Bedford
Square, meals were served in the Club dining room; in the
Exhibition Room above, with its decorative Adams ceiling
and frieze, displays of one kind or another were held
almost monthly—exhibitions of John Galsworthy's first
editions, of the work of German Private Presses, of books
representing the flower of French printing. The idea of
making a Committee of the Club responsible for the
selection of "The Fifty Books of the Year" (in a typographical sense) took first effect in 1928, and was soon
firmly established. There were some, indeed, who suggested that the Club arrogated to itself in this matter an
authority it did not possess; but establishment lends
authority, and in two or three years the "Fifty Books"
exhibition was recognized and respected. The method of
selection was ingenious. A system of marking was adopted,
for paper, typographical design, binding, relation to price,
and general impression, by which it was possible for a
book published at half a crown to be chosen, as well as one
published at twelve guineas. The exhibitions gave
particular encouragement to the development of brighter
and more interesting bindings for English books: and there
is no doubt that over a period of years they had a generally
beneficial effect by increasing the taste and intelligence

used in English book production, an effect increased by the simultaneous exhibition of a selection of books printed in the United States.

The Club blossomed modestly: but its Secretary flowered like an orchid. In his flat on the second floor startled guests were received in a sitting room filled with shagreen and silver furniture, with walls and ceiling stippled in green and dull silver, chairs, sofa and carpet in varying shades of green. A square lighting fitting flush with the ceiling cast a cold aquarium light upon the room. In the library next door some thousands of books were now housed, each author's works being allotted a differently-coloured fancy paper: the more valuable books were enclosed in paper-covered board cases: and upon the spine of each was affixed a small label exquisitely written in my brother's hand which told the name of the author, the title of the book, and, in the case of first editions, the year of publication. My brother's time was now divided between social engagements and the Club's affairs, in the handling of which he was assisted by two competent secretaries.

The Club's prosperity, however, was in a financial sense illusory. The first year's working in Bedford Square showed a paper loss of nearly £2,000: and it is difficult, at this distance of time, to see why rational people should have thought that the Club, in these new premises, could ever pay its own way. There is much force in the remarks made by Sir Shane Leslie on the difficulties inherent in running such a Club in this country:

> As a Club it lacked the importance of the Olympian Athenaeum where the greatest literati could lunch and browse and meet their fellows, and on the other hand (it) was too imposing for the pale and haggard hordes of "literary ghosts" and research-agents who haunted the British

Museum. In any other country it would have drawn from
all literary categories, but in England it drew neither the
writers nor the collectors.

although his further remark that "I hardly met a soul
there, and only A.J. striding about with incessant conversation and exhibiting brilliant shows of books kept any
life in the building at all" is a little exaggerated.

In the booklet issued when the Club hoped to buy
Topham Beauclerk's house, three pages are devoted to
"financial details". The Secretary's ingenuity, and his
optimism, can be detected in these pages, which show
budgets for 1,000 and for 2,000 members. If the Club had
1,000 members it could run a periodical, and still make a
small yearly profit; and if "the anticipated membership of
2,000" was reached, the profit would be £4,500 a year.
But in fact, as the Secretary regretfully reported at the
end of the first year's workings: "The budget presupposed
a membership roll of 600 as a minimum to ensure a
balance of profit and loss. The Club did not then possess
that requisite minimum of members; and that minimum
has not yet been reached." An adverse balance, the Secretary continued, must recur in the following year; but he
said cheerfully that the loss should be cut by half. It was
essential to gain time "until the natural accretion of
members brings us to financial stability". The £7,500
Debentures remaining unissued represented working
capital locked up beyond the Club's reach. What could
they do to redress this loss? He suggested four possibilities:
the sale of further Debentures (which proved to be impossible); the raising of a loan from the bank (which would
require security); the creation of life members; and an
invitation to members to give money. He ended this
report of a year's workings by expressing the hope that

the Board would not think it necessary to contemplate liquidation.

The Board may have contemplated liquidation: but they adopted neither this course nor any other, beyond offering to create life members of the Club on a basis of 70 guineas for town and £50 for country members. The step had little effect on the Club's finances, and the passage of another year in which a loss of over £1,500 was incurred, made it impossible for the Board of Directors any longer to ignore the fact that some steps must be taken to secure the Club's financial position. This was, indeed, desperate: but that fact could hardly be gathered from the elegant circular sent out which was signed by the Secretary, and contained more of his ingenious monetary calculations.

The circular reviewed briefly the work of the Club, and congratulated the members on the fact that "they have helped to create an institution which, a hundred years hence, will still be bearing fruit of their planting". The Club had "passed from juvenility into adolescence, and our position now is that of the young man who, for the first time in his life, finds himself the master of a household." It was necessary to ensure the future by making certain of the present; necessary for the members to support the Committee with "something more than the simple annual subscription".

How could this be done? A variety of propositions, more or less attractive, were laid open to the members. They could take up some of the Debenture issue still unsubscribed. (And here, in a wholly typical phrase it is observed that "If every member who does not hold a Debenture would acquire two, we should have sufficient capital for our purposes"); they could, on the other hand, voluntarily surrender any Debentures they already held.

The Ingenious Financier

They could bring in new members (and here again "If every existing member produced one acceptable candidate the Club would have no difficulties"); if they were unable to bring in new members, they could at least bring visitors, and ask them to stay to luncheon, which would reduce the loss on the kitchen accounts. They could buy some of the Club's publications ("Sales of stock provide liquid capital"). And—the point is an important one, and caused a great deal of trouble—they could guarantee an amount of £100 towards a Club loan. In the words of the circular:

> Until these debentures are sold we must borrow. Our Chairman, Dr. G. C. Williamson, has very generously offered to deposit his personal securities with our bankers, if members in return guarantee him against final loss in units of £100. As the debentures are taken up the guarantors will be released. It is extremely unlikely that events will be so untoward that these guarantees will require calling up.

And once more the characteristic form of persuasion is observed: "If forty members will sign and return the guarantee form enclosed, our immediate needs will be more than filled."

This appeal had little result. A few members bought books, one or two bought Debentures; but the kitchen accounts continued to show a loss, and new members came in slowly. Although, as the appeal rather pathetically said: "A membership of 800 does not seem a high percentage of the populations of England and the United States to hope or work for", that membership was never achieved. The most urgent question, however, was that of the guarantees to cover the securities which Williamson deposited in the bank, and on which the Club obtained a loan. These were pursued by A.J. with considerable pertinacity, and in the course of a month he collected £100 guarantees from several of his friends.

The course adopted by the Club—that of borrowing money from a bank on securities which were in turn secured by guarantees from a number of people who were sometimes little-known, or even unknown to the owner of the securities, and who had in any case been assured that it was "extremely unlikely" that their guarantees would be called upon—can hardly be regarded as sound financial practice. In retrospect, it seems astonishing that a Committee containing two or three business men were prepared to accept it. But the enthusiasm of youth is infectious to men of experience; and to back that enthusiasm, and to support the Secretary's visions of the Club of the future, they saw such evidence of the increasing influence of the Club in the present that any thought of the guarantees being called in must have been as remote from their minds as it was from those of the guarantors. The guarantee itself was a sufficiently curious document. By its terms the guarantor, on condition that Williamson obtained an advance not exceeding £3,500 from the Bank, agreed to pay him £100 "or such proportionate part of £100 as such sum bears to the amount owing to the Bankers". Some dozen guarantee forms were signed at the time of the appeal and more were signed later; among them were some signed by the Secretary. With these guarantees placed in a tin box in his safe, Williamson rested, for the time, content.

It is necessary now to consider a little more closely the figure of the man who made the generous loan which played a large part in the tragi-comedy of the Club's oncoming collapse. Williamson's photographs show a trimly-bearded donnish figure, with a long straight nose and keen eyes behind small egg-shaped gold-rimmed spectacles. He observed a Victorian courtesy, streaked at times with Victorian curtness; he suffered from an asthmatic complaint that took him to Torquay during the early months of the year; he was at once touchy and generous, and he combined the rashness of giving security which he emphasized that he could not afford to lose with an anxious caution about the safety of his loan.

Williamson's interest in the affairs of the Club had always been an active one, and was now at its height. For some months of the year his activities were, however, confined to correspondence, as visits to London to attend Board and Committee Meetings increased his asthmatic troubles. From his home in Guildford he bombarded A.J. with a regular stream of letters, on all sorts of subjects. What was a fair price for first editions of *Pickwick* and *Vanity Fair*, with the original advertisements? How could one be sure of getting the right advertisements? How much should he give to the Kitchen Fund at Christmas? How much would copies of the *Memoirs of the Chevalier de Faublas*, *Justine*, *Straparola*, and other erotica (which an acquaintance of his had for disposal) be worth? His interest in the Club embraced all of its major activities, and he even found time to concern himself with minor ones. He was much disturbed by a theft from the Club's petty cash. "The information that you gave me yesterday is disquieting and distressing. Moreover, pardon me for being frank (we know each other sufficiently well for me to be frank) it involves the existence of some laxity which I deeply regret. . . . Would it be within the province of the Chairman to promulgate a definite instruction that every night the cash takings should be deposited in the safe?" All these, and many other, queries the Secretary dealt with blandly and efficiently; he also performed such services as giving an (unsuccessful) tip for the Derby.

A. J. A. Symons

Williamson had been somewhat worried about the safety of his securities; but he was reassured by the thought of the guarantees in his safe; and correspondence between him and the young man in whom he rested such confidence moved from finance back to such subjects as the worth of a copy of *Fleurs du Mal* containing "a manuscript copy of the poem, which I don't think is very likely to be in Baudelaire's handwriting", and of a Beardsley print called "Black Coffee". At times, and particularly with the approach of winter, Williamson felt gloomy, and regretted the difficulty of finding the "help of some person of very large means interested in books". Generally, however, he was moved by A.J.'s diurnal cheerfulness. "Next year will probably see the end of all our troubles", the Secretary wrote at the end of 1930; and at Christmas an interchange of gifts was made on the friendliest terms. "Let me thank you again", A.J. wrote, "for the beautiful, elaborate (or should I say elabradorite?) pin, from which I shall never be separated and which I wear even in my pyjamas. *If you can suggest a way by which I can wear it in the bath please ring me up at once.*"

My brother had reason to feel pleased with himself, for he had just completed an arrangement which provided the Club with the periodical which had for so long been promised, and which showed his business ability in its most favourable light.

One day a slim and rather shy young man called at 17, Bedford Square. His name was Desmond Flower, and he was the son of Sir Newman Flower, Chairman of the large publishing firm of Cassells. Young Desmond Flower had entered his father's publishing business very recently; and he was fascinated by that side of it concerned with biliography and book collecting. He wanted, in fact, like many other

The Ingenious Financier

young men, to edit a periodical; and instead of starting something completely new, he wished to take over an existing magazine. His choice fell on the *Bibliophile's Almanack*, which Oliver Simon and Harold Curwen had produced for two years, and then allowed to lapse. Oliver Simon lent his help in the preparation of the new magazine, and one of the first things he said was: "You should get an article from A. J. A. Symons." It was with this intention that Desmond Flower called at Bedford Square.

"I was shown", he says in a memoir of my brother, "into the front room on the first floor, magnificent in green. A.J. knew precisely how to receive people. He greeted me with courtly distance, so that I dared not accept the invitation to be seated; he thawed with calculated precision until by the time I found myself lounging over the edge of the sofa with a glass of sherry in my hand I felt that the First Edition Club was a home from home. By that time also a more far-reaching metamorphosis had taken place: my poor little *Almanack* had become the official organ of the First Edition Club, under the joint editorship of the two of us."

The process was, in fact, a little more complex than is suggested here. The two young men might make plans: but on A.J.'s side at least, the plans had to be approved by a Committee. A name had to be found and, after some hesitation, the *Book-Collector's Quarterly* was chosen to replace the original *Bibliophile's Almanack*. Terms had to be arranged with Cassells, who were to publish the periodical; and A.J. drove such a good bargain that Williamson, at least, thought there must be something wrong about it. His secretary wrote:

I am desired by Dr. Williamson to say that he will be glad if you will arrange to have a few minutes' *quiet* conversation

A. J. A. Symons

with him, undisturbed by telephone calls and visitors, when he comes up on Wednesday, because he is not at all comfortable about the Quarterly, he cannot in the least understand why any publisher should be likely to make a present to the Club of three hundred copies of a new magazine, without any remuneration in return. It seems to him inconceivable that, without any advertisement or remuneration, they should place all these copies at the disposal of the Club, and still more inconceivable if they are prepared to do it four times a year. He is convinced that there is a serious snag somewhere.

In reply the exultant A.J. said: "I warn you that I shall expect your congratulations. For what seems to you unlikely is actually a fact." The *quid pro quo*, he said, was twofold. The periodical would have the prestige of being the Club's official organ; and also "they receive, without any noticeable disbursement in cash, the editorial services of a trained expert, i.e., me". He did not fail to point out that "This stroke for the Club is a sacrifice by me, since if the Quarterly did not go free to members, I should be paid for editing it; whereas, since it does go free, I shall not be paid." Under the joint imprint of Cassell and the First Edition Club, and printed at the Curwen Press, the first number of the *Book-Collector's Quarterly* appeared in December, 1930.

This *Quarterly* comes into being (said A.J.'s editorial in the first number) in a time of trade distractions, when men's minds are agitated by economic difficulties afflicting all nations alike though not equally. Such a time may seem to some an unfortunate one in which to ask for a hearing. The editors, on the contrary, believe it to be a very good one. The heady speculation which has marked the last few financial years is obviously at an end; and every office, workshop, and stock exchange throughout the world is adjusting itself to a more rational relation of credit and conduct. What better

84

opportunity could offer for the collector to set his house in order?

The first number, which was gathered together remarkably quickly, contained an article by Edmund Blunden on the pleasures of book-collecting, a piece by Holbrook Jackson on Burton's *Anatomy of Melancholy*, and a lengthy section called "Notes on Books". A.J. contributed the editorial, some notes on the Club, a review of Holbrook Jackson's *The Anatomy of Bibliomania*, and an article called "The Book-Collector's Apology", which is perhaps the best of the many articles he wrote on bibliographical subjects. He tells, charmingly, of the way in which he became a book-collector:

> I myself became a book-collector (I was already a reader) when a schoolboy of fourteen years, by the simple act of buying two different Lives of Shelley. I read them both, and, noting contradictions, desired a third. It was then that the shadow of the "first edition" first fell across my path. There *was* a third Life, by John Addington Symonds, on my bookseller's shelves, but it was fifteen shillings, five times as much as either of the others, though in itself a slimmer and less valuable looking volume. The enhancement was due, I learned, to this book being a *first* edition. Why that should weigh so heavily I could not then understand, yet accepted; but my confusion was doubled when I found that my other, cheaply purchased, Lives were first editions too. The explanation given, that "they" "collected" works by John Addington Symonds, whereas the other Lives were only books, left me astonished, even when I learned that "they" were the book-collectors and booksellers of the West End (I lived in a distant fringe of London); I bought something else.

He told how, as his acquisitions grew more numerous, visitors to his home called it "quite a collection", and of the hours spent "arranging and re-arranging it, some-

A. J. A. Symons

timcs classifying by authors, sometimes by subject and affinity, sometimes, less reasonably, by mere height." His curious way of ensuring that his books were actually read and not merely collected, is worth notice. His shelves were in a perpetual state of flux; and he used to take the lefter-most book on the top shelf, and, having read it, pass to its neighbour, hoping to read through the whole case. He castigated the habit of collecting books which are merely fashionable, and advised collectors not to take their views ready-made. The concluding paragraph of the article is worth repeating, both because it is admirably written, and because it is an echo of the kind of ingenious special plead-ing he would advance in conversation:

> There is a modern school of medical philosophers which has explained, to its own satisfaction and in a vocabulary of its own invention, the inwardness of our outward actions, the secret causes of our desires or hopes. Complexes, inhibi-tions, repressions, sublimations: of such stuff, it is said, are our sleeping and waking dreams made; in our directest doings we act or react from wishes of which we are not conscious. So runs the code. But not even the most dogmatic expounder of this new heraldry has ventured to assign any (beyond the obvious) motive to the beneficent activities of the book-collector. The bibliophile, as the centuries have shown, is to his hobby born, and can best be explained in his own terms. Behind all the paraphernalia of bibliography, behind the bookshops, auctions, exhibitions, catalogues, collations and research which define the collector's efforts, is the single fact of a love of books.

The second number of the *Book-Collector's Quarterly* recorded editorially "Letters of congratulation which have reached us from near and far.... Our circulation has already reached to the third thousand, and we hope that by the conclusion of our first year we shall have reached to the fifth." The periodical maintained its declared intention of casting a net wide enough to include all kinds of book-collector by putting between the covers of one issue articles as diverse as those of Alfred Fairbank on calligraphy, Vyvyan Holland on fashion plates and Desmond Flower on the history of *The Fleuron*. This diversity of aim was appreciated. The periodical was, in its own world, a success.

The relations between the two editors were extremely friendly; and Flower has recorded that he never enjoyed anything more than the four years he spent in struggling with the periodical, and with his co-editor. Those who co-operated with A.J. in any enterprise, literary or commercial, were likely to experience a mounting intoxication caused by the bubble of ideas that rose from his effervescent mind, with intervals of dejection brought by the recognition that he was unwilling to lend himself to the practical work of carrying through most of these ideas to a conclusion. A division of labour was arranged between the two editors, by which A.J. wrote the editorials, and suggested and arranged most of the contributions; Flower wrote some articles, dealt with the printers and made up each number. This arrangement had the advantage for A.J. that he was able to extend the area of his acquaintance, and that he had no need to concern himself with distasteful matters of routine; it had the disadvantage for Flower that he was exposed to all the vagaries of his co-editor's brilliant mind, and to his extravagant unconcern with dates and times.

"My great difficulty", he notes, "was to get anything out of him. A solemn promise that I should have some proofs back the next day went for nothing. When at last I had extracted the proofs from him he would ring up the next day impatiently inquiring when printed copies would be ready. At other times he would produce a brilliant editorial—such as the attack on the Dean and Chapter of York for their sale of incunabula to America—with bewildering speed, often written on the first scraps of paper which came to hand. To my embarrassment I once received an article written on the backs of a number of drafts of an appeal to his friends for funds when the Club was in low water."

Flower also soon became aware that his co-editor's love of an ingenious, and profitable, financial transaction, had made A.J. a number of enemies. A letter to a bookseller in the Midlands asking for an item from his catalogue on approval, brought Flower the reply that he could have it, if he was prepared to give an assurance that he had nothing to do with Mr. A. J. A. Symons. A question to A.J. about the matter brought no exact reply but only a mischievous look, followed by an expression of boredom and the words: "I remember the case. A stupid fellow." In spite of his character as the disciple of one who, within his chosen field, seemed to have read all books and to possess all knowledge, Flower was uneasily aware that it was necessary for him to stay continually alert "To ensure that A.J. did not perpetrate a business deal which, while perfectly legitimate, nevertheless benefited only one person, who would not be myself".

It is certainly true that A.J.'s ingenious financial arrangements were designed primarily to benefit himself; but they had generally the secondary effect of benefiting the other person involved in the transaction. There are, to be sure, all kinds of benefits; no Marxian economist, A.J. believed that he was conferring a benefit upon a collector when he sold him a rare book, at a rare price, to complete a rare collection. The original purchase price of the book seemed to him an irrelevant consideration. It was a joint benefit of this kind—a material one to himself and a

The Ingenious Financier

spiritual one to Desmond Flower—that he envisaged by the transaction into which, in spite of his alertness, Flower was lured.

It was A.J.'s habit to disarm friends who might possibly feel some irritation with him by an invitation to dinner, the gift of a book which they had mentioned casually in conversation or the provision of some information that they needed, which he had unearthed personally with a good deal of trouble. A typical story (though I do not know that she felt any irritation needing assuagement) is that told by Doris Langley Moore. A.J. shared with her an enthusiasm for the work of the artist Henry Moses, and he displayed perhaps too unrestricted a glee when he bought for fifteen shillings a Henry Moses book for which she had just paid three pounds. When however, some weeks later, he discovered that his copy was a finer one than Mrs. Moore's, he presented it to her with the inscription: "After forty days in the wilderness Moses reached the promised land."

In response, then, to Flower's exasperated enquiries for the delivery of editorials or the return of proofs, A.J. would ask his co-editor to try some wine which he had just discovered, or to dine with him at the Sette of Odde Volumes; or he would be full of information about Ernest Dowson. He had communicated to Flower his own enthusiasm for the work of this Nineties poet, and now he offered him a remarkable Dowson "find", made some little time before; nothing less than a black leatherette notebook with marbled endpapers, containing forty poems of Dowson's that had never been published, and variant versions of many other poems. A.J. had bought this notebook very cheaply; and it gave him, of course, a powerful position with regard to any fresh edition of Dowson's poems. He had made tentative arrangements with two publishers, one of whom wished to print a limited edition of the unpublished poems, while the other proposed to issue the poet's complete Works. Both publishers contemplated paying A.J. £100; this sum was to include a considerable amount of creative work which, as always, he felt some reluctance to do. What a splendid arrangement it would be for both of them if Flower bought the notebook and, fired as he was with enthusiasm for Dowson's work, produced the Collected Poems himself. A.J. bent his energy to procuring that desirable consummation.

> As I am now committed to Wilde (he wrote to Flower), and in addition propose to issue, this year, through the Club, a bibliography of Moore, and there is also the Quarterly, it is not easy for me to settle with Gregynog and Lane, though I could do with their money. . . . How would it suit you, or your revered father, or your venerated firm, to buy the manuscript book from me for £300? It could then lie fallow, or you could edit it yourself.

The book, as A.J. observed, was well worth £300, judging (perhaps rather deceptively) by the "current rate of MS. Dowson poems"; its original cost to him, however, was not much more than one-tenth of that figure. But the bait was tempting, the notebook was purchased, not for £300 but for something near it, and Desmond Flower speedily found himself involved in a series of intricate financial transactions by which he made loans to A.J. on his motor-car and advanced money on manuscripts which he felt little inclination to purchase. "Would it suit *you* to take over the Dowsons, and set them (or £100 of them)? against the motor-car money? That would leave you free to pay Elkin Mathews and so square up everything." Such a note, unintelligible at this period of time, indicates how thoroughly Flower, in spite of his caution, was entrapped in the web that the ingenious financier was spinning round himself.

In Flower's case the issue was a happy one. (Although in other cases it was not so happy.) His loan was, after a lapse of time, repaid, and Cassells *did* publish an elegant edition of Dowson's Collected Poems; an edition in which Flower paid tribute gracefully to "Mr. A. J. A. Symons, for to hours of delight and wonder spent among his books and to evenings of even greater delight and wonder graced by his conversation I owe the fact that I have been able to undertake the interesting task of preparing this edition".

This transaction was one of several in which my brother engaged in an attempt to allay the storm of debts that threatened to break over his head, without reducing his personal expenditure or abandoning luncheons and parties in favour of literary work. He was less dismayed than infuriated by the period of trade depression with which the Thirties opened; such conditions gave no scope to his talents. He adhered, not quite consciously, to a Stevensonian optimism which made him think that any check in material prosperity must be merely temporary; and he applied this view to his own and to the national economy. When placed in a difficult financial position, his reaction was the defiant one of a swimmer who finds himself out of his depth and swims onward to a raft instead of returning to the shore; although the analogy is inexact, because in A.J.'s case no raft was visible, and swimming onward was purely an act of faith. This kind of faith he possessed abundantly. Was it not perfectly possible, after all, that another Dowson notebook might come his way to-morrow?

Retrenchment of any kind was distasteful to him, but

A. J. A. Symons

in one form or another it became inevitable; and at last he decided to sell the library of Nineties books and manuscripts which he had collected over several years. The sacrifice was a considerable one but when he had decided that it was necessary, he made it without hesitation. The Catalogue prepared by Elkin Mathews had an elegant Aubrey Beardsley drawing on the cover, and contained an appreciative note on the collection by Holbrook Jackson. The choicest items, Jackson suggested, were those labelled Beardsley, Corvo, Dowson and Lionel Johnson. The Beardsley section contained an original pen-and-ink drawing for Leonard Smithers' Catalogue, valued at £105, a proof of the suppressed design done for *The Savoy* of John Bull shown in a state of sexual excitement, and several of Beardsley's posters. The section given to Baron Corvo contained the holograph manuscript of *The Desire and Pursuit of the Whole*, the original manuscript draft of *Hubert's Arthur* (both of these books were subsequently published by Cassell), and seventy-one venomous letters from Corvo to Grant Richards which were valued at £300. The Dowson treasury ran to forty-seven items, half of them with Dowson's own autograph. Many minor figures of the period were just as fully represented. The whole Catalogue contained over a thousand items, and the total value put upon them by their owner was more than £3,500.

The realization of such a sum would have paid all of his debts, and left him with the considerable financial resources which he never, in his lifetime, possessed. I am sure that he never had £1,000, unencumbered by debt, to his credit in a bank. Whenever he obtained considerable sums of money he used them to buy books, to buy clothes, or to lay down some wine; he was constant to his often-expressed belief that personal property could

be both beautiful and useful, whereas money consisted
merely of paper and metal pieces which were not, in
general, of an appearance aesthetically pleasing. He was
always annoyed, I think that there should be any relation
at all between these pieces of paper and the possession of
books and pictures, and if his book sale had realized £3,500
it is likely that the money would have been quickly
metamorphosed into possessions.

By his own standard of optimism the sale was not a
success, although it could not justly be called a failure. The
time was not propitious for selling books, or anything
else; and the American book-collectors on whom he had
placed great reliance because the rate of exchange enabled
them to buy English books cheaply, had their own troubles.
In America as well as in Britain the number of unemployed
swelled. The poor went on the bread-line and the rich
lost some dividends and cut down their expenditure upon
such luxuries as books. The sum of £1,000 realized by
sale from the Catalogue was, in these conditions, not
at all a bad one, but it spelled disaster for A.J. With the
failure of the sale he was no longer disturbed simply by
the necessity of cutting down expenses. He was faced,
instead, by the likelihood of the loss of home and income;
the sums of money involved were not large but, for him,
they were vital.

CHAPTER VIII

THE CATASTROPHE

D URING 1931 the fortunes of the First Edition Club
declined steadily in fact, although not immediately in appearance. In a desperate attempt
to increase the membership the Club held more, and more
varied, exhibitions in the first half of this year than at any
time in its history; and in a time of commercial prosperity
these carefully-planned exhibitions might have had a
considerable beneficial influence. But the weight of
economic circumstance, and of expenditure, was too great,
and as the year passed even the bravest optimism was
necessarily dimmed.

In January the Club held an exhibition of "Books
Illustrating the Art of Good Living", a subject in which
my brother had become increasingly interested through
his friendship with André Simon, who had collected these
books. The books shown included a leaf from Gutenberg's
42-line Bible, containing Isaiah's prophecy of the vine; a
number of controversies between wine, beer and cider;
and the Rent Book of the Monastery of Polling, in Upper
Bavaria, showing the machinery of Estate administration
in the late fourteenth century. The Exhibition included,
also, several accounts of food and drink purchased in great
households of the past. The most interesting of them was,
perhaps, the household account of King Henri II of France
on January 21, 1552. The day was one of abstinence from
meat, but the establishment purchased pike, roach, carp,

gudgeon, crawfish, a sea turtle, oysters, soles, cod, white and red herrings, and four vipers, as well as twenty-five pints of red and twenty-five pints of white wine for the six Royal children.

In February the Club showed an exhibition of the printed work of John Bell, founder of the *Morning Post* and several other newspapers; it was opened by Lord Riddell, owner of the *News of the World*. An exhibition of Illuminated Manuscript Books, and one of modern German bookbinding was followed by the Fifty Books of the Year and a display of the copy books of English writing masters of the seventeenth and eighteenth centuries. These exhibitions, all of them displayed within the first seven months of the year, testify to the Secretary's activity. Club publications announced as "in the Press" included an account of Swift's Library by Harold Williams, a translation of Meleager by Baron Corvo, Aubrey Beardsley's Letters to Leonard Smithers, an account of the rarest ancient Irish books by Shane Leslie, a bibliographical catalogue of the Exhibition of Printers' Specimen Books held by the Club in 1925, two peepshows by modern artists, and a special edition of a treatise on English Writing Masters by Ambrose Heal. The last-mentioned of these books was the only one published during the year: most of them were delayed for a very long time, and some were not published at all. The comedy of the Nineties Bibliography was carried a step further by the announcement in the *Book-Collector's Quarterly*, through a double-page spread in the advertisement pages, that the book was "Now in the Press. In order to expedite production, publication will be made in three compact volumes, instead of the single-volume form originally contemplated. Price to pre-publication subscribers, six guineas." Foyles had long ago lost interest in the book,

A. J. A. Symons

and resigned themselves to a certain loss on it (a loss which
they perhaps offset to some extent, in their minds, by the
help my brother gave them in preparing the publicity
material for their Literary Luncheons, which were just
then being launched); and my brother approached
publisher after publisher, in an attempt to obtain the
financial backing for the Bibliography which he was unable to provide himself. Some contemplated publication,
but all at length drew back; and he turned to Fisher, whose
fortunes had changed considerably, and for the better,
in the past few years, with a scheme which gave no
indication of his real financial plight, but broached ideas
for publication of the book which were, as usual, ingenious
and plausible:

> This election is a frightful nuisance; and its coming at the
> present time has considerably disturbed my plans. At the
> present moment I am arranging (amongst my other occupa-
> tions!) to issue, in three volumes, my long-famed Biblio-
> graphy. There are two reasons why I want to get it out in
> that way. The first is that, by producing a volume a year, I
> can reduce what remains to be done to three reasonably sized
> jobs; and the second, equally cogent, is that on the appear-
> ance of vol. 1 I can get back the £350 I have already paid on
> a/c of work done to the printer. But unfortunately the im-
> minence of this wretched election has scared off Secker, the
> publisher, with whom I had virtually come to terms; and I
> have no hope of fixing up a similar arrangement elsewhere
> for weeks, till people are satisfied which way the cat will
> jump over all this political business. This has created a situa-
> tion of some difficulty for me. It occurs to me that you may
> care to help me out of it in one or two ways. (1) Would you
> care to have a dip at getting your Brazil Traction loss back
> by coming in as sleeping or financial partner in the publishing
> of the 90's book? In that event I should abandon my search
> for a *publisher* as partner, and issue the book on my own a/c
> (or rather on ours) through the Club. Over a period of three
> years we should each make from £500 to £1,000 profit

The Catastrophe

(total, not annually). I won't quote the figures in detail at the moment, but roughly it will cost £2,000 to produce 1,000 copies of the three volumes saleable at 6 gs. Allowing 33⅓% trade discount the revenue accruing from the edition if exhausted would be £4,000. Two years ago the whole edition could have been sold in six months. Now I expect to sell half (500) in 12. A sale of 450 copies will cover costs, and thereafter every copy sold will be almost 100% profit. No large sum of capital, moreover, will be needed, as (a) the revenue from 1 volume will help to finance the next; and (b) I already have 200 orders, gained by preliminary prospectus years ago, which could easily be increased when once the book is really ready. But I cannot finance the book myself now, because so far from being able to put up more money when needed, my domestic economy makes me want to withdraw the £350 I have already put up. Hence, in return for financial support I will gladly part with a share in the return. Of course there is no absolute certainty of return, but I have now published, through the Club, nineteen books, and made a profit on each, so that (failing revolution or some chaos of that sort, when nothing much will matter) I am confident, certain (in my own mind) to do as well with this, given time.

Nevertheless, since there is an indisputable element of the speculative in the scheme, you may feel it is a risk which a professional publisher should take. In that event I shall be more than grateful if you will help me in another way. My immediate problem will be solved if I can cash in even half of the £350 sunk in the book. Can you advance me this amount, for the time being—say six months—so that I can either conclude a new arrangement with a publisher, or get the book forward through the Club? Needless to say I should not even suggest this if I were not utterly confident of repaying you.

Perhaps Fisher did not share his friend's confidence about the profit on the book. In any case he expressed himself unable to advance the money, and in spite of the *Book-Collector's Quarterly* announcement the Bibliography still remained in proof form.

A. J. A. Symons

At the same time that my brother was attempting to improve his personal position by this move of expansion, moves of retrenchment were being made by the Club. In February Williamson was wintering, as usual, in Torquay, and A.J. wrote to him after a Committee meeting. The problem was, he said, that the Club was facing a yearly loss of approximately £1,400. What was needed was £20,000 capital, with no liability attaching to it. Unfortunately there seemed no hope of obtaining that. The Committee had agreed that at a time of national crisis a general appeal for the First Edition Club would not meet with approval. They were thrown back then, Lord Esher suggested, upon what he called, "the ingenious exercise of the wits of the Secretary".

What did the Secretary propose? His suggestions were sharp and sensible. They must abandon the catering, which cost £350 a year. The dining room and garden room must be let "to a solicitor or some other respectable person". They must declare a moratorium of debenture interest. And they must have a whip round among the members, asking them to contribute £10 each. These suggestions were certainly drastic but, A.J. said, so far from inducing pessimism, they "filled him with the greatest cheerfulness". When these steps had been taken the Club would be able to stand on its feet, and what, after all, would they be asking of the members? No more than a modest tenner a head!

Williamson's reaction was far from cheerful. "It is all very terrible", he wrote, "but I am sure it is right." Nevertheless the whole thing upset him; and, typically, his concern with the major difficulties of the situation did not prevent him from attending to points of detail. Would they be able to keep the garden? The lavatory must be retained—the tenants must be satisfied with use of it. Who would pay for towels? Who would attend to the boiler? Who would cook for A.J.? Many similar questions agitated him; and he signed himself, "Yours very sorrowfully, very gloomily and very sadly". He slept badly through worry; and while he lay awake at night fresh points occurred to him, which he embodied in daily letters to the Secretary. They must be sure not to let the dining room for more than a year. Lord Vaux had written him a very worrying letter about the debenture position. "I believe that when we send out our terrible ultimatum we had better register every letter so as to be *quite certain* that every Debenture Holder *especially* and if possible every Member has it and we must enclose forms and *envelopes* or we shall never get replies".

In March the circular letters were sent out; and the anxious Williamson, and the equally anxious Secretary, waited for results. It is hardly surprising that they were not good. The 400 members had already been subjected to one appeal; now, in a time of trade depression, they were asked for money, and those of them who had bought debentures were told that they would receive no interest. Some members wrote indignantly or sarcastically about the debentures; some resigned because of the loss of the dining room facilities; very few subscribed the "modest tenner" for which they were asked. Williamson became seriously alarmed, and urged A.J. to approach the few rich people who were interested in the Club. In particular Lord Riddell, who had opened the John Bell exhibition, must be approached. He could not run the risk any longer of being upset and un-nerved by the affair and, he pointed out to A.J., "after all, it is your home and occupation that is at stake, and not mine." Lord Riddell was approached; but he replied that he could not enter into engagements which involved expenditure of time or money, and ended

A. J. A. Symons

his letter with the philosophical observation that it is
better to be a live dog than a dead lion.

Once again, however, both my brother's and Williamson's spirits rose as creditors momentarily ceased to
press, the Fifty Books of the Year exhibition obtained a
good deal of publicity, and A.J. found some more
guarantors. He produced the ingenious suggestion that
guarantees should be "taken at 15 per cent discount"—
that is, for a guarantee of £100 Williamson should allow
the Club to draw £85. Williamson grumbled a little,
but complied; and a crisis was averted.

But not for long. Before the end of the year it was
evident to all the Directors that the Club could not be
carried on in its existing form. At a meeting which was
more regretful than stormy it was decided to appoint a
Receiver, wind up the Limited Company, and if possible
continue the Club at Little Russell Street. Williamson
did not attend this meeting, but his letter of acknowledgement shows his relief at what he took to be the end of the
affair, and the freeing of his securities.

> You are a very brave man, because it concerns you more
> intimately in some ways than it does anyone else, and I think
> that the scheme you have drawn up does much credit both
> to your heart and your head. . . . It is, of course, a backward
> step, but in these times of very severe financial stress we have
> to take backward steps, and to economise in directions that
> one has not hitherto even considered. It will be a severe blow
> to Mrs. Symons, and a serious one to you, it has meant some
> pluck on the part of both of you to have dealt in such broad
> fashion with a very complex situation, but the result is
> excellent and admirable, and I welcome it with enthusiasm.

A few days later, on the eve of departure to Torquay,
he felt less elated. They must, he said, get a substantial sum
for the lease, for "It will never do to have to apply to our

guarantors." In any case, he looked to A.J. to protect his interests, because he could not afford to lose any money; and as a further protection, when he departed for Torquay, he put his affairs into the hands of his solicitor.

The winding up of the Company did not, however, work out as Williamson had expected and A.J. had hoped. The lease was not sold for some time, and then it was sold at a loss because of trading conditions; the Debenture Holders were forced to accept a settlement of 2s. in the £; and the question of the guarantees (of which the signatories had been assured that "It is extremely unlikely that events will be so untoward that these guarantees will require calling up") became acute.

The solicitor acting for Williamson felt, naturally, no particular reluctance in approaching the guarantors; equally naturally my brother was anxious that they should not be worried. Against Williamson's murmurs of indecision—it was necessary, he thought, to write to the guarantors at once—and in the face of A.J.'s protest against such an action, the solicitor briskly drafted, and sent out, a letter asking the guarantors to pay the amounts they had promised. The guarantors were approached with delicacy—but still, they were approached. To Williamson's horror very few of them replied; and his distress was increased by the fact that the more carefully his solicitor considered the form of guarantee, the more difficult he found it to decide whether the document was susceptible of legal action. Williamson's letters to A.J. were backed, and perhaps at times prompted, by the advice of his solicitor who naturally felt none of Williamson's tenderness for the First Edition Club, its secretary, or its guarantors. They reveal a growing anger, and sense of the injustice done to one whose actions had,

A. J. A. Symons

as he observed, been moved only by a desire to help the Club and its Secretary. All the money spent had been for A.J.'s advantage, and, but for Williamson's help, where would A.J.'s occupation and livelihood have been? What, also, about the Secretary's own guarantee, which had reached the figure of £500? "You certainly will have to pay up something and it ought to be substantial". He cannot have been soothed by A.J.'s letters in reply, in which he saw himself as the injured party.

If I may say so, you do not seem to realize at all how very lucky you are. You are the only director of the unfortunate Company who has not had to pay very dearly over this matter. Esher has lost £1,000 in Debentures, given £500 to the creditors, and guaranteed £300, which he will ultimately have to pay. Lord Vaux has lost £500 and paid £300 to the creditors. Ehrman has lost £350 in Debentures, has given £200 to the creditors, and guaranteed £200. I myself have had to take over responsibility for any loss the Club may hereafter make, and lost £500 on guarantees, as well as the loss there is certain to be this year.

You, although you were a Director of the Company, and Chairman of the Committee, have lost far less than any of us, even supposing that there is ultimately a deficit of £250 or £300 on the loan. I am very glad, for your sake, that it is so; but, in view of the fact, I think you ought to make a very special effort to keep faith with those who, on the strength of your assurances, have made, so recently, sacrifices to keep the club going.

What A.J. called "keeping faith" was an agreement by Williamson to allow his securities to remain in the Bank at the Club's disposal, and to withdraw the request to the guarantors to make payment. Instead he received a letter from Williamson's solicitor asking for confirmation of the fact that Williamson's resignation from his Director-ship of the Club had taken effect. He replied acidly: "It is the present wish, of course, of every Director of the Company to resign; and when these matters have been cleared up, steps will be taken to that end."

But, as he must gradually have become aware, he was fighting a losing battle against the energetic solicitor. One by one the unhappy guarantors paid up; and the solicitor demanded payment also from A.J. It was in vain that he said he had recently been unable to find a cheque for £10, that he was much the poorest person involved in these transactions, and that he had been virtually ruined by the turn of events. "I must have time", he said, "and if I cannot get it your client will be the loser as well as myself." But the solicitor pointed out that he had property in Clapham and at Finchingfield in Essex (where he had taken a house, in circumstances to be recounted); that he lived in comfortable circumstances and kept a car; and that he possessed the assets of the First Edition Club (which he had bought from the Receiver by mortgaging problematic advance royalties from his projected biography of Oscar Wilde and by obtaining a loan on his Life Insurane). He had no intention of leaving A.J. scot-free to pay nothing until some unspecified future date, but intended to recover whatever money could be obtained from him. Pressed, some will think justly and others uncharitably, to this far end, A.J. made a statement of his resources which shows the small margin upon which he precariously maintained himself, and his total lack of any financial backing; it is also a good example of the delusive clarity of what may be called his financial literary style, exemplified already in his letter to Fisher about the Bibliography:

> I appreciate that you require amplification of my position (he wrote to the solicitor), and I am prepared to deal not only with the points you raise, but also with any other that you may feel inclined to put. I do not instantly put you in touch

with my solicitor, as I have no wish to incur any expense whatsoever at present if I can avoid it. If it becomes necessary I will do so, but I hope to obviate the necessity by this correspondence.

You say I have property at Cedars Road, Clapham. That is true. There is, however, a mortgage of £1,100 thereon, which I am being pressed to reduce, and cannot do so (the mortgage holder has agreed to leave the matter as it stands in view of the circumstances). The property is in the possession of my mother, who discharges the outgoings. Otherwise I should be forced to abandon this property.

The house at Finchingfield is not mine. I pay £60 per year rent for it; and though that seemed cheap when I took it, I doubt if I could find anybody willing to take it over at that price to-day. I may mention also that my rent is in arrears there, though I hope to pay it up shortly.

I have, as you say, a car. I began to purchase this on the hire system nearly two years ago. In March of this year, being several instalments behind, the hire-purchase company repossessed themselves of the vehicle, and in order not to lose the whole of my previous payments, I had to pay at once the remaining balance, both due and not due. That being utterly beyond my power, I was lent £100 by a friend for the purpose, on the security of the car; which, however, would not, if sold, realize the amount of the loan, which is still outstanding.

The assets of the Club are (or will be) legally mine. I have contracted to buy them for £500 from the Receiver. Of this, £250 remains to be paid. It will, I trust, very largely be set off (this remaining £250) by the sum which will become due from the Receiver to me by virtue of the debentures I hold. It can, therefore, be agreed that in effect the club belongs to me. Its assets consist of (a) furniture, suitable for that purpose only (as showcases), of next to no sale value: (b) stock of publications, which I cannot convert into cash save very gradually, and (c) goodwill. The goodwill is obviously contingent on the club being able to be carried on. Until December next it is a liability, and not an asset at all. The subscriptions for the year were very largely spent in conducting the Club for three months at Bedford Square:

The Catastrophe

and now, in order to continue it until January next, when the subscriptions again fall due, I shall have to borrow money, if I can. Unless you, on Dr. Williamson's behalf, take steps against me, I imagine that I can; but it is, of course, not certain.

Now as to the debit side of my balance sheet. At the moment of writing I owe Barclay's Bank over £500. As securities they have (a) a life-policy valued in March at £88; (b) personal guarantees from Mr. H. V. Marrot and another. I also owe the Royal Bank of Scotland £501, covered by (a) a personal guarantee and (b) a charge on moneys becoming due to me from the sale of books (this as to 50% of the proceeds of such sales) and (c) a lien on the first proceeds of the sale of my Wilde edition and royalties thereon, when it is published.

In addition to these, I have a considerable number of debts, all of comparatively small sums, which aggregate to a by no means negligible total. To meet these I have arranged that they shall be paid off by degrees, through my solicitor, from the 50% proceeds of sale of books which is not allocated to the Royal Bank of Scotland.

Over and above these I have been forced to contract a number of personal loans during recent months. I owe nothing, however, to moneylenders.

Under my guarantee to Dr. Williamson I owe £450; and the guarantee I have given in respect of 17 Bedford Square will, in my opinion, end in a loss, and therefore liability, of £350.

Against all this, I have a certain amount of furniture and personal effects, worth to-day probably a sixth of what I paid for them; i.e., well under £500—probably not more than half that sum.

You will appreciate, therefore, that if you, as Dr. Williamson's adviser, think it the right course to take action against me, I shall have no recourse but to file my petition. In that event, my bankers will, of course, recover from my guarantors, who will then figure as creditors for the sum they have paid. My total liabilities will amount to a considerable figure, and I cannot see how any creditor would get more than a shilling or so in the pound.

A. J. A. Symons

The case is an impressive one: but A.J.'s artistic sense of balance, as well as his inherent optimism, did not permit him to leave it at this point, which might have shaken even Williamson's solicitor. His revelation of the reverse of the medal partly nullified his own case:

> That being so, and my position being so difficult, you may naturally ask why I do not file my petition at once, and so escape from the net in which I am confined at present. As it is my purpose in this letter to make the whole situation clear to you, I will anticipate the question, and answer it at once.
>
> Though I have many creditors, no one of them is pressing me now, or is likely to press me, unless you force me to commit an act of bankruptcy. To take my liabilities in the reverse order to that in which I have set them out:
>
> 1. My co-guarantors of Bedford Square, realizing my utter inability to pay, have reconciled themselves to bearing my proportion between them, and have given this resolution effect to the extent of already paying my share of the rent that has fallen due.
> 2. The personal friends who have lent me money, whose good opinion you may be surprised to find I still retain, sympathize with my position, and do not even ask for interest. Naturally they expect to be paid when times improve; and, though you may not think so, they will be paid.
> 3. My general debts have been reduced already, and these creditors realize that I am doing what I can.
> 4. The Bank of Scotland will receive part of what is owing to them this year, and will wait for the Wilde edition to provide the rest.
> 5. Barclay's Bank have asked for a reduction, but are not very materially concerned over my account, as their guarantee from Mr. Marrot covers them.
> 6. Under my agreement with the Receiver I am under heavy penalties if I do not carry on the Club until the end of the year: but these only arise in that contingency, which I am positive of averting unless Dr.

The Catastrophe

Williamson acts against me, in which event they will merely swell the list of my creditors.

7. The motor-car transaction is a static one, and can be dealt with later.
8. The interest on the Cedars Road property is paid to date.

The point arises, what can be done for Dr. Williamson if he does not disturb the very delicate *status quo*. It is here that your action in the matter of the guarantors has been harmful to me. At present my sole income (or, rather, hope of it, for at present I have none) lies in the surplus that may exist between the revenue of the Club in a normal year and its diminished expenses for that year. Every defection from membership therefore takes three guineas at once away from the amount available to me for any purpose whatsoever. As you know, a number of guarantors have already resigned, and I am fearful that others will follow suit. However, it cannot be helped, though I want you and Dr. Williamson both to bear the circumstance in mind. . . .

In conclusion, let me say that though I am, of course, distressed that Dr. Williamson should be forced to wait, I am certain in my own mind that if he does, he will be paid every penny that I owe him. To my mind, the sympathy should come from him to me. The loss falls on me, not on him, ultimately. I entered on these guarantees in the hope of saving the Club, of which he has been for many years chairman; and, very largely as a result of my action, the Club has been put on a basis which, if he gives it time, will make it a permanency.

The solicitor stigmatized this letter as "the most deplorable document, of its kind, I have ever read" Nevertheless, it had some effect. We do not know what Williamson thought of it, or whether he was impressed by A.J.'s remark in a letter to him that "I have cut my expenses down to a minimum. A sandwich at a bar contents me in place of lunch; and I no longer take guests to the Odd Volume dinners." It was, in any event, agreed finally, although, by Williamson, reluctantly, that he would make a choice of the books remaining from the Elkin Mathews sale to the value of the debt. Even here A.J., salvaging something from the wreck of his fortunes, made an audacious proposal which Williamson accepted. He sold the books to Williamson at 20 per cent below list prices; and half of the money went to pay the debt, while half was paid to the Club funds.

The settlement in terms of books was protracted over a period of years, because of continual squabbling about the value of individual items, and Williamson's reluctance to place my brother's own high valuation upon Corvo items (and my brother's valuation, it should perhaps be said, has been fully justified).

The most notable feature of the First Edition Club catastrophe is not the small sum of money involved, although that is sufficiently remarkable; nor the fact that the Club's affairs were trusted so implicitly to a young man of thirty; but that, at the end of it all, A.J. emerged with the loss of very few friends. Those who knew him recognized the fact, which cannot be conveyed easily in this plain recital of fact, that idealism and ingenuity were woven inextricably in the character and actions of this young man who never finally decided what he required of life. There is, as one of the characters in *Citizen Kane* observes, no trick in making a lot of money—if all you want to do is to make a lot of money. But A.J.'s aim was never finally to make money; he valued it only as a symbol of success in the intricate game of chance which he made of life. Such enormous, and unsuccessful, gambles as those of Clarence Hatry and Jimmy White fascinated him, and he viewed their careers as spectacles which could be regarded with complete abrogation of the moral sense;

he envied the magnitude of their conceptions, and sometimes even the dramatic nature of their downfall. "The
gambler", he said, "wishes always in his heart to lose. He
is only content when he is ruined." He was never nearer
to complete ruin himself than at this time: pertinacity
and luck pulled him through, still, miraculously, owner
of that battered property the First Edition Club; still,
surprisingly, able to claim many friends.

His relations with Williamson, in their later stages,
were certainly marked with some acerbity. "When this
transaction has been completed", my brother wrote, "I
shall have handed over books value £563, and £70 in
cash, for the privilege of having helped the First Edition
Club, Ltd. That is my share of the loss, and it is quite
enough." He remarked that the thought made him feel
depressed. He received a reply from Williamson's secretary: "Dr. Williamson is sorry to hear that you are
depressed. He can assure you that he is a great deal more
so." But on the rare occasions when the two men met
Williamson felt a generous sympathy for his friend's
position, and an admiration for his talents, that overcame
his other feeling of indignation at what he considered
betrayal. He never resigned his membership of the Club;
and it was, after all that had happened, A.J. whom he
asked to catalogue his library, with its many valuable
association copies, after his death. But that task was
never performed, for the asthmatic Chairman, who was
an old and sick man in 1930, outlived the sprightly
Secretary, who seemed to be on the threshold of a new
career.

It was a career, certainly, that had received a setback.
The Club could no longer provide him with an income:
and he was forced to the attempt to make a position for
himself in a field where all his self-confidence fell away,

and he was left at the mercy of a perfectionism which made him uncertain of his talents, and unsatisfied with their performance. He attempted, now, to make a career by writing.

CHAPTER IX

THE QUEST FOR CORVO

H E turned to writing. But he flinched from the kind of creative effort involved in writing a novel or a play. He was still, in those fields, inexperienced; whereas his attempts to write the biographies for his Nineties book, buttressed by his studies of Baron Corvo, Edgar Allan Poe and Emin Pasha, had caused him to give much thought to the problem of producing a biography which should have the shape of art as well as the realism of life; he had embodied some of his ideas on this problem in an address to the City Literary Institute. When, therefore, at this nadir of his fortunes, he turned to writing as a fresh career, he took biography as his field: and the first subject he chose was the life of the explorer, Henry Morton Stanley.

My brother never attempted to write seriously about any subject that held for him less than a vital interest; and although, at a cursory glance, the life of the "short, square-headed, self-confident young American" would seem to hold few attractions for a Bloomsbury bibliographer and dandy, there were in fact several threads that drew my brother to Stanley. The explorer had realized many of the ambitions which A.J. held suppressed throughout his life, fulfilling them only in mimic form when pondering the difficulties of generalship over an Ordnance Map, or writing a report for the Race Game of his activities on the Turf. He was delighted by the career of such a resolute "man of action" as Stanley, whose vivid life might (he felt) by a turn of time and circumstance have been his own. It was one of his strengths as a biographer that he was able to make a close imaginative identification of his own character with his subject's, experiencing vicariously another's struggles and temptations, yet standing sufficiently far outside them to be able to make an analysis of character and motive. He felt in himself Stanley's self-command and astonishing will-power which "overruled everything", and drove him through such travails as "A forest where ants stung like wasps, where gorillas seized men and bit off their fingers one by one" and where, frequently, the white companions who accompanied him died. He felt a link, further, with this man who was deliberately mysterious about his education and antecedents, who although born of Welsh parents called himself an American, and who took the name of Stanley in preference to that of Rowlands, with which he had been born. He used in this book, with some modification, part of the study of Emin Pasha which had already been published: and he was fascinated by the contrast between Stanley and Emin, extrovert and introvert, the direct, self-reliant, ruthless explorer with his "strong love for the centre of the stage" and the pliable, negative, enduring figure of Emin. The two men represent, he said, "Those types of human ability between which repulsion is a natural law". And his final judgment of Stanley is applicable as much (or even more) to himself as to the explorer:

His personality and will, and the achievements which were based on them, remain as a memorable testimony to the development which lies within the reach of all who possess by birth—or can acquire—sufficient self-control to withstand adverse circumstances and triumphantly support the privilege of life.

In its combination of a smooth style with intelligent compression *H. M. Stanley* is a model short biography, although it is not free from the intrusion of the kind of attempt to attain a "period" atmosphere which my brother had mocked in his address to the City Literary Institute on "Tradition in Biography":

> Shelley was then nine years of age and Wordsworth twelve; George IV was King, Canning Prime Minister; and though ten years had passed since the battle of Waterloo, the Corn Law Repeal Act had not yet been framed.

This "method", as he said, required almost as much patience to write as it does to read: but is there not a hint of it in his own opening phrases?

> In the January of 1871, when the German armies were encamped round Paris waiting for the city to surrender and half Europe was trying to foresee the consequences of Napoleon the Third's downfall, a short, square-headed, self-confident young American, giving his name as Henry M. Stanley, disembarked from a small whaling brigantine at the island of Zanzibar.

The book was published in Duckworth's inexpensive "Great Lives" series. It was received amiably, but with no particular critical accolades, and earned its author no more than the first small advance on account of royalties. Such a result was not encouraging: but, with the First Edition Club temporarily moribund, and no other regular source of income available, my brother set to work on another biography, and this time a full-length one. Oscar Wilde was the obvious subject, a subject to which he was already contracted, and on which he had collected, through years of research, an enormous mass of material: but there were several reasons which made it difficult for him to settle to his book on Wilde. The most potent was the fact that he had already mortgaged his future royalties, in the way already described, so that the book would be of little help in satisfying his creditors; another was the opposition of Lord Alfred Douglas to certain material which my brother felt it essential to include—an opposition which was not diminished, but rather lent additional point, by the fact that poet and biographer were on the friendliest terms, and addressed each other in letters as "Bosie" and "Ajaccio"; a third was my brother's haunting feeling that his knowledge, although exceedingly comprehensive, was still far from complete. He looked instead to a theme that was both ready and congenial, and set to work on the full-length picture of a character he had already sketched —Frederick William Rolfe, Baron Corvo.

When he added Corvo to Stanley in his list of biographical studies my brother accepted, I think, the limitations of his own nature. He showed in everyday life such a rare dramatic sense, he told stories so effectively and with such power of invention, that it was easy to imagine him as a successful practitioner of some other form of art. But he lacked insight into the character, or interest in the actions, of other people except as they afforded an opportunity of matching their characters against his own, or of placing them as the central figure in dramatic events; and he had, I think, in his early thirties come to realize this, although he never acknowledged it. The hero— frustrated or victorious, but always lonely—was the figure that held attraction for him, and he endowed this hero, who for him was typical of the ambitions, although

not of the achievements, of mankind, with a measure
of freewill hardly less great than that granted by an
Elizabethan dramatist, or Thomas Carlyle.

Very unwillingly he became cognisant of modern
psychology, very reluctantly he accepted some of its
inferences about the unconscious motives of his heroes'
actions. He discovered also with surprise, and rejected with
indignation, the political determinism which is a feature
of modern Socialist theory, and which replaced his view
of the members of the Gironde in the French Revolution
as romantic, noble and tragic moral figures, by a con-
temptuous dismissal of them as political ignoramuses out
of touch with their time. The opening lines of his study of
Emin Pasha embody with characteristic bravura the view
of life that he always expressed publicly:

> "Circumstances", exclaimed Napoleon, in one of those
> boasts that have the emphasis of the theatre in their elo-
> quence, "Circumstances!--I *make* circumstances!" This is
> the strength of the strong, the strength of Mussolini and
> Bismarck. Such destiny-defying power must always delight
> our dramatic sense.

The gesture of the falling Titan who defies the world
was one that constantly fascinated my brother; and he
pondered at times whether "Ajax" would not be a more
suitable and symbolic name for him to adopt than the
letters A.J. which he had chosen. But self-confidence was
mixed with self-distrust in his character. He suspected a
certain vulgarity inherent in his tendency to dramatize,
and the reluctance he always felt to mark a sheet of paper
with a pen was magnified many times by the idea of
producing fictional works whose course would be wholly
dependent upon his own taste and judgment. He felt
biography to be safer ground; for here at least a personal

taste could be justified by the odd patterns of life, and the task of selection and arrangement was one that he could approach with confidence.

The story of Frederick William Rolfe will be familiar to readers of *The Quest For Corvo*; I summarize it here for the benefit of those who do not know my brother's book. Rolfe was a Catholic rejected for the priesthood, of homosexual inclination, who died in Venice, at the age of fifty-three, in 1913. He wrote several books of which five (*Stories Toto Told Me*, *In His Own Image*, *Hadrian the Seventh*, *Don Tarquinio* and *Chronicles of the House of Borgia*) had been published at the time my brother's biography appeared; and these were so little known that Rolfe's name was unmentioned in Holbrook Jackson's book chronicle of the period *The Eighteen Nineties*. Rolfe was litigious, quarrelsome, poor and frustrated; he adopted, as a compensation for his rejection as a Catholic priest, the imaginary Barony of Corvo; he wrote, in a beautiful script, much that was venomous, imaginative, and merely odd; his life was full of self-created mysteries and miseries. This was the man of whose life and works my brother went in quest.

"My quest for Corvo was started by accident one summer afternoon in 1925, in the company of Christopher Millard." Those are the first words of *The Quest For Corvo*; and, like much else that my brother said and wrote, they have an imaginative, rather than a factual, truth. I mean by this that Millard, the grey-haired, disreputable, handsome bookseller and bibliophile who produced under the pen-name of Stuart Mason a bibliography of Oscar Wilde's writings, may well have lent A.J. Frederick Rolfe's *Hadrian the Seventh* on that day when they talked together of unjustly-neglected books in Millard's little garden; but this assuredly was not the first work of Rolfe's that my brother had read. He describes vividly the impact which a first reading of *Hadrian the Seventh* had upon him; and how Millard then lent him the pornographic letters which Rolfe had written from Venice in the last year of his life. The contrast between the generous human aspirations of *Hadrian* and the gleeful perversion of the letters makes an admirable opening to the book: but the effect obtained is one of literary conjuring rather than of literal truth. "The secret", A.J. remarked to Edward Wadsworth, "lies in the sequence"; and I am not implying here any criticism either of my brother or his book, but showing simply one instance of many in which he was able to turn his dramatic sense to good use. The encounter with Millard seemed to him a good stepping-off place for his tale, and he used it accordingly.

A.J. became interested in Rolfe, as one of the strangest artificial orchids of the Nineties, when he first projected his Bibliography; he was in correspondence with Shane Leslie (to whom *The Quest For Corvo* is dedicated) and had read his biographical account of Rolfe in *The London Mercury*, and the stories which Rolfe contributed to *The Yellow Book*, some two years before that afternoon in Millard's garden. Admiration of Rolfe's writing, and interest in him as a character, moved my brother conjointly; and, with his usual enthusiasm, he set himself to discover something of the history of this neglected writer.

The paper which he read to the Sette of Odd Volumes has already been mentioned; this paper, which had its germ in one of the Nineties biographies, was a pencil sketch rather than a finished portrait, but it holds one or two points of special interest, both in literary style, and in its treatment of the subject. In manner this essay paid tribute to that biographical convention of the twenties (which is not, unhappily, altogether dead even in our own day) which permitted a writer to produce whole paragraphs, and even pages, backed by no obvious factual authority and consisting generally of an ingenious use by the author of fact and conjecture for his own purpose:

> This mysterious Baron actually appeared at Harland's Thursday afternoon tea-parties in the Cromwell Road. Tall, priestly-visaged, eagle-nosed, clean-shaven, middle-aged, clothed in plain blue serge or white drill, reticent, unsmiling, wearing strange rings and using stranger words, he was obviously eccentric and a man of parts. . . . Probably he would have told you that he had starved in England, and that the Welsh had treated him less kindly than the Scots; he might have referred to his paintings, or explained that he was a tonsured clerk who had received the minor orders. . . .

And so on. In A.J.'s case conjecture had generally a firm basis of fact: but by the time he came to write *The Quest For Corvo* he had realized the opportunities this convention gave for slipshod and weakly imaginative writing, and, within obvious and necessary limits, he abandoned it in favour of a more factual approach, just as he purged his writing of the plague of hyphenated epithets that mar the passage I have quoted.

It is very probable that A.J. intended at this time to write no more about Rolfe than this essay. He said himself that after the death of Millard in 1927 the "Quest" ceased altogether; and although he sometimes turned over reflectively the files and papers in Rolfe's handwriting that he had purchased from the "Rev. Stephen Justin" (the pseudonym used in *The Quest For Corvo* for a clergyman who befriended Rolfe in his last days at Venice), it is unlikely that he would ever have attempted a full length study of him, but for the intervention of Mr. A. J. Maundy

Gregory, who came to see him at the First Edition Club
one fine spring morning.

> Mr. Gregory (or, as he was formally announced, Mr.
> Maundy Gregory) proved to be a plump, rubicund, middle-
> sized man in the fifties, with an expensive flower in his
> buttonhole, an air of constant good-living, an affable smile,
> a glittering watchchain, good clothes and (as I noticed when
> he sat down) very beautiful boots. His business was briefly
> stated. He had read the works of Baron Corvo with fan-
> atical admiration . . . and meeting Mr. Leslie by chance,
> had been advised by him to seek me out as the source of
> further knowledge. . . .
> With a curious and rather attractive diffidence, my visitor
> asked if I would consider selling him one of my less im-
> portant treasures. He could not hope, he conceded, that I
> would part with any of the major manuscripts; but perhaps
> I could spare a fragment or a duplicate? Money was no
> object, he added almost regretfully, as he turned over again
> the leaves of *The Weird of the Wanderer* in Corvo's beautiful
> handwriting. Actually I had no particular wish to sell any-
> thing that morning; but something in his hint that he was
> immensely wealthy, a peculiar challenge in his eyes as he
> made it, prompted me to pass him, more in jest than in
> earnest, a small poem of Rolfe's composition and in his
> hand, and say "You can have that for £20." Without hesi-
> tation Mr. Maundy Gregory's hand went to his pocket; a
> thick gold-edged wallet appeared and was opened; four
> five-pound notes were taken from an impressive wad; and
> "I am most grateful to you", he murmured.

Maundy Gregory had just that sense of the effectiveness
of a theatrical gesture, and just that touch of flamboyance,
which appealed unfailingly to my brother. His sleeve links
were platinum balls covered with diamonds, he wore a
black pearl in his tiepin, he would produce on one occasion
a gold cigarette case that was a gift from the King of
Greece, and on another, one that had been given him by

A. J. A. Symons

the Duke of York (now King George VI); he used a
private taxicab instead of a private car, because a taxicab
passed unnoticed, whereas a car was easily recognized; he
sat in a vast red chair in the Whitehall office from which,
he confessed, he conducted a world-wide campaign against
Bolshevism; his desk was covered with indicators that
buzzed, or flashed with coloured lights. "He told me that
he lunched every day at the Ambassador Club, never
alone, and that every day at a quarter to one two bottles
of champagne were put on ice for him. I learned that he
possessed two yachts, a house in London, another on the
river, and a flat in Brighton. Without in the least boasting
he let me know that his library contained many rare
books, his cellar much fine wine. Of all these things he
spoke quite calmly, and with a friendly, flattering assumption that thenceforth I should share in them." A.J. was
hardly surprised when, after a long lunch at the Ambassador Club, Maundy Gregory looked round the magnificent but now empty restaurant, and whispered confi-
dentially, "Of course, this place belongs to me."

For nearly three years my brother did share, if not in the
yachts and the house on the river, at least very frequently
in Maundy Gregory's company at lunch; or, as Sir Shane
Leslie puts it, in the lonely hand of double dummy
that A.J. played by himself, the dummies (so called
because they were dead) were Baron Corvo and Oscar
Wilde, and the fourth chair was occupied alternately
by Shane Leslie himself, and Maundy Gregory. At the
end of this time the bubble of Maundy Gregory's fortune
burst, and some of the secrets of this remarkable man were
revealed when he was found guilty of attempting to
obtain a bribe as an inducement to procure for a retired
naval officer the grant of a knighthood. It was said, in the
case discreetly presented on his appearance at Bow Street,

that many similar complaints against him remained unheard; he pleaded guilty, and was sentenced to two months' imprisonment in the second division. A receiving order in bankruptcy followed his release, and he left England to spend the remainder of his life in exile.

Such was the end of the extraordinary career of one who was reputed to have organized before the First World War a detective agency employed in advising large hotels of the antecedents and activities of guests arriving from abroad; who claimed to have been a member of M.I.5, in control of 1,000 agents, during the War; who later planned, in his capacity as editor of the *Whitehall Gazette*, the restoration of many exiled royalties—plans which, in spite of their unsuccess, earned him such decorations as that of the Grand Cordon of the Royal Montenegrin Order of Danilo to add to his many other esoteric honours, such as that of the Grand Cross of the Equestrian Order of the Holy Sepulchre. This bright, falling star moved briefly across the panel of my brother's life; and deserves, in his own right, a separate biography.

At the end of the twenties no shadow of the disastrous future seemed to touch this plump and fabulously wealthy figure, who had time to spare equally for promoting the restoration of deposed royal houses and for finding the lost manuscripts of Frederick William Rolfe. Few of his lunches with my brother were without an element of surprise; at one of them, for instance, Maundy Gregory pulled an envelope out of his pocket, laid it on the table, and invited my brother to guess its contents. These proved to be a passport issued to Mussolini at Milan in 1921, nine months before the March on Rome; with the generosity that characterized him in all their relations, Maundy Gregory gave the passport to my brother, with the remark that he should add it to his collection of interesting documents.

A.J. was astonished and delighted, in almost equal measure; but astonishment and delight increased when, some time later, at another lunch, this unexpected Maecenas placed in his hands a bound copy of *Don Renato; or an Ideal Content*, one of the five existing copies of a printed but unpublished work of Rolfe's (it still remains unpublished), which one of his agents had salvaged from a rat-haunted cellar. A week later Maundy Gregory produced the manuscript of a translation of the Songs of Meleager which Rolfe had made with Sholto Douglas, together with the blocks made from Rolfe's drawings done to illustrate the songs. Modestly the figure of mystery disclaimed the magical powers which A.J. was almost inclined to attribute to him—with money, he said, one can do anything; and he exemplified his belief in this tried platitude when one day he summoned my brother to his Whitehall office and said that he would like to buy the scandalous letters Rolfe had written from Venice. Greatly daring, A.J. set their value at £150, six times what he had paid Millard for them. "So far from demurring, my host questioned (without the slightest irony) if I was asking enough for such remarkable documents; and on being assured that I was, opened a drawer of his desk and from a thick packet handed me fifteen £10 notes. The packet was not noticeably diminished by the transfer; there must have been at least £5,000 on that table."

Maundy Gregory's money was behind the most fantastic of all pieces of Corviana: the Corvine Society, whose declared objects were "To honour his memory, recommend his writings, and explain away his life." The Society had no headquarters, and the members performed no duties; its activities were confined to two astonishing banquets held at the Ambassador Club, and paid for by the Treasurer. It is needless to mention the

Treasurer's name. Details of the food and wine consumed, and of the words spoken, have been preserved in
two elaborate descriptive booklets. The proceedings were
reported by A.J., who was Secretary of the Society:

> The Second Corvine Banquet was held on December 12th,
> 1929, in a Special Room at the Ambassador Club; and, as
> before, its keynotes were magnificence and mystery. Of the
> five members three were present; and the unnamed but able
> Treasurer also graced the table, which, as before, was gar-
> landed with white and yellow flowers, the Papal colours, in
> honour of one who was a Pope in imagination, a Baron in
> fiction, a Genius in life.

The guests—seventeen were present at the first banquet,
and thirty at the second—included Lord Berwick, Pro-
fessor Tancred Borenius, Professor R. M. Dawkins,
Vyvyan Holland, James Laver, Shane Leslie, Wyndham
Lewis, Maundy Gregory, Francis Meynell, T. Sturge
Moore, Ralph Straus, T. Earle Welby, and of course A.J.
The toast wine was Corvo Gran Spumante, and at the
second banquet the guests drank also Vodka, Tio Pepe,
Montrachet 1916, Chambertin 1915, Pol Roger 1919,
Chateau D'Yquem 1922, Croft's 1904 and Courvoiser
1811. These wines and spirits were companions to an
eight-course meal which included Turbotin Corvo; and
after such a meal the guests were, perhaps, prepared for
such opening words as those spoken by Shane Leslie,
speaking as or for the Grand Master of the Society:

> Whether I rise to address the companions or the com-
> mentators of the late regretted and regrettable Baron of that
> Title which none has challenged, because none has claimed;
> whether you are frankly hostile or freely admirative;
> whether you have come from a purely intellectual desire to
> indulge in the Corvine Cornucopia or from attraction to

the vinous Symphony composed, decanted and degusted by one of the great Masters of Cellarage; whether, indeed, you have only come from a curious spirit in the hope that you might penetrate the impenetrable and possibly learn the identity of previous or reigning Grand Masters, or to decipher the symbolism which has made the handscript of the General Master Secretary a feature at so many trials of forgery,
Greeting!

A.J.'s own speeches on both occasions show very well the capacity for formal, weighty and original humour which often underlay, and accentuated, the Victorian gravity of his manner. They show also his delight in any activity that could be regarded as a game. The opening of his first speech as Secretary is a model in its kind:

I regret to inform you that the Secretary was stopped this morning while attempting to leave the country with the Portland Vase. He has explained the matter to everyone's satisfaction, including his own; but the experience has left him somewhat shaken, and he cannot be present. . . . He has sent me a vast batch of papers, which are headed on the front page, "Report upon the Present State of Corvine Studies." I am bound to confess that they make extraordinary reading. The first fifteen pages are taken up by an analysis of the works of Mr. Ronald Firbank, Mr. Shane Leslie, and the late Robert Hugh Benson, showing that all three owe most of their ability, and a considerable number of their epigrams, to a profound study of Corvo's books. Following this are five pages of statistics regarding the number of motor-cars in Ireland, the relevance of which entirely escapes me; and then comes a brief essay, the whole point of which seems to be that since the discoveries of Einstein, there are two forms of measurement—rectilinear and corvilinear. With this the so-called report ends abruptly.

And this was the opening of his second report:

You,
are bidden to a banquet to be
held by the Corvine Society on
Thursday June 27th 1929

Compliance with this mandate should
be confirmed to the secretary of the society
at 27 Conduit Street, whereupon you will
be informed of the time & place of meeting
& the costume to be worn.
During the evening, the Grand Master,
or one deputed to speak for him will
proclaim a eulogy of

Baron Corvo

and subsequently the secretary, or one
speaking in his place, will report on the
State of Corvine Studies

A. J. A. Symons

The method and policy of this Society have hitherto been shrouded in mystery; but by the command of the Grand Master, it is my privilege to-night partially to lift the veil from our amiable secret activities. First, concerning the Society itself. Membership is open to any proficient student of the work of Frederick William Serafino Austin Lewis Mary Rolfe, sometimes known as Baron Corvo. The test of suitability is a formal examination paper, copies of which can be obtained on application to the Secretary, such applications to be made after an elaborate lunch or dinner provided by the prospective candidate. Election is performed by secret ballot, the Grand Master voting alone in a room so darkened that his right hand knoweth not what his left hand doeth. This method has been found to work quite well, despite the fact that a candidate is sometimes unwittingly blackballed by the very, and indeed only, person who can sponsor him. An elected candidate is required forthwith to pay the sum of £1,000 to the Treasurer, which sum is instantly invested in wild-cat shares. The interest, if any, so provided, is taken as the equivalent of an annual subscription, and forms the basis of the Society's vast wealth. In the event of death, divorce, bankruptcy or the performance by any member of any other act displeasing to the Grand Master, the £1,000 deposited by that member is instantly forfeited. It will be seen that membership of the Corvine Society is a deterrent from divorce, bankruptcy, evil manners, and even from death. Actually, no member of the Society has ever been known to die; and this mutual immortality is both a matter of observation and belief.

The carefully-calculated beat and intonation of his voice is in these words. They were designed to be spoken; but they are also admirable written examples of the development of humour by an incongruity between manner and subject which is not common in our literature (Johnson's is perhaps the perfect specimen in this kind).

Maundy Gregory's interest in the eccentric figure of Corvo had faded, even before his own disgrace; the

Corvine Society met no more; but, with such a background of incident, how could my brother refuse this easy, and quickly-rewarding theme that had been lying for years, so to speak, in his lap?

The theme, then, was settled: but not the approach. It had proved possible, years before, to convey Rolfe's story comfortably in five thousand words; and although much more information about him had been gathered since that time, it would not be easy to transform this essay into a full-length book. It was obvious that Rolfe's quarrels, when extended from paragraphs in an essay to chapters in a book, might prove merely tiresome to many readers. Moreover, my brother had no taste for the "standard biography", which he had condemned in his lecture on "Tradition in Biography" already mentioned. English biography, he suggested, had lamentably failed; in beauty, "for what biography could be re-read for the pleasure of its form alone"; in truth, "for biography is still a form of panegyric". So far as it had a tradition, it was a bad tradition, that of attempting a completeness which was not merely undesirable, but impossible.

Since any biography must in its nature be a selection, whether made by unguided instinct or self-conscious technique, the biographer, my brother suggested, should accept the limit of his art. His objective was "not to record, but to reveal"; and his revelation could not hope to be more, and should not be less, than the truth about his subject as it was filtered through his own mind. The objection that such a responsibility encouraged the biographer to distort reality he dismissed by saying that "The artistic conscience has its own honesty", and that the biographer would accept "the convention of truth".

A. J. A. Symons

There was, he maintained, no other biographical convention—there were, therefore, as many ways of writing a biography as of telling a story, for a biography was indeed a life story; the true biographer would pick his subject and his method with equal care, choosing them "As a dandy chooses his suit, remembering cut and tone as much as texture; and his subjects should fit his talent as the suit fits the dandy's body: exquisitely".

This address was the most brilliant of his pieces of special pleading for the kind of writing which he felt himself able to perform. Some of its revolutionary suggestions are now accepted commonplaces, but the freshness with which they are put makes it possible still to read them with pleasure. It is clear that he had himself in mind in the peroration, in which he outlined the qualities to be desired in the biographer of the future:

> We may take Mr. Strachey as the forerunner of the biographer of the future, who, though not unmindful of learning, will not be a pure scholar, for the scholar is more interested in scholarship than in humanity. Nor will art alone, not even the art of writing, claim his sole devotion. Eternally curious, he will know men and books and cities; possess the quick assimilative promptness of the legal mind, and the judicial balancing calm of that mind also; be avid of personality, and rate men as what they are, rare and curious flowers of character, interesting both when they conform and when they differ from the general standards of law and virtue. If he accomplish all these things, and possess as well a sense of the theatre and a sense of style, he may even, in his own right, deserve a brief biography.

His book on Stanley had hardly satisfied the requirements of this address; but he designed that the story of Frederick William Rolfe should do so.

After much thought, he decided to tell the tale of Rolfe's

life in the form of a detectival adventure, in which the storyteller's pursuit of the elusive and enigmatic Baron should be entwined with the Baron's own tragic life. By that means he could avoid the chronological approach which he found distasteful; he could maintain the interest of the narrative with comparative ease; and he could introduce all the strange characters, from Millard to Maundy Gregory, who had taken part in the quest. He discussed the idea with several friends, before he began to write; and he outlined it also to his family. I made the objection (which was made also, no doubt, by others) that he would not be able to maintain such a framework throughout the book. The detective interest was certain to flag after a few chapters, and when it faded the book might collapse. He listened with flattering attentiveness, but he was not convinced. "We shall meet that difficulty when it comes", he said, and chuckled. "You will find that I have a few surprises up my sleeve." And he began to write the book, choosing as his starting-point that summer afternoon in Christopher Millard's garden.

The first four chapter headings, "The Problem", "The Clues", "The Newspaper Attack" and "The Reluctant Brother", show how closely he adhered to this detective story theme. But his ingenuity was never merely mechanical; the web of fine threads from which *The Quest For Corvo* is made has the half-deliberate effect of revealing and contrasting the author's personality with that of his subject, and this contrast gives additional depth to the picture of the lonely, frustrated, and almost continuously unsuccessful Frederick Rolfe. When he had written seven chapters, however, A.J. realized that he could not carry the detective element through to the end of his book: and the tact and skill with which the quest was pursued in the opening chapters is balanced by his discernment of the point at which the formal pattern should be abandoned. A less sensitive and perceptive writer would have adhered rigidly to his original design; A.J. relegated it to the background, delicately and successfully, in a note prefixed to Chapter 8:

> So far, I have set before the reader (not an analysed summary of my researches but) an account of the search itself; and I believe that in regard to a man so exceptional as Rolfe this exceptional method is justified. Truth takes many forms; and the dramatic alternation of light and dark in which my inquiries discovered Baron Corvo has, I am convinced, more value as verity than any one man's account. ... At the point in Rolfe's life which my narrative has now reached, however, that method ceases, for the moment, to be advisable.

He found, as always, great difficulty in the act of putting down words on paper in any satisfactory order. His method of composition was curious, and lengthy; he avoided alteration as much as possible, preferring to re-write whole passages in the beautiful rounded script which he had now developed, when disturbed by a failure of balance in a phrase. He always used a fresh sheet of foolscap paper when he began to build this new verbal structure, and in consequence his manuscript drafts consisted very often of many sheets of paper, on each of which a paragraph, or sometimes only a sentence, had been written. I have seen myself three manuscript drafts of the first page of *The Quest For Corvo*, each differing in a few words; and it is very likely that half a dozen other drafts were written before he found a form that satisfied him. This fastidiousness retarded him always in the production of any serious literary work, and he was delayed further by his practice of reading chapters of the book to those friends who would, he knew, prove attentive listeners.

He read exceedingly well, and the friends were always charmed; their praises stimulated, he said, an easily-discouraged pen. Like others I was awarded the privilege of having the first chapter read to me (it was, in A.J.'s mind, a kind of badge of honour to be selected as a listener; his wife, who received many such badges, always encouraged him to read to her); and I heard some of his telephone conversations—"All I can tell you about the book, my dear fellow, is that it will be unlike any other biography ever written." During the summer of 1933 the pile of manuscript grew so quickly that he became almost alarmed for the merit of his work. "Think of it", he wrote to Harold Fisher, "I have written, or put together, 75,000 words! I am permitted another 15,000; and as Corvo would have said, 'As long a space as possible will not be a page too much'." He added that he much missed the benefit of Fisher's advice and criticism, and said wryly that his fate would be to write an annual biography to balance his annual deficit.

Bulletins concerning the progress of the book were sent to other friends from time to time. It was completed in a little more than six months from the time when he had written that first manuscript page; he wrote the last chapter in the garden of his friend Philip Gosse's house at Steyning, sustained by his host's Turkish cigarettes. He did not, however, conceive of his part in the book as finished with the delivery of the manuscript, as a common author might have done. The proofs were delivered to him, chapter by chapter; every proof was altered, and then sent hastily to friends so that their opinion of its merits might be obtained. One of his early friends, Ian Black, received several such advance extracts, accompanied by urgent notes. "This chapter, 'The Nowt of Holywell', has given me more trouble than any other. I revised it from

galley to page. You may find a little difficulty in connect-
ing it up. I have had to complete the proofs with typescript
at one point, but you will see how it dovetails." Page
proofs, already checked, were sent to friends for re-
checking. Excisions and additions were made up to the
last possible moment—when, in an attempt to convey
his own sense of urgency, A.J. wrote to Black: "The page
proofs are rushing through the press!"

At last, early in 1934, the book was published—very
fittingly, by Cassells, who were associated with the Club
in publishing the *Book-Collector's Quarterly*; and the
author sat back and awaited the critics' reactions to what
he had called, on the title page, "an experiment in
biography".

It is a fascinating, and faintly disturbing, experience to
turn the pages of a press-cutting book of fifteen years ago.
How distant seems the world in which a book review one
thousand words in length was a commonplace, in which
publishers' advertisements extended over two columns
and eight inches, in which friendly notices helped to
secure a book its second edition. To-day an author is
happy if he gets twenty short reviews, where before the
war he would have expected sixty long ones; shortage of
space in papers prevents publishers from taking more than
a small fraction of the advertising space they took before
the war; lack of paper makes second editions almost
bibliographical rarities. We shall not return, in any easily
visible future, to those days when inflation, rather than
compression, was the reviewer's task; but looking through
the reviews of *The Quest For Corvo* contained in one of
my brother's elegant press-cutting books (he kept,
typically, a book for each of his several occupations) it is
difficult to adjust one's bare present-day standards of a

The Quest for Corvo

"successful book" to those days of profuse illustration and big black type.

There can be no doubt, however, that *The Quest For Corvo* was greeted warmly. A.J. had provided material for the lively journalists who handle a book as a news story, by the chapter at the end in which he described his meetings with Maundy Gregory. This story was seized upon by *The Star* ("A Prince of Spenders"), the *Daily Express* ("Maundy Gregory in his Glory") and the *Daily Mail* ("Maundy Gregory's Lavish Feasts") in a way which had very little to do with the merits of A.J.'s biography, but undoubtedly had an effect on sales. The book obtained considerable notice, also, from those who had known Rolfe and had fresh tales to tell of him, under such titles as "Genius Who Lived in a Welsh Workhouse" and "Charlatan-Genius Whom Aberdeen Kicked Out". This merely sensational success was backed by the solid praise on literary grounds of such diverse critics as Desmond McCarthy and Graham Greene, Harold Nicolson and Mary Butts, Peter Quennell and David Garnett; and although some reviewers looked unfavourably upon Rolfe himself, as a man and a writer, and suggested that the subject of the quest was hardly worth the pains that had been spent on its accomplishment, there were few who failed in admiration of the ingenuity of the author's method, and the skill with which he had carried through his account to the end. Several reviewers referred to the "new mode of biography" by which "he holds up the mirror also to his own fastidious and amusing self"; and if Graham Greene thought that an endeavour to reproduce the emotion of the moment had led A.J. to include "a good many paragraphs of amiable gossip, on such subjects as the quality of Mr. Shane Leslie's hock, which are below the dark dignity of his record", his view was balanced

A. J. A. Symons

by that of David Garnett, who said that the book's merits
"Reside in its being the story of how the author first came
to be interested, of how he sought and pieced together
the scraps of information which came into his hands."
John Hayward wrote a London Letter in *The New York
Sun* in which he observed that the career of the author, as
well as that of his subject, presented certain enigmatic
features. "Symons has often laughed at me for suggesting
that he is a bit of a 'mystery man'. But I still like to think
that there is something a little mysterious about his
numerous activities and diverse contacts. . . . I have begged
Symons to write 'The Quest For Maundy Gregory'. If
he refuses, I threaten to write 'The Quest for A. J. A.
Symons!' It would make a fascinating story!"

A second edition of the book was called for, and then a
third; American publication by MacMillan late in the
year brought the delighted author more friendly reviews,
although the book had a smaller sale in America than in
this country. The success of the book made him at once a
figure of importance in English letters. He was asked to
compose an entry for *Who's Who*, which he wrote with
his customary care, and read aloud to his family for
approval. He gave his recreations, in this first entry, as
"Talking, amateur forgery, and searching for lost manuscripts of Baron Corvo". His pleasure in the appearance
of his name among those of the rich and the famous must
have been marred, ever so slightly, by the necessary
reve ation of the Christian names which he had always,
from his childhood, disapproved. He had concealed them
successfully by called himself A.J., an abbreviation which
he used so consistently that most of his friends did not even
wonder what was hidden behind the initials. These who
did wonder had, formerly, been left in doubt; but now
his name was at the mercy of their discovery, and laughter.

The circumstance must have disturbed him: for seven years later he jettisoned the offensive "Alphonse" in his *Who's Who* entry, substituting the romantic "Alroy" a name at once suitably patrician and possessed of a respectable literary parentage in one of Disraeli's heroes.

The book brought him also many new friends—and he was a man who always welcomed new friends. He received a shock when, one day, a letter came through the post addressed to him, which seemed quite plainly to be in Rolfe's handwriting; it proved to be that of a man who had received some letters from Rolfe in childhood, and had been so struck by the beauty of their script that he set himself to copy it. Many other letters came to my brother after the biography was published: some from men who had known Rolfe, and wrote to contribute their own impressions of him; some from those who felt sympathy with him in his priestly ambitions, or his homosexual habits; some from people who offered various explanations of Rolfe's life and downfall; and, most of all, letters from people who had been dazzled by the strange story that my brother told, and were curious about the personality of the writer who had dealt so ably with such an odd subject. Even now, half-a-dozen letters are addressed to my brother every year, from those who have read the book for the first time, and are eager to know something of its author.

Every one of these letters received an answer. A few of my brother's correspondents were invited to lunch; some were told tactfully that the author of *The Quest For Corvo* was not a Catholic, and was not personally interested in his subject's sexual foibles; with some correspondents my brother engaged in protracted correspondence on points of Corvinity. He kept, and valued, all of these letters; and he valued particularly the several occasions when a reading of his book turned dislike or indifference towards him into admiration and friendship. He had thoughtfully provided himself with a considerable number of first editions of the book, and with their assistance he continued through a number of years this process of turning enemies into friends. The most notable case of conversion is that of James Agate, who had met A.J. on two or three occasions, and had shown a distressing lack of appreciation of his personality, and unawareness of his talent. More than five years after its original publication a first edition of the *Quest* was despatched to the recalcitrant critic with, as Agate wrote in his letter of acknowledgement, "a dedication and letter all in that beautiful handwriting like an Elizabethan farmhouse". In the same letter Agate noted: "I have begun the book and am a leeeetle bit put off by the sacerdotality of the chichi." But, he said, "I have only got as far as page seven or so." Another letter followed on the same day:

> Symons,
>   Am now at p. 27.
>   Boswell's Johnson is a better book.
>
>   J.A.

And another:

> Dear A.J.A.S.
>   P. 50.
>   *Only* Boswell's Johnson, etc., etc.
>
>   J.A.

And two days later another:

> My dear Symons,
>   (Half-way through)
>   But it's magnificent. . . .

And in another week a final verdict:

The Quest for Corvo

Dear Symons,

I have now finished *Quest for Corvo*. The book's existence at all is a miracle. First there was the right kind of curiosity to be aroused, second it had to be aroused in the right person, and third there had to be the original Corvo. Well, the hat trick came off. . . .

As for your share in it I can only repeat what Harland wrote to Rolfe about his *Chronicles of the House of Borgia*, and talk of the "labour and learning, imagination, humour, irony, wit, perverseness, daring, the tremendously felicitous and effective *manner* of it." Now are you satisfied?

The flattered author was entirely satisfied. "I walk about in a state of mental flush which is, I am certain, intolerable to all my friends. From time to time I pull from my pocket one of your numerous encomia, which I study with an absorbedness so thorough that even strangers are almost forced to ask what I am looking at. The slightest enquiry (even the raising of an eyelid) suffices; at once I read aloud, in a resounding voice, the nearest favourable phrase— usually twice. What is the proverb about killing by kindness?"

Within a few days A.J. was writing letters to "My dear Egomet Bonmot", and observing as a P.S. that "In case the question never crosses your mind, please note that I am willing (and, indeed, eager) that you should make use in *Ego* of any letter I ever write to you" and as a P.P.S.: "And if you do so perhaps you had better remind your readers that Egomet Bonmot, the name by which I now regard you, was originally devized for himself by Thomas Griffiths Wainewright, the murderer, critic, friend of Charles Lamb, and star contributor to the *London Magazine*."

Such was Baron Corvo's power of creating good will among men, after his death.

A. J. A. Symons

The method by which *The Quest For Corvo* was constructed has, after all, been emulated very little by later biographers. It is fair to say that the book was, in the best sense, a biographical *tour-de-force*, and that the method employed could be used successfully only by such a natural self-dramatiser and born emotional conjuror, as A.J. It would have failed under the treatment of a less serious, less fastidious, more self-indulgent hand.

But *The Quest For Corvo* was not designed as a model for imitation. It proved triumphantly what its author wanted to show: that a biography could be imaginative without inaccuracy, that cleverness need not be synonymous with chichi, and that an unorthodox treatment is not necessarily unsound. The Penguin edition of the book has reached a sale of well over one hundred thousand copies; and it is likely to be rediscovered with no diminution of enthusiasm by successive generations of writers and readers; for in its balance and fine sensitiveness, in its careful omission of material, however rich, which would have destroyed the Corvine figure in the carpet, and above all in its style, formal yet easy, solid yet graceful, sufficiently ornamented without a hint of fretfulness, it is a work of art.

CHAPTER X

WINE AND FOOD

IT is impossible now to call back details of the particular
meeting of the Sette of Odd Volumes at which
Brother Prattler (Maurice Healy) introduced to
Brother Speculator the ebullient and erudite literary
gourmet, André L. Simon. Did A.J. make on that occasion
one of his elegant and elaborate speeches in which the
phrases were, as some listeners thought, almost too
carefully studied, by which the guests of the Sette were
gracefully denigrated? Was it the evening on which he
was permitted to "mislead the company" (as the menu
put it) on the subject of Emin Pasha, Governor of
Equatoria? Or did he talk of Edward Irving, that strange
preacher who founded a Church in which many of the
believers were granted the gift of tongues denied to the
preacher himself? The details of the evening are lost:
we know only that the meeting took place in the late
twenties, and that the occasion was an important one to
both men, although they did not know it. It is likely that
Simon was impressed by A.J.'s youth, wit and assurance;
and it is almost certain that the talkative, but still ever so
slightly gauche, Secretary of the First Edition Club, was
immensely impressed by the worldly knowledge, the
florid but genuine enthusiasm, and above all by the
astonishing knowledge of matters gastronomic and vinous,
possessed by his companion. André Simon had for many
years taken wine and food as his province, and on the

ground of his choice he moved as a master, with an un-
rivalled knowledge of the great cooks and dishes of the
past, exploring in the present with an enthusiasm undulled
by repetition the infinitely varied pleasures of the table.
His energy was abundant. He was an admirable after-
dinner speaker, with a suprising gift of metaphor; the
dignity of his personal appearance was enhanced by the
crown of thick white hair which stood erect like pins
above his square and smiling face; and he was the author
of books on the proper treatment and dignity of wine and
food which gastronomes regarded as classics in their kind.

The first meeting, whatever the impressions of the
participants, was succeeded by others. The bibliographer
presented a copy of his *Anthology of Nineties Verse* to the
gourmet, who expressed his thanks charmingly. The First
Edition Club showed the exhibition of Simon's wonderful
collection of books on "The Art of Good Living" which
has already been described on page 94. The gourmet was
entertained in the delightful flat on the top floor of 17,
Bedford Square, and perhaps it seemed to him, as it seemed
to many of A.J.'s friends in those days, that this young
man had solved the problem of living several lives at
once, and enjoying them all. It was flattering to him, too,
that this intelligent *littérateur* should sit as a neophyte at the
feet of the master of good living. Simon willingly assisted
his pupil's vinous education and A.J., who had travelled
abroad for only a few weeks, and could not speak any
foreign language, learned to appraise the "demure self-
confidence" of *Domaine de Chevalier* 1920 and the "majestic
finality" of *Chateau Margaux* 1870, and to speak severely
of English cooking.

One cold dark winter's day early in 1931, A.J. sought
respite from the troubles of the First Edition Club at
lunch with Simon. There were three other guests, Maurice

Healy and Sir John Squire among them; and the fare, the host tells us, "Was simple for those gold-standard days: a plain omelette, plain but *baveuse*—as Baker, our Cellarman, a Cockney and former pugilist, cooked admirably; a thick piece of fillet of beef, grilled, underdone and tender; and a ripe Wensleydale cheese." The party ended the meal with a bottle of Haut-Brion 1874 instead of port; and this wine was so good that "it brought forth an enthusiastic outburst from Squire who declaimed against the neglect of old Professor George Saintsbury, a man who would have so dearly loved such a beautiful wine a few years back, but who was now wineless and nearly sightless, worse still, almost friendless, at Bath." It was agreed that they must give him a dinner. When, however, Squire wrote to the Professor, this amiable project received a check; for he declined to attempt the journey to London, and even expressed himself unwilling to attend a lunch at Bath. The enthusiasts, however, were not to be dissuaded from their resolution to hold a dinner by the mere fact of the chief guest's unwillingness to attend it. One day several admirers of George Saintsbury were gathered together at the Connaught Rooms, and the meeting carried with applause Maurice Healy's motion that a small dining-club called The Saintsbury Club should be founded. The membership was limited to fifty, and it was publicized in the Press as "London's most exclusive Club." The Committee of five included A.J. who served, in a capacity now familiar to him, as Secretary.

The Club had been formed to honour Professor Saintsbury: but not necessarily to honour him as a man of letters. A.J., indeed, distressed Simon one day by passing judgment "in exquisitely chosen words, and in a kindly but quite definite manner, which scorned the possibility of an appeal, upon Saintsbury's colossal literary output. . . .

'Unfortunately', he said, 'He can't write English' ''. There is an element of high comedy in the fact that the members of the Saintsbury Club were not called upon to honour, nor even to have read, the *History of Literary Criticism*, that encyclopaedic work in which the great critics of the past lie embalmed in academic pedantry; they were required merely to respect the *Notes on a Cellar Book* in which the Professor had recorded, with characteristic conscientiousness, the wines he had enjoyed during half a century. Perhaps the Saintsbury Club may seem, to some, a mere excuse for eating and drinking; it has survived to the present day, and Vyvyan Holland has taken A.J.'s place as Secretary.

It was partly the success of the Saintsbury Club that put into Simon's mind the idea of forming a Society of Gastronomes, and by this time he was sufficiently friendly with A.J., and had sufficient respect for his alert intellect, to talk over the idea with him. A.J. glowed with optimism and enthusiasm, as he always did when a new and romantic idea was put before him; and the collaborators talked about ways and means. At first they thought of launching a Wine Society, analogous to the Book Society, in which members received one wine a month, selected by a committee of experts, for one guinea a year. This proved impracticable: and the partners finally decided to found a Wine and Food Society, whose primary declared object was to raise the standard of cooking throughout the country. Membership cost one guinea a year, and the chief inducement offered to join the Society was the "practical demonstrations of the art of the table" promised to members in the form of lunches, dinners and wine-tastings. Simon was able to make the necessary arrangements with wine-merchants for these functions.

Neither of the partners was anxious to risk more than

Wine and Food

the minimum of financial outlay on such a speculative venture. The office address of the Society was 6, Little Russell Street, so that its office was in fact that of the First Edition Club. It was agreed that A.J. should handle all the correspondence; and it must have occurred to him that every member of the Society was a potential member of the Club. With no office expenses, therefore, and a simple arrangement between the partners regarding sharing of profits, the Wine and Food Society was launched in October, 1933, with André Simon as President and A.J.A. Symons as Secretary.

The announcement of the Society's formation (it claimed at the outset less than a dozen members) had a mixed reception. The depression of two years before was not yet forgotten; the standard of living of the English working class was wretchedly low. Should a society devoted to the niceties of eating and drinking be started at a time when so many were unable to fill their bellies? *The Manchester Guardian* was ironic about those attending the first "practical demonstration" organized by the Society:

> Weaned from the crudities of roast beef and roly-poly pudding, their first demonstration of the higher life will be "a luncheon with an Alsatian menu" where all the food and wines will come from Alsace and the cost will be only ten shillings. Only the incurably insular will be inclined to reflect that many a housewife could do the whole family rather well on ten shillings and without going any nearer Alsace than the village shops which she ordinarily frequents.

The *Guardian* concluded that while "To discuss food with affection—at the right time and season—is not without its charm . . . whether it should be discussed in public and at the top of one's voice—particularly in a world where a

143

large number of people cannot get enough of its simplest forms—often seems a little open to question."

The *Guardian's* objection, put with varying degrees of urbanity or wrath, has been made at intervals during the Society's existence. If, in fact, the Society's chief concern was to raise the standard of cooking in Britain—a motive which *The Manchester Guardian* and other critics must have applauded—they went about it in a very odd way. During the whole of its existence the Wine and Food Society has made little attempt to give practical advice to the working-class housewife; it has made no attempt at all to set up those bureaux of advice and practical assistance which might really have transformed, in pre-war days, the nature of English cooking; its members, from the President and Secretary downwards, are open to the charge that they have educated others merely by setting an example in good living themselves, without moving on to the mundane ground of ways and means. The Society could more properly be regarded as a luncheon and dining club for those over a certain income level, than as an organization bringing light into the dark places of the English kitchen. Or let us be more urbane, and say that the Society's *obiter dicta* were appreciated in Kensington rather than in Keighley, and that A.J.'s remark that they would offer "education in good living for people who cannot afford to go to the most expensive restaurants" excited a greater percentage of gastric juices in Streatham than in Stockport.

It was essentially to the middle-class that the Wine and Food Society at first hearing made its appeal—to the man who wished to drink wine rather than beer or spirits; to the bank manager and his wife, the cultured stockbroker, and generally to that considerable army of men and women anxious to impress their friends, and to indulge the snobbery inherent in all of us, by showing cognizance of a wine's name instead of pointing to a number on a Wine List. The professional and semi-professional section of the middle class had made few sacrifices in the depression, and were well prepared now to make believe that no depression had ever disturbed the even tenour of their lives. Within a month of the first announcement the Society had 230 members. Within three months it had 500—more than the First Edition Club had obtained during the whole course of its existence.

It would not be true to say that this early success embarrassed the partners, but it imbued them with a very lively optimism. A.J., indeed, unquestionably felt, as he felt several times during his life, that his fortune was made. He had lived at Clapham ever since the retreat from Bedford Square, and every morning he entered my mother's room smiling, and announced the number of epicurean sheep who had entered the gastronomic fold on the previous day. He was up at seven o'clock on these mornings, and out of the house before eight; during the day he devoted himself to the Society's business with his customary exuberance. One newspaper correspondent who went along to see him was so much impressed by his eloquence that he signed a membership form after a quarter of an hour's conversation, in which A.J. explained earnestly that food and drink need not be expensive; that the Society would encourage every hotel in England to stock two sound but very inexpensive wines, one red and the other white; that such important delicacies as English cheeses must no longer be scandalously neglected. The neophyte had been transformed into an authority on wine and food, and at almost daily luncheons with prospective members he gave them advice on the conduct and condition of the cellar which, he assured them, could be put down at a trifling expense. Returning from these luncheons, he laid plans for a quarterly periodical, and discussed its form and shape with his old friend Oliver Simon, dealt with correspondence, and with all kinds of queries, and infected his partner with some of his own conviction that within a year or two the Society would count its members not in thousands, but in tens of thousands.

Certainly the Society's first function, the Alsatian lunch, was a great success, and the tasting of Madeira and Malmsey wines which followed it was also approved by the members, who had the opportunity of tasting ten different wines including an 1808 Malmsey and a 1790 Reserve, at the small cost of half a crown. More than 300 people attended both the Society's third and fourth meetings, which consisted of a Savoyard dinner with Rhone wines, and a "Rabelais" luncheon of dishes from Touraine, and wines from Rabelais' birthplace. A tasting of Empire wines followed, held perhaps as much to placate those who accused the Society of a prejudice in favour of Continental wines and cookery as from any intrinsic admiration of Empire wines in themselves; a note supplied to the members said: "There is a strong and, it must be confessed, a well-earned prejudice against Empire wines in the minds of many who have tried them in the past." The membership still swelled daily, and was given fresh impetus by the publication of *Wine and Food*, the Society's own magazine, which was distributed free of charge to all members. This periodical has been published quarterly down to the present day, in spite of the vicissitudes of bombs and rationing, which have threatened respectively the physical appearance of the magazine, and its frequent editorial implication that spiritual satisfaction need not await the Kingdom of

Heaven, but can be attained by the fortunate upon this earth through the pleasures of the table. The magazine was edited by André Simon, who was also responsible for obtaining most of the contributions. A.J.'s part was almost exactly the counterpart of that allotted to Desmond Flower in the *Book-Collector's Quarterly*—he did most of the production work, saw the magazine through the press, wrote occasional articles, and was responsible for some of the editorial notes. The advertisements in this excellently-produced magazine were often almost as interesting as the editorial contents. The Hinds' Head Hotel at Bray-on-Thames (Mine Host: Barry Neame) matched very well the tone set by the Society's President and Secretary, with their full page advertisement in the first number:

> All food in its due season is cooked for each customer, our specialities being buttered shrimps, Cornish oysters, hung beef, sorrel, artichoke and giblet soups, salmon and lobsters, soles, turbot, mussels, whitebait, trout, mullet, fish pie, soused herrings, roast duck, boiled chicken with gammon, chicken pie, jugged hare, calf's head, saddle of lamb, marrow bones, sucking pig, asparagus, cheese souffles, and anything else that the customer desires and we can supply.

After this, the statement of Professor Henry E. Armstrong, F.R.S., in the same number, that we were in the middle of a "great social revolution", that the Society had the opportunity of "co-operating in a colossal social enterprise", and that *"An era is upon us when food must have full scientific and ethical consideration and the social economies of supply must be the common care"* strikes a modern note— a note, almost implying that something in the nature of present-day "planning" is desirable—which seems curiously out of place. But the articles on "J. Pierpont Morgan's Cellar Book", on the virtues and defects of the

1933 vintage, and the recipes for "chicken with tarragon" and *"duckling à la Bordelaise"* recover the appropriate tone; and the "Memorable Meals" feature, in which Members of the Society were invited to give an account, for publication, of the most notable meals of which they had partaken during the past three months, more than redressed the balance. Some of the remarks in this feature reached, as we shall see, a point of deliberate esoteric gastronomic criticism which made them easy subjects for parody, and even on occasion gave an effect of parody to the notes themselves.

The first issue of *Wine and Food* was planned when the venture's success was still uncertain. By the time it appeared, the Society was firmly established as a thread in the post-depression fabric of English life. Its veneration of wine had been praised by the *Temperance Quarterly* which observed that "The man who savours his glass in Christian fashion seldom drinks to excess; he does not profane a sacred thing"; and it had made a wise concession to criticism by holding an English Day in André Simon's beautiful garden at East Grinstead where the guests considered such English dishes as Roast Surrey Fowl, York Ham, glazed tongue, pigeon pie, veal and ham pie, and roast fore-rib of beef. Luncheon was accompanied by beers from Whitbread and Watney, and Barclay's London Lager, and was succeeded by a cricket match in which Wine (captained by Francis Meynell) defeated Beer (a team drawn from the Staffs of the Brewery Companies) by seven wickets.

Here, then, was a new and delightful way to fortune, and A.J. walked down it gaily; there would be plenty of time for writing books after his fortune was made. At the end of a year the Society had more than 1,000 members, and its first birthday was celebrated by the

Wine and Food

most sumptuous and elaborate banquet held in Britain for more than a hundred years. The occasion of the banquet was the centenary of Marie-Antoine Carême who knew and served, among others, Napoleon I, George IV and the Emperor of Russia. Carême was chef to the Prince Regent for eight months, and because of this it was decided to hold the banquet at the Royal Pavilion in Brighton where, more than a hundred years before, the Prince Regent had said to his chef: "Carême, you will be the death of me; you send in such appetizing fare that I cannot help overeating", and the master chef had replied, with admirable sophistry: "Sir, my duty is to tempt your appetite; yours, to control it." A special number of *Wine and Food* was given to Carême's life and achievement, and again a note of veneration was touched in his praise. "Carême", Andre Simon observed, "was a true apostle. Apostles cannot be beaten"; "Carême", declared M. Eugene Herbodeau, chef at the Carlton Hotel, "was a great artist and a great teacher"; and Ambrose Heath gave details of dishes "dignified by the description *a la Carême* in the language of cookery."

At the Royal Pavilion, then, A.J. delivered his cheerful Report of the Society's first year of working; other speeches were made; and then the members visited the kitchens and saw a few of the dishes which they were to taste in preparation on the great revolving spits, before the fire which had not been lighted for half a century. Two hundred people, who had paid two guineas each, sat down to eat in the vast E-shaped Chinese dining-room, lighted by thousands of tallow candles in eighty great candelabra. They found in front of them twelve knives and forks, and an equal number of glasses; the menu for their meal had been modelled with great care on dishes served by Carême to the Prince Regent. The forty-two courses, with their sixteen specially chosen wines and liqueurs, were provided in two services, in the custom of an earlier day. Some, like the boar's head and the two models in iced sugar of *"La Temple de l'Amour"* and *"Le Frégate 'La Gourmande'*," were designed for admiration rather than consumption; but although one person present denied indignantly that the meal had been "the banquet of a glutton or a wine-bibber", being merely "the dinner of people who took trouble to ensure that everything was artistically right", another was astonished by a thin young man on his left who sampled two of the four kinds of soup, all the six *hors d'oeuvres*, both sorts of fish, the veal and the chicken among the four *entrées*, and even the generally neglected boar's head, in the first service alone. The service of the dinner took two hours and a half. Afterwards a concert of chamber music by Arne, Boyce, Handel and Vivaldi was given in the Music Room. "The lateness of the hour", said the decorous report in *Wine and Food*, "Made it necessary for a number of the diners to forgo the final pleasure of the concert, but those who were able to remain were richly rewarded."

When the Prohibition Act was repealed by Congress the partners decided that it was time for Simon to go to the United States, to spread there the gospel of good living. A farewell banquet was given to him at the Savoy Hotel, which was attended by the Ambassadors of Spain and Portugal, and the Rumanian Minister. On this, the first of several visits to America, Simon organized Branches of the Society in some of the larger cities, branches which materially increased the revenue of the Society, and the circulation of its magazine. In his absence, A.J. was left in sole control. He arranged functions and tastings, in addition to handling all administrative work,

and the business of the Society occupied more and more
of his time. During 1934 the members of the First Edition
Club might have forgotten the Club's existence, but for
the regular appearance of the *Book-Collector's Quarterly*;
for the Club published no books during this year, and its
only exhibitions were one of English Bookbinding, and
another of the Fifty Books of the Year. The quarterly
remained: it published some admirable articles, including
a piece on William Morris by Holbrook Jackson, an
article by Thomas Balston on the various series of illus-
trated books published in the Nineties, a complete number
given to English bookbinding, and a brilliant summary
by A.J. of the position arising from the publication of
John Carter and Graham Pollard's *An Enquiry into the
Nature of Certain Nineteenth Century Pamphlets*, the
astonishing exposure of forgery in high bibliographical
circles which was published in that year. It was plain,
however, that the Club could not flourish through its
quarterly magazine alone; obvious also that the sales of
the quarterly were bound to diminish while the Club itself remained inactive. A few members were gained
through the Wine and Food Society; but, indirectly, more
were lost, for many members considered receipt of the
quarterly an inadequate return for their three guineas'
subscription, and resigned, some of them writing indignant notes. The Club's fortunes took a further turn for the
worse at the end of the year when Cassells reluctantly
decided that they must cut their losses, and cease to back
the *Book-Collector's Quarterly*; and after the late publication
of one more number, financed by A.J., in which he
observed that "The reason for delay lies in a change-over
as regards the purely *business* side of the Quarterly", the
periodical ceased to appear, although its impending revival
was several times announced.

A. J. A. Symons

The definitive biography of Oscar Wilde which was to follow *The Quest For Corvo* also remained at a standstill. To the friends who reproached him with neglecting his talent, my brother replied that he was in fact taking the quickest way possible towards its full use; that, for the first time in his life, he saw a glimpse of the chance of freedom from everyday labour, and that through the imminent, vast success of the Society, he would be left free to sit at home and write. In the meantime, all literary projects were postponed, while he dealt with the rising tide of members. He arranged that functions should be held in duplicate, to avoid overcrowding; he tried, as far as possible, to reach a personal relationship with every member; his life became more and more nearly a solid block of social engagements. He dined out three or four nights in every week, and as Secretary of the Society, and gastronomic expert, he considered it a duty as well as a pleasure to attend the country house parties to which he was frequently invited.

Life could hardly have been ordered more pleasantly for him, in the sense of physical enjoyment, than it was in those days. He preserved always, no doubt, a sense of detachment about the value of the life he led; and he paused, between luncheon and dinner engagements, to write such letters as the long and helpful notes he sent to his friend Philip Gosse, who was planning a book about the pleasures of a retired and rural life (it was published under the title *Go To The Country*), in which A.J. observed that

> The moral behind the whole book would be the possi-
> bility of leading a reasonable, dignified, happy life instead
> of the disappointing emptiness of most retirements or the
> hectic round of unrooted and unenjoyable enjoyment by
> which so many people avoid contemplation of their disap-
> pointment with themselves and with the universe.

Wine and Food

But it would be an error to think that, at this time, he was much occupied by the idea that his own career could possibly be an example of the evasion which he recognized, and condemned, in others. The joy with which he yielded to new facets of life was unending, and he became an expert in gastronomy with all the zest he had given, much earlier, to the Race Game, and a little later to sailing that yacht of which he knew so little down from Maldon to the sea. In these days many London *restaurateurs* were pleased to see his tall, slim figure moving among the tables; nightly he entertained, or was entertained by, old friends who found his pretensions amusing and lovable, and by new ones who thought his deliberation of speech and readiness in argument impressive, and slightly terrifying. The gravity of his manner grew, and his announcements on the merit of food and drink were made as those of one conscious of the care that must be exercised in pronouncing a judgment which was final, and from which there could be no appeal. In the dark, carved rooms of Vintner's Hall he was to be seen; there, in front of a row of tables covered with slim Moselle bottles and flanked with sawdust-filled spittoons, he matched his taste with that of experts who had been drinking Moselle for years. At Bristol the Committee of the Saintsbury Club was given a literary wine luncheon by Harveys, shippers of fine wines, and there he drank an 1870 Chateau Margaux, "a giant, bearded like the pard", as another luncheon guest observed, "but good natured and sweet tempered, though not yet quite as smooth and soft as I think it may still be in years to come." Mornings and evenings were filled with such engagements. "I have hardly time", he said, "to dress in the mornings or to undress at night." His wife saw him only at weekends, and his family hardly at all. Many of the private feasts which he attended were carefully organized in advance, like the occasion on which Barry Neame ("Mine Host" at Bray) commissioned A.J. to find half-a-dozen friends who were strange to the delights offered by the Hind's Head Hotel, and bring them down for dinner. The meal lasted for more than four hours, from the time when the company sat down to sorrel soup to the moment when, after "Barry Neame had told us the story of his early years, and (James) Laver the tale of his first book, and Curtis Moffat taken a photograph of ourselves at table, we were amazed to find midnight past". Less lengthy, but equally well organized, was the luncheon at which Percy Muir, acting as host, brought together A.J. and Hugh Walpole, "two book-collectors sharing a fanatical interest, not only in the writings of Baron Corvo but in the literature of the Eighteen Nineties generally", and set before them a replica of a meal given to the Sette of Odd Volumes in 1895, when Max Beerbohm first dined with that body. Sometimes, however, a meeting might be not the less delightful for its impromptu nature, like the occasion on which Curtis Moffat telephoned A.J. and asked him to come over, on the staff's night out, for the serious purpose of comparing two bottles of Lafite '65. Here the curtain was rung down a little before midnight, "the right time for a good dinner to end", as A.J. observed approvingly; and in spite of the staff's absence the host and single guest ate salami sausage, smoked salmon (a mistake—"we were glad to clear our palates with potatoes baked in their jackets, slightly salted and peppered"), cold grouse, Cheshire cheese and walnuts. The Lafite '65 survived its trial with honour. The first bottle was "delicious—not ethereal—but fine-spun, with no suspicion of faultiness, beautiful in colour, and with a delicate yet pervasive bouquet." The second bottle whose waxed top was impressed with the letters "B.R." was a long way behind the first when it was opened, but after it had been given more air "improved, and came up hand over hand like *Rainbow* overhauling *Endeavour*". More elaborate, but equally typical, was a meal at Richard Wyndham's home at Tickerage Mill in Sussex where grilled lobster was eaten, "not boiled at all, but kept alive until needed, then killed by a knife through the head, cut in half, and grilled". This meal was accompanied by a dazzling assortment of wines—it began with two sherries and ended with a potent Curaçao, "pungent and inviting on the nose", whose "gross orange flavour had been etherealized by time". The details of this, and many another, meal has been preserved for us: but the conversation is lost. We can be sure only that A.J. played a major part in it, and that he turned it dexterously in the direction of his own knowledge. He left no Boswell, so that we shall never know whether his deep, resonant voice was heard in friendly dispute about the merits of his favourite romantic poets, or whether he told in detail the strange facts of a forgotten legal puzzle which he made as interesting as fiction, or whether he defended his newly-found view that Sheridan le Fanu was the finest novelist of the past fifty years; any more than we can be certain whether it was on this occasion that he wrote a complete page of forgeries in Wyndham's Visitors Book, reproducing exactly on the right hand side of the page the entries made by other visitors on the left, and adding to them his own signature.

Some of his friends viewed his gastronomic career with distaste. He replied to them rather sharply that he had no sympathy with the typically English Nonconformism or Puritanism that prompted their remarks; or he said more amiably, and with a kind of endearing naive cleverness, that these vast meals, however enjoyable in themselves, were regarded by him quite rationally as a means to an end—and that the end was making his fortune.

He never, at this or any other time, made a fortune: and the Wine and Food Society, although its success in the first year of its life exceeded the most sanguine hopes of either partner, never provided him with that fairly considerable settled income which seemed certain in the flush of its first remarkable success. The membership did not greatly increase, during A.J.'s lifetime, beyond that obtained at the end of the first year.

The Society's impartial view of the English catering trade was partly responsible for the moderation of its success. A scathing attack delivered by one of the members in a speech at the first General Meeting annoyed the Hotel and Restaurant Association; the support of the trade was never given fully to the Society's activities, and the project of blessing certain hotels with the Society's approval could not be carried out. As A.J. noted sorrowfully, when the Society had been in existence four years: "Our most important failure is that we have still failed to capture the confidence of the hotel world . . . the official body, the Hotel and Restaurants Association, since our inception has viewed us with a mixture of suspicion and hostility. Unfortunately the hotel industry in general, and those who guide the Association in particular, seem to see in the natural desire of the Members of the Society for better food, better attention, and more reasonably priced wines, an open attack upon their whole foundation". This was a subsidiary reason for the Society's inability to achieve large membership: but the prime cause lay in the temperament of the two partners in the enterprise.

I have said already that the Society was designed to attract the great body of middle class support from which a membership of 10,000, or more, might have been obtained. It failed finally to do so because the taste of the President was too good for him to make the necessary concessions to popular vulgarity; and the taste of the Secretary had been educated by the taste of the President. An editorial in *Wine and Food* (written, again, in the Society's fourth year of life) at last recognized this fact:

> Disarming criticism is difficult when one set of critics accuse us of having ceased to be an *élite* and become a mob, whilst others blame us for being too highbrow and ignoring the masses. To those who think that our doors are open too wide, our answer is that an *élite* is not a *clique*, and that we cannot hope to achieve what our Society was founded to achieve unless we have the power of numbers at the back of us. To those who tell us that our bounden duty is to the masses, and that we could be certain of an immense volume of support did we but address ourselves to them, we can but confess that we do not feel equal to the task. . . .
>
> Our helplessness with the brainless majority, both rich and poor, does not mean that we have no, or but little, interest in questions of nutrition for the poorer classes of the community. On the contrary. We fully realize that the poorer the home the more essential it is to avoid waste in cooking, and that it is very important to teach the humbler housewives how to make the best use possible of the food-stuffs within their means. We are also fully aware that, when it is good, plain food is best, and that English food can be both plain and best. But if we go to the trouble of importing out-of-the-way wines and staging exotic meals, it is not merely to give to our Members and their friends opportunities, nowhere else to be had, of appraising the cooking and wines of different countries; it is also, and we may say chiefly, to introduce just an element of novelty likely to rouse more interest in and attract more attention to our Society, its aims and its work.

As President and Secretary recognized this parting of the ways, the articles in *Wine and Food* were written, more

A. J. A. Symons

and more, not merely for a minority, but for a very small
minority of the membership, conscious of its own gastronomic culture; the recondite nature of many of the subjects, and the tone of airy superiority in which they were
treated must have frightened away more prospective
members than it attracted. Lunches and dinners gradually
became fewer, better, and—more costly. For some time
neither partner fully understood the implications of the
attitude they had adopted, and a large increase in membership seemed to them axiomatic; but A.J., at least, realized
it more and more as the years passed and the novelty of
sitting at the head of a table lost a great deal of its savour.
He understood, too, that the same kind of fastidiousness in
his own character had prevented him from making the
First Edition Club the great popular success it might have
been in less sensitive hands. When, during the war (to
anticipate a little) the Society fell on hard days and André
Simon wistfully suggested that in the hands of a publisher
the Quarterly might greatly increase its circulation, A.J.
rebuked him for wishful thinking:

> The trouble is that you are too much a true gourmet and
> connoisseur to win the comprehension or confidence of
> that Hampstead housewife who could give it (the magazine)
> the circulation for which you long. Your gastronomic con-
> science is too strict; you are too conscious of high standards
> to tolerate mush; you have the fatal defect of sincerity (fatal,
> that is, if you want the rewards that go to the ——'s and
> ——'s). You are a luxurious, cigar-smoking, wine-loving
> gourmet, who wants the best, and has been able to indulge
> his preferences (very rightly!) up to the present time. You
> have drawn to yourself a circle of contributors who feel
> more or less as you do in these matters, and produced a
> magazine calculated to understand, sympathize with, or
> learn from it. I am not in the least blaming you. Most of the
> work I have been allowed to do—the organizing of exhibi-

tions of Polish, Czech, French, German, Dutch, American printing in this country, the showing of English printing abroad, the establishing of new standards of book production, and much, much more—has met with even less recognition and reward than your efforts for the Quarterly. The lack of recognition does not make me feel that what I did was wasted, though, like you, I feel rebellious at the unequal scales in which my work and that of others has been weighed.

He recalled sadly that the *Book-Collector's Quarterly* had proved an unsatisfactory commercial proposition for a publisher "after four years, during which the magazine never paid a farthing, in cash, kind, or 'office expenses' to either editor; during which it was, in a modest way, advertised in the press; during which it drew on the foremost contributors in its own line and printed a body of material of permanent interest"; and he concluded with a truism which in his younger days he had been gallantly reluctant to admit, that intelligence and good taste will not ensure popularity. "For a popular success you must touch a growing audience—an audience growing with the times, like the motor-car conscious audience since 1918, or the radio-listening audience since 1926." Neither President nor Secretary ever had this kind of success at heart enough to achieve it fully; and although in the early days of the Society A.J. was very happy to sit down to the same dinner four nights running (for some of the Society's meetings had to be held in quadruplicate as membership grew), to discuss the wine and food again and again with the same earnestness, and to build repeatedly the same smooth pyramid of conversation in similar unintellectual company, this occupation palled with the passage of months and years.

By a queer turn of events the Society has gained, since

A. J. A. Symons

the end of the war, something of the audience which its sponsors expected in its first years. "As soon as peace conditions are restored", A.J. wrote to Simon in 1940, "the audience will be waiting". He was right: and they have waited with the more eagerness because of the restrictions placed upon luxurious eating and drinking. The very name of the Society is to-day a kind of lure to many severely-rationed Englishmen and women, who regard exotic and intelligently-prepared food with a tenderness which they did not at all feel for it in the past. To-day, when the Society can no longer offer Alsatian and Savoyard meals at half a guinea, and wine-tastings at half a crown, its membership is larger than it ever was before the war: but only one of the founders has lived to see its late and curious blossoming.

CHAPTER XI

FINCHINGFIELD

―――

IN these days A.J. left London on Friday evening, or sometimes (to his partner's slight annoyance) on Friday morning, and motored down to the red-brick house at Finchingfield in Essex, which has already been mentioned but not described. From his boyhood the possession of a house in the country had been one of the chief objectives of his life. "No man", he assured a friend, "is complete without a country property"; and when he discovered one he became lyrical in its praise. He had been house-hunting in Essex with a friend, in his wife's absence on holiday, and the results of the search had been disappointing, for the most promising of the properties, although inexpensive, resembled too much the box-like structure of Cedars Road:

So we decided [he wrote to his wife] not to look at any more, but to find a place to put up at. Then I thought we'd look at Finchingfield, the village Iris Barry had said was so fine. We found our way there, left the car outside an inn, drank cyder, and then strolled round the corner down the hill to see the place. My God! we rubbed our eyes. All I.B. said was perfectly true. It's as good as Broadway. It's as good as Lindfield. It's as good as Chipping Campden. It's *marvellous*. We gasped. In the sunshine it looked like a scene in a play. Everything unbelievably neat, tidy, and unspoiled. We looked down from a hill at a confluence of roads, a bridge, and a river which expands into a duckpond; the most delicious village green; and charming houses. Slowly we walked down, and then on the left A HOUSE hove into view. Georgian; red brick; situated slap facing the village green; lovely windows; good door. "Now if *that* had been to let. . . . " I said, and then we both stared at a small board. It was! It is!

We went inside. It's on a slope. This is it. [He made a pen drawing in the letter.] There are, as you see, two doors; an iron railing in front. Date about 1780 and looks it. Marvellously built. Well; we went inside. It's like this. [Another drawing.] There is one noble (but not too large) bedroom with powder closet (which would make a wardrobe or dressing room), two other good bedrooms, and one small one. It is a noble house. At the back there is a long garden (almost as long as Cedars Road but not so wide) in which are roses, peaches, nuts and vegetables (all thriving). And the rent of this lovely Georgian house (the attics, I forgot to say, are superb) the rent, my child, is 19s. 6d. per week. Rated at £27 a year—about £12 10s. to pay.

Such enthusiasm was irresistible: and, in any case, he did not mean to be resisted. In the flushed days of 1929 when he first discovered the house, with the expansion of the First Edition Club (he felt comfortably assured) round the corner, £1 a week seemed a trifling liability. It was true, of course, that the liability was not, finally, merely £1 a week. There was no bathroom, and no lavatory, and these had to be installed. The two front doors proved an inconvenience and one of them was bricked up. Furniture had to be bought and oil lamps, carpets and cutlery and linen. The barns were renovated, a gardener hired, and a maid. All of these things were clearly indispensable elements of a gentleman's country property, and neither A.J. nor Gladys was inclined to be niggardly in such matters.

But still the house remained a fragmentary and incomplete affair until the collapse of the Club at Bedford Square, with its attendant consequences, enforced economies. Gladys, immured, at this time quite contentedly, in this remote Essex village, now used all of her considerable tact and taste in decoration to make Brick House a pleasant and even a notable home. Her husband loved it more and more. It was, as one of his friends remarked, the castle he defended against the attacks of creditors during the most unstable financial period of his life, when he maintained himself, almost miraculously, among a storm of debts. Nothing in his life gave him more pleasure than the occupation, and later the ownership, of this red-brick house. He would expatiate to friends on the advantages of living in Essex, and particularly in Finchingfield. There were no golf-courses, he said, so that one was spared the possible visits of that scourge, the golf-bore; no one lived nearer than four or five miles—an easy distance for one's friends to travel by car, but too far for undesired casual callers to wander in; the fact that the nearest railway station was several miles away conferred, in some ways, positive benefits for those who owned a car. Essex was not, like Surrey, filled with stockbrokers, and property, although much less expensive than in that overcrowded and over popular county, was immeasurably more attractive. Here, for a few thousand pounds (and now a wistful look might show in his eye, and he might look faintly discontented with his, after all, rather *small* red brick house) it was possible to own a mansion. But for those of his friends who remained irreconcilably urban, he would add that if Essex did not please them, even country property in Surrey was better than no country property at all; for only property could give a fitting background to a man's life.

There can be few of his friends who did not, at one time or another, spend a weekend at Finchingfield; and the experience, although beyond question impressive and pleasurable, might also be in some ways an ordeal, or at any rate a trial, from which few emerged altogether triumphantly. For in the later thirties, when the Wine and Food Society had relieved A.J.'s most pressing financial problems, he spent a great deal of money on Brick House. It remained a charming and comfortable home: but it was also quite plainly the house of a man of taste, or indeed of tastes, in several subjects—a man who flatteringly assumed that your knowledge and appreciation were equal to his own.

Thus the visitor, soon after arrival—after, perhaps, drinking a glass of sherry which he treated with more respect on being assured that it was the ever-reliable Tio Pepe—would be asked whether he was amused by mechanical toys. Such a question, except for the hardiest spirits, admitted of only an affirmative answer; and this led to a tour of inspection of perhaps two or three dozen of the hundred Victorian musical boxes that were in every room of the house. Tiny boxes, in appearance like cigarette cases; great boxes like grandfather clocks, called not musical boxes but polyphons, with an enormous disc replacing the clock-face; boxes that looked like miniature organs; boxes that played four, six, eight or ten tunes. The tour of inspection might be interrupted to gaze at the late-Victorian picture of a family group that hung in the entrance-hall—a picture, the host might say, that combined the talents of Daumier and the miniaturist; and he would vary his observations on the history and virtues of musical boxes and on the splendid solidity of Victorian painting with an eagerness for the expression of his visitor's opinion on these subjects which was equally flattering and intimidating. The pause was not a long one, for there was a great deal to be seen within the house: the

5,000 books which lined the study, landings, and even the bathroom and lavatory; the astrological maps, and the Chinese paintings on glass, the foliage of which he likened, on the authority of Edward Wadsworth, to the foliage of Vlaminck; the Bristol glass paper-weights and the Victorian card-cases. But perhaps, he would suggest courteously after a while, the visitor was weary of staying indoors; perhaps he would care to look at the garden.

The garden was pleasant, but less remarkable than its owner's pride in the produce—apples and pears on one side of a tiny stream, and on the other side neat rows of vegetables ("We shall eat Finchingfield asparagus to-night"). On their return the visitor might be moved to exclaim at the splendour, in appearance and condition, of the two fine barns that flanked the back of the house. Obligingly the host would lead the way into one of them: and there the visitor would see, perhaps with a mixture of pleasure and distress, an enormous, finely-roofed and soundly-floored room and, in the middle of it, a large table tennis table. Here, A.J. would tell his guest, Finching-field had played and defeated Toppesfield, in spite of the playing wiles and acute generalship of Toppesfield's finest player, Francis Meynell; and, laughingly, he would suggest a game. If his visitor did not warm to this sugges-tion he would offer to play with his left hand, and with one eye closed. When he had won—he was altogether quick of hand and eye—he would comfort the guest by saying that he had two younger brothers who could give him ten points start in a game of twenty-one.

A visit to the cellars was an indispensable prelude to dinner. Dark, low, and slightly dank, they were toured by candlelight. The selection of wine at the guest's disposal was displayed. What would he choose to drink with dinner? Sometimes the visitor capitulated weakly, and left the act of choice to the host: but A.J. preferred that an expression of opinion should be given so that he could, like a conjuror, exert his mental prestidigitatory skill by diverting his visitor's choice to the wine which he had already marked as suitable. A visit to the cellars, like everything else at Brick House, held certain disastrous possibilities. Doris Langley Moore has described one of them. "On one occasion I carried down to the cellar after him a pair of Regency decanters which he had just bought and was freshly delighted with, and I was clumsy enough to let one of the stoppers fall out and break to smithereens. He touched the highest point of courtesy in his convincing reassurances to put me at my ease, but oh! the dreadful moment it was!" At dinner the wine would be treated with a deep, and to the irreverent faintly comic, respect, especially if other vinolaters were numbered among the company. The host's proboscis would hover above the glass, he would murmur "A splendid nose", or "A little light on the nose, I think", and his challenging glance would pass round the table. Other heads would be pushed forward reverently above glasses but there were few, outside a coterie of intimate friends, who dared to question the rightness of a decision made with such certainty.

Conversation was a necessary concomitant of dinner: and indeed it flowed during the whole day. All of his friends agree in praising A.J. as a talker; yet they have found difficulty in capturing the essence, or the phrases, of his conversation. His vigorous delivery, his manifest delight in argument and eagerness in rebuttal, his retention on difficult occasions of an unruffled temper and smooth, well-constructed, perfectly grammatical phrases, his apparently spontaneous enthusiasm or his fully-considered scorn, all these were part of an effect that was greater by far than their sum. His phrases seemed memorable, but

when recounted later by others in cold print they acquire
a Jamesian ponderousness which they hardly possessed
in delivery and which, somehow, does not give a full or a
right flavour for those who knew him. Most of the
elements in his conversation are, thus, distinguishable,
yet they do not make up his talk; and the threads of his
sophistical arguments, the detail of what he said, has
passed with his death into irrecapturable fields of memory.
His conversation, in recollection, suffers the fate of that
of many other men who have impressed by their presence
rather than by their paradoxes.

We can still summon up, however, some of the general
characteristics that delighted, awed, amused and infuriated
his friends and enemies. He had no use for small talk, and
little taste for gossip; he disliked the appearance of apathy
or boredom: and his own conversation embodied the
reverse of these qualities. He brought the full force of his
intelligence to bear on every topic discussed; he would
seize a disputed point (perhaps not at all the main point)
in argument, and worry it until his opponent gave up the
battle in despair. Conversation with him became almost
always a struggle between opposed points of view, conducted upon his side with an unfaltering courtesy and
friendliness, which concealed an eagerness to take advantage of every opening or error. He talked for victory, or if
the assembled company was too timid or wary to give
battle, he indulged in elaborate monologues on subjects
close to his heart. These subjects were varied, and some of
them were odd, but he chose them generally with a mind
to the interests of his listeners. He could talk with lawyers
on the injustice of certain famous prison sentences or the
expediency of judicial flogging, with an etymologist like
C. K. Ogden on a point of grammatical construction or
on the debasement of our language that might be brought

about through Basic English, with such experts on the psychology and history of clothing as James Laver and Doris Langley Moore on the influence of clothes on character. He talked, also, to tease, and would often adopt deliberately an attitude likely to irritate the professional "expert" on any subject. Since I edited a verse magazine that was firmly modern in taste he would discuss with me T. S. Eliot, whose work he praised with a deliberate disregard for his serious reputation ("An admirable comic poet, my dear Julian—although inferior, as you no doubt realize, to Hood"); and he never revealed the irritation that my brashness must have caused him, when in return I dismissed his favourite Shelley, and praised the work of Ben Jonson.

His knowledge was, generally, not deep but wide, and he was rarely at a loss for a happy analogy. If the talk moved in fields rendered distasteful to him by his own ignorance he would divert it—but the change was carried out so skilfully as to be imperceptible, frequently, to the other people in the circle of talk. Thus a don, launched happily on such a subject as the art of the Cinquecento might find himself drawn into a discussion of the old chestnut: "Does beauty exist merely in the eye of the beholder, or is it inherent in the thing seen?"—in which A.J. would eagerly espouse the latter cause. He would argue, with every appearance of sincerity, that Edgar Allan Poe possessed the most profoundly original mind of the nineteenth century; express his warm appreciation of the benefits wrought by the Code Napoleon; or turn a historical argument on Cromwell and the Levellers into a dissertation on the generalship of Prince Rupert of the Rhine. A talker's memorial is of its nature impermanent: but few who sat round a dinner-table with him will forget his flashing intelligence, his out-of-the-way knowledge and, playing over all his conversation, the good-natured attempt to draw out the less glib or more sullen of his companions so that they too could shine—as, it must be added, secondary stars. After an evening of wine, food, and such conversation, the guest retired by the light of oil lamps (gas and electricity were unknown to Brick House) to sleep in one of the four-poster beds. The day had been a stimulating, but also an exhausting one. It was sometimes a comforting thought (if the visitor had come for a weekend) that the following day was Sunday— traditionally a day of rest.

Such tradition, however, was not often observed at Brick House. The host rose early and ate his usual breakfast, which comprised a great mug of very weak, almost milkless tea, and some dry toast (he never ate butter, except when it was cooked with food) with Cooper's Marmalade. He then retired to his study, leaving an injunction that he should be called as soon as the visitor appeared in the breakfast room. The sound of his type-writer might be heard tapping in the study, but the visitor would have been wrong in the ingenuous supposition that he was typing the long-awaited successor to *The Quest For Corvo*. He was engaged, instead, in the daily round of answering letters from friends and duns (bills were paid once a year at Finchingfield—"Such", he observed, "is the custom of the country gentry"), or purchasing additions to his library from booksellers' lists.

Late rising was not encouraged. Those guests who dallied too persistently would receive a polite summons when a musical-box tinkled gaily outside their door. Breakfast, for them, would be a more ample meal than for their host; when it was finished (always supposing they had not adopted the evading tactic of going to Church) they would be asked what they would like to do during the day. This question gave an illusion of freedom of choice, like that other question about the wine: but in his mind the host had already decided that a call on one or another neighbour would interest the visitor, or that there was a particular old house for sale (to be reached by a five-mile walk) which should be seen by host and guest alike. If the visitor expressed positive disapproval of these suggestions, A.J. was prepared to accept modifications of them, providing they allowed him some congenial form of mental or physical exercise. If, in response to his question, the visitor said that he would like to do nothing, a faint shade of displeasure might cross his face, to vanish as quickly as it came. He did not care for such a negative reaction.

If the day was fine, and the visitor moderately amenable, it was likely that he would find himself walking in the Essex countryside—a countryside that he had perhaps not suspected of possessing particular charms, but which his host viewed with proprietorial pride. Nothing delighted him more than an unwary hint that his guest considered Essex flat. The Sunday walk, which was conducted always at a cracking pace, would then contain a surprising number of gentle rises, and at the end of each of them A.J. would ask triumphantly: "Does *this* seem to you flat?" or "I see that you show signs of exhaustion. Clearly they cannot be accounted for by any contour of the landscape, for we know that it is completely flat." A.J. had the very slightest acquaintance with natural history, so that his customary accompaniment of a long walk was an intricate or simple verbal game—a game which, again, any moderately amenable visitor would certainly be bound to play. Sometimes the games were as simple as the identification of poetic quotations, or a variant of the ordinary child's spelling bee; for subtler minds there were more complicated pastimes. Even the simpler games were likely to bring the visitor back from his walk feeling physically and mentally tired, and fully ready for a glass of the ever-reliable Tio Pepe.

After the Tio Pepe, luncheon; and this (like dinner the night before, like almost all the meals served at Brick House) was unpretentious and delicate, rather than ornate. A.J. refused to have tinned foods in the house; he would—and in wartime, did—live on vegetables alone if necessary, rather than resort to tinned food. He was not finicky, nor hard to please; and the circumstances in which meals were prepared at Brick House—cooking was often done on an oil stove—made this fortunate. Luncheon was likely to comprise a good soup made from stock, meat or poultry cooked simply but well, with whatever vegetables were in the garden; and a portion of fine Stilton or Blue Cheshire cheese. The guest, if he were a member of the Wine and Food Society, would perhaps notice with some surprise that although A.J. might enter the kitchen frequently during the morning, although he might look seriously at the soup stock, or display a faint judicial perturbation about the meat, the gourmet's only practical part in the preparation of luncheon was the mixing of a salad dressing, a process attended with a pre-parative care and a fine anxiety that seemed dispro-portionate to the critical mind.

Sunday followed the pattern of Saturday—although this theme was subject to variations. Sometimes a friend would be summoned specifically for the display of a talent; and he was expected to show it in a satisfactorily impressive manner, for his arrival had been advertised by A.J., and his talent stressed. A heavy weight of responsi-bility rested on this friend, for he had become, during the period of his stay, part of Brick House; like the vegetable garden and the Essex landscape he had, temporarily, gained importance in A.J.'s eyes. Thus my brother Maurice and I were advertised as table tennis players against whom any local talent would show very poorly, and it was lucky for us that we were able to help Finchingfield to victory over Toppesfield. Less fortunate was Desmond Flower, who rashly expressed to A.J. his interest in cricket. Interest in a game was, for A.J., synonymous with playing it well, and he can have had no other thought than that his friend would be delighted with a chance to shine in person, and to reflect glory on his host, when he spoke of Flower's ability to local cricketers. Flower received a letter saying: "You play for Finchingfield on Saturday"; and A.J., whose interest in cricket was not greater than that of Henry James (who, during Rye cricket week, always sat in the tent talking to the ladies with his back to the cricket) came to watch. Flower's tale of what followed is unhappy, but not untypical:

> I can guess the kind of thing he said to the Club Secretary over the telephone, for I found myself unduly prominent in the batting order. I am an indifferent performer at any time, and I did not excel on that afternoon. After scratching at the wicket for some time I was dismissed. A.J. was waiting for me when I walked back to the pavilion and he was not pleased. He indicated that I had not only practically closed every door in Essex on my insignificant person, but had as good as proved him a liar. I was glad when we left that unhappy field to console ourselves with champagne in the garden at Brick House.

But the visitor lacking this special talent, who had been invited for a customary weekend, would be expected to play, on Saturday or Sunday evening, one or another elaborate game. Some of these games have been described already, but others had by now been discovered, or invented; Caballo, in which a number of metal horses were

propelled rapidly along a strip of green baize by the turning of a handle; Monopoly, which A.J. played with
devilish energy and concentration ("It brings out all one's
worst instincts", he said with a chuckle); the old game
"Squails", which he revived, or "Nyner", a combination
of bagatelle and shoveha'penny. He even attempted to
revive the old War Game, spurred by the interest of his
friend Percy Muir. "It was his ambition", Muir said,
"To initiate a sufficient number of neighbouring friends
into the game to permit of a grand assault on Braintree. . .
Insufficiency of aptitude, time and patience eventually
disqualified me from being seconded as A.J.'s chief of
staff, and similar disappointments reduced him to his own
resources." Occasionally an exceptionally hardy guest
would refuse outright to play a game; and then, although
nothing would be said at the time, and A.J. would not
fail in courtesy towards him, it was likely that at some
time during the weekend that guest would feel the full
weight of his host's powers in argument. A.J. never apppre-
hended fully, I am sure, just what those powers were, for he
was not often willingly asperous, and his weightiest remarks
—like those made to Desmond Flower after the failure at
cricket—were tinged with self-ridicule: but this was not
realized by those who provoked him, and his playful
savagery, like that of a large and intelligent cat, his piling
of epithet on epithet, his relentless tearing to pieces of an
incautious statement, reduced more than one unhappy
feminine victim to tears.

But such scenes were rare and, at Brick House, they
were almost unknown, for, although what has already been
said may sound like evidence against him, he was a
lavishly generous and thoughtful host. It should be
remembered that many of those who visited Brick House
regarded the amusements he favoured with positive

enthusiasm (as I did); or they were so much impressed by his personality, engaged by his fervour, and delighted by his conversation, that they participated willingly and even with enjoyment in games that they would have played nowhere else. It was not likely, for example, that anywhere else would his friends have cared to engage (with his enthusiastic family) in the house game, in which every player was armed with a toy pistol firing balls of tissue paper, and in which Vyvyan Holland's "epic and successful defence of the back staircase when his side had been seriously depleted by casualties" was well remembered by another participant; or in the more boisterous variant of the game played with two barricades of furniture placed in the hall, behind which sniping took place and in which, again, Holland distinguished himself by flinging handfuls of bullets into a trench with the cry "Machine-gun". The uncomfortable moments were very few, and the compensations for them many. Desmond Flower's hurt spirit was soothed by champagne and conversation, and Doris Langley Moore's embarrassment was brief, although acute. The weekend visitor, when he returned to London on Monday morning, would perhaps remember with pleasure the wine and food, the conversation or the country walk: but much more sharply, and for a longer time, he would remember the clothes, the talk, and the personality, of the old-young man with dark hair and bright eyes and discoloured teeth who had been his host; of whose past so little was generally known, and of whose future so much was varyingly predicted; whose friends and enemies were busy in making of him, to his own delight, a man of legend.

The position in which my brother envisaged himself, as a man of property occupying a country residence,

required that he should interest himself in the affairs of
the village. He did so; and in his own view at least was the
ruler of a kind of cultural squirearchy in that part of Essex.
His reputation in the village suffered somewhat from the
fact that he very rarely went to church, and also because of
complications in his personal life which are told in a later
chapter. These events would have been more than
balanced by the realization of a projected visit from Queen
Mary, to look at his collection of musical boxes; but
unexpected events intervened, and the visit was never
made.

It was in his capacity as public guardian of Finchingfield interests that A.J. exerted himself by writing a letter
to *The Times*. "It has recently been found necessary", he
wrote, "to bring electricity to the village. Electric light
and power rank high among modern amenities, and their
introduction is welcome." (The tinge of regret is clearly
visible). The electricity company, he went on to say,
wanted to use overhead cables, carried on poles; but "in
consideration of the payment of £100 towards its
increased expenditure", it had agreed to lay underground
cables in the centre of the village and in other parts where
the erection of poles at short intervals would disturb the
village's character. The letter ended:

> The Company has very generously agreed to wait a year
> for the receipt of its promised contribution, for the payment
> of which I have given a personal guarantee, in order that
> the admirers of this beautiful village may have an oppor-
> tunity of assisting in its preservation. May I therefore beg
> the courtesy of your columns for the purpose of inviting
> subscriptions towards the promised £100 from those who
> share the desire to preserve, in its present unspoiled condi-
> tion, this superb survival among the villages of England.

The optimistic guarantor had no doubt that he would
get his £100, but, as had often happened before, his

optimism was unjustified. He suffered from the measure of his success. The cables had been run underground; the Green was saved; and he was able to collect only a quarter of the sum he had guaranteed. The Electricity Company was amiable but insistent, and his refusal to have electricity installed at Brick House did not render them more liable to sympathize with him. The incident ended in a defeat for his perennial optimism.

He was never, I think, accepted in local society on his own terms; nevertheless, he placed a value upon his position in the village which was so extravagant that he did not care for other members of his family to visit the village pubs. This self-importance was irritating, but it was complemented, and for those with a sensibility able to appreciate his self-involved irony largely cancelled, by his own clear knowledge of what he was doing. In the summer of the late thirties he lent Brick House to his friend Ian Black for a few weeks, and the letter that Black found awaiting him in the hall on arrival shows both my brother's unreadiness to take himself or his possessions lightly, and his concern to cast a sheen of humour over a characteristic which he recognized as something less than positively endearing:

First of all, welcome. I am delighted to think that while I am walking, pack-laden, across unknown country, you will be here to stroke the cat and cheer the house up. It will take you a few days to settle into the routine, but once you find out the ways of the household you ought to be as comfortable here as I am.

Various small points.

(1) I.E.B. reserve. I find, alas, that there is no more Hermitage, when my store is exhausted. But I have put out 6 Dopff Alsace wine (white, cremant, dry) and 12 St. Croix du Mont (white, sweetish) and 6 bottles of claret (Lynch Bages 1924, Grand Corbin 19—and Ausone

1931—this last the best wine of a bad year). For these I propose to charge you 4s. a bottle—cost price to me—but don't mention the price to St. Denis or others. I have also put out 3 bottles of Aloxe-Corton 1929, a very reasonable burgundy, at 6s.; 3 Yquem 1929 and 3 Irroy (champagne) 1923 at 9s.; and 3 halves of Perrier Jouet 1926 at 4s. 6d. (½ bottle). I hope this is sufficient. Writing this reminds me of sherry. If I remember, I will put out 3 bottles (all I have here) of La Riva Fino (7s. 6d.). This is the only sherry on the market *bottled* in Spain. It is light, and *very* dry. You may not care for it, but you can easily order ordinary sherry to come down.

(2) Be careful of lamps. They tend to burn up when first lit. If they do, and turn the mantle black, turn down and then up gradually. They will burn the black off slowly. It is a good thing to acquire the habit of turning down lamps if you leave them burning in an unoccupied room.

(3) Visitors book is in the greenroom. The bookcase is unlocked save for the side sections: the same key fits both. These are locked only because the doors fly open otherwise.

(4) I have put most of the musical boxes away, as they are fragile in unexperienced hands. But there is the table model on landing (don't change the cylinder), the drums and bells model (in perfect order: don't let it run down in the middle of a tune, but stop and start it by the switch provided) and another in the oak room.

(5) I have put away the snuffboxes, as these are irresistible to the souvenir-fiend. You may not number any among your acquaintances, but on the other hand you may entertain them unawares. These two precautionary measures don't reflect on you (I need hardly say) but are meant to make your responsibilities lighter.

(6) Despite appearances to the contrary, the books are arranged, or are in process of arrangement. If, therefore, those taken out are replaced as they were, I shall be grateful. But failing this, let them be piled for me to put away later. This will be no trouble to me at all.

(7) Suckling and Kitty will do anything you ask within their power. He is a most excellent car-cleaner: she is an

excellent plain cook. Between them they can do most
things if warned in time.

(8) If there are any household necessities needed (such as
more sheets, etc.) Kitty will buy them and charge to me.
The garden should yield ample vegetables. Other comes-
tibles you will buy as you want, I presume. The lettuces
are excellent now, and Kitty makes admirable salads.
Investigate the *white* fraises des bois. These are a special
sort, and never gored—a novelty. They are always
small. This has been a shocking year for fruit, alas, and,
in common with my neighbours, I have no apples.

(9) Don't expect too many hot baths too quickly too early.
But treated properly the boiler is very efficient. I suggest
a pre-dinner bath for somebody.

(10) Watch the kitchen fire.

I can't at the moment think of any more cautions or
problems, but over the week-end I shall be at The Lee 342
(Great Missenden, Bucks.).

oh (11) Tours of the countryside.

Don't miss (a) Saffron Walden. Go via Thaxted: you
can return via Gt. Sampford.

(b) a longer expedition is via Clare and Cavendish to
Long Melford (the hall is wonderful).

(c) Braintree and Bishops Stortford are best for shops.
Early closing on Wednesday.

Such a "walk in unknown country" was part of his
yearly holiday—and frequently, indeed, the whole of it.
He would eat and drink simply and moderately with
chosen companions, walk enormous distances, look at
fine houses, talk incessantly, and forget, like a boy, all
debts and difficulties. He preserved a record of one such
walking holiday, taken with Richard Wyndham and
David Tennant; and it is interesting, both because it shows
the dandy, the gourmet and the painstaking host in a
different but not less characteristic light, and because it
reveals indirectly the powers and the limits of his physical
and spiritual observation.

Finchingfield

The three friends set out from Great Yews, on the top of Whitsbury Down, six miles south of Salisbury. They planned to follow the ridge which stretches through Dorset, and to strike the sea at Weymouth. A.J., who loved oddly-named villages, "cherished a secret desire to visit an obscure village of which I knew (and know) only that it has the romantic and improbable name of Rime Intrinseca", and he observed that "Dorset challenges my favourite Essex in the charm and quaintness of its place names, with Toller Porcorum to set against Shellow Bowells, Cricket Malherbie against High Easter or Wendens Ambo". At the end of a day's walking, sharpened by lack of lunch, he remarked on the excellence of the meal they obtained for two shillings each, "Rabbits swimming in an appetising half-stew-half-sauce, garnished with good carrots and floury potatoes", followed by English cheddar, fresh lettuce and household bread. On the next day he viewed with sceptical interest the products of anthropological research in the local Pitt-Rivers Museum, and remarked on the beauty of the Benin bronzes whose "Impressive, V-lipped, broad-nostrilled faces look beyond the visitors to the surrounding English landscape, so demure, safe and parklike, and call up another land of torrid sun and dangerous, thoughtless life". But most of his record tells of food and drink consumed, and of fine houses looked at; he appreciated only the most broad and extensive aspects of nature, and could hardly tell an oak tree from an elm. It was one of the deficiencies in his nature that he loved contrived, rather than natural beauty.

There is no doubt, however, of his zest for fine architecture, and for architectural detail. He admired the two rows of symmetrical thatched cottages which form the whole of Milton Abbas and the old house at Binghams

Melcombe, "a small, delightful stone medley, with a chapel built into the general block, and a self-composed air of having withstood many generations and events without ever having been worried by either"; the long, many-windowed, unsmartened house at Cruxton, an English monument underlined by the stream which moves peacefully behind it, and the fine gatehouse of Frampton Court, "which started a pleasant argument on the folly of 'functionalism', that depressing apology for the optically incomplete"; the beautiful houses on the front at Weymouth and an equally beautiful chemists' shop at Bridport. He loved them all, and longed to possess them, or something like them. When he returned to London and to absorption in gastronomic, instead of architectural, detail, and then went at the weekend to Brick House, he found himself sometimes faintly dissatisfied with his surroundings. Brick House was pleasant, even delightful: but there were, after all, houses of greater architectural distinction, larger houses, houses more suited to the successful man he had become, or was becoming. There was one particular old Wren house which he had looked at with his wife; and one evening, after such a walking tour, he sat in the large room at Cedars Road which was kept for his weekday occupancy, thinking of the pattern of life which he still imagined himself capable of controlling, and wrote to her about it:

> Somehow, to-day, I am fascinated by that old Wren house. (Don't be alarmed—I haven't taken it; I'm not expecting to take it. But you know that I like to daydream, to "meditate"; and to-night, having no real work to do, I'm "meditating" on paper, to you. But it is only meditation.) Well, then, I am fascinated by that old Wren house; this is my musing.
>
> It is after dinner. At dinner we drank a pleasant young Burgundy. All has gone well at the Club; and I am in a very

Finchingfield

good mood. The soft light of the shaded lamps throws a restrained glow on the panelled walls, which are emphasized in their broken lines by slight shadows. Coffee; a cigar; no brandy or liqueur: we keep them (in that ravishing cupboard from Newport), but we keep them for other people. Or no; sometimes you take a sip of some honey coloured distillation, while I sample an old madeira, full of grape and sunshine. But on the night I am describing we don't feel like madeira or liqueurs; so we go from the dining room to the library.

To get there we pass through the hall, and I look up with fond pride (as I always do) at *the* staircase. It is worth looking at; a wonderful staircase. Twisted strings, square newels, wide steps, a lovely turn, lit from above with the gleam of polished mahogany, by the panelling of the landing. But we don't stop; we go on to the library.

What, what, *what* a room. Longer than the long room at the First Edition Club; lit by four superb chandeliers; with decorous side lights gleaming on the backs of red, blue, green, orange, brown and gold books. Books all round in orderly array; every one in its exact place, and not a thing which is notable in English missing. A room, a collection, to dream about; a room to make the young, who hunger for books and beauty, dizzy with delight.

Comfortable chairs; well placed lamp standards (how clever Mrs. Symons must be with her shades); a noble double desk. We sit; and I read to you an old poem, explaining as I go.

> Now winter nights enlarge
> The number of their hours
> And clouds their storms discharge
> Upon the airy towers.

The first two lines are very good; a noble way of saying, not that the days draw in but, that the nights lengthen out. The second pair are not so good, but pass.

> Let now the chimneys blaze
> And cups o'erflow with wine,
> Let well-tuned words amaze
> With harmony divine!

A. J. A. Symons

Good? But it gets better.

> Now yellow waxen lights
> Shall wait on honey love,
> While youthful revels, masques, and courtly
>   sights,
> Sleep's leaden spells remove.

How charming the first two of those lines above are! "Now
yellow waxen lights" (candles of course). But they are all
good.

> This time doth well dispense
> With lovers' long discourse;
> Much speech hath some defence,
> Though beauty no remorse.
> All do not all things well;
> Some measures comely tread,
> Some knotted riddles tell,
> Some poems smoothly read.
> The summer hath his joys,
> And winter his delights;
> Though love and all his pleasures are but toys,
> They shorten tedious nights.

A fine poem. Campion wrote it over two hundred years
ago.*

As for the rest of the house, you must fill it in for yourself; the other long room (called, affectionately, the Gallery), hung with pictures, with paper weights and treasures,
suitably displayed. And the noble bedrooms. Everything
that a fine old mansion should have. Your own sitting
room, of course, with your own case of special books in it.
What does it matter to those who live inside this loveliness
that Charing Cross is four miles away, that outside is the
place that men call Clapham? We live inside, not out. And
there is a garden.

Sometimes —— and —— are with us. Sometimes there
are other faces. The house has become famous, and it is a
privilege to visit it. Vincent often dashes over after dinner
from Wimbledon (three miles away) for a glass and a chat.

* An error. Campion died in 1619.

Finchingfield

Well well well. Something of all this can be got even though we don't take the Wren house. I am spending Sunday house looking with Carl. He is eager to see the old house, and I shall show it him. But I shall say that it is too far out, and too grand; we shall look at Chelsea and Kensington and Baker Street and even Bloomsbury. But I shall always have a certain sentimental interest in that old house.

News. I got seventeen members for the Society to-day. I have had a rushed but pleasant day.

Well well well. You must be patient with me, my dear. The unusual and grand have always fascinated me, and always will. I live very much in my head, and I am abstract and undemonstrative. I like people, and I like talking. I like things, and like some things you don't. But behind all that burns a constant love for you, which is only dimmed when you try to get me to take up your standard instead of trying to take up mine.

This is a vague long letter. I have let my pen run away. Suddenly I feel tired. But I am cheerful and confident. *Be so too*. You will enjoy your life with me if you trust, a little more than you sometimes do

Your own

A.J.

But as the years went by and he became more and more engaged in the work of the Wine and Food Society he slipped further away from his hopes and aims in the past; and from his wife, who could not refrain from recalling to him the trail of debts and broken resolutions that lay behind him. We often think that we are conquering society, when in fact we are adapting ourselves to its remorseless vulgarity, its fathomless destruction of our own idealism.

CHAPTER XII

MUSICAL BOXES AND PROTEAN
SCENES

———————————

ONE of the difficulties inherent in the construction of any biography (it is one that surely occurred to my brother, but which he excluded from his ingenious essay on the kind of biography he wished to write) is the fluidity, richness and disorder of life. The biographer imposes retrospectively the design of art on a life which, if it is like most lives, was lived scramblingly and without clear dedication; he forces a pattern of consistent conduct upon a human being who, if he was like most human beings, was by turns mean and gracious, intelligent and foolish, reasonable and unjust. The biographer is involved, above all, in falsities of time and place. Since he is writing a biography and not a daily journal, he presents events in a continuous sequence rather than piecemeal as they occurred, he makes small distortions of reality (like that involved in the opening of *The Quest For Corvo*) to procure—quite legitimately, he assures himself—dramatic effect. These things are unavoidable and, indeed, desirable elements in the construction of any biography which is conceived, however clumsy may be its execution, with the firm order of art rather than the shapelessness of life.

My brother's career, after the founding of the Wine and Food Society, was a gallimaufry of memorable meals and, generally abortive, publishing schemes; of week-end

visits, and ideas for books which remained germinal; of
friendships easily made and often neglected; of hours and
days spent in collecting Victorian card cases and glass
obelisks and snuff boxes and protean scenes and musical
boxes; and, among all these occupations, of an energetic,
though not unremitting, attention to the affairs of the
Wine and Food Society and the First Edition Club. He
followed twenty different threads of interest every day,
where an ordinary man follows two: and the justification
for certain small distortions of chronology which are
involved, for instance, in labelling a chapter "Wine and
Food", and then recounting the fortunes of the Society as
if they were the simple and exclusive interest of my
brother's mind, is that a wholly chronological approach
would be tedious, and a diurnal one bewildering. Against
a background of wine and food his personality flowered,
slowly yet fantastically. He became widely known, not as
a bibliographer nor as a biographer, but as a dandy and a
figure of legend.

It was the Society's success, and the consequent increase
in his social self-assurance, perhaps, that led him to indulge
unstintedly a natural dandyism. He bought many suits,
and dozens of ties, few of which bore an unexciting pattern. All of his suits were expensive, and those made for
town wear had invariably very long jackets and brief
double-breasted waistcoats. Most of his clothes were very
obviously hand-made, and he was genuinely shocked
when Vyvyan Holland told him that he never paid more
than a guinea for a shirt, and that he possessed only two
pairs of cuff-links. "Some people are puzzled", he once
said to me, "by the fact that although my shirts and ties
are sometimes a little extravagant, the total effect of my
appearance is that of absolute sobriety. They fail to observe
that any small extravagance in the rest of my dress is

A. J. A. Symons

offset always by the perfect plainness of my suits"; and he continued with an elaborate gastronomical analogy about the happy combination of rich and plain fare. It is true that his suits were always quiet in pattern, and that he never wore a suit with a stripe or a check; but their cut was often extravagantly individual. He continued, to the distress of his conservative friends, to wear double-breasted waistcoats long after they had become unfashionable, but although he was often what in another man would have been called overdressed, he carried his unfashionable, or over-fashionable, clothes with such an air of conscious virtue that many who would have laughed at others wearing the same clothes, were impressed by him.

This elaborate care for his dress was combined with an equal concern for his physical appearance. He knew that his slimness, his absolutely upright carriage, and his great height were good features, and he used them well. He was aware also that his nose was too large, his mouth too thin and his forehead too low for orthodox good looks, and he was much concerned with the preservation of his thick black hair and his exceptionally large, soft and white hands. This care for his appearance often seemed excessive to his friends; and when he sensed that this was the case he was capable of going to extreme lengths in order to fulfil the extravagances which they irritably expected of him. Thus on one occasion, when staying with a friend who was annoyed by A.J.'s exact dandyism, he came out attired for a walk to Chanctonbury Ring in a dark tight-fitting overcoat, black pork-pie hat and black kid gloves. When it was suggested to him that the gloves, at least, were otiose, A.J. replied that he wore gloves always to protect the soft white skin of his hands; and, taking off the gloves, invited his host to pat them and assure himself of their fine texture.

Musical Boxes and Protean Scenes

As he became more widely known socially, several stories were told of his mysterious past, and of a life said to be full of scandals and secrets. Most of the people who met him for the first time through the Wine and Food Society thought of him as a playboy, a man of independent means who was pleased to be foppish. They heard with surprise of his literary and bibliographical activities; and then some rumours of the collapse of the First Edition Club reached their ears, and they learned that so far from being a man of independent means he was apparently dependent on literature and gastronomy for his income. What was his background? A few friends knew part of the story, but none knew all of it, and hints and half-truths are almost always more interesting than facts. The legends about him grew: he was an adventurer who had made and lost several fortunes at horse-racing; he was a dealer in books who had started a Club to cover his professional activities; he made a living by forgery; he was a gambler who had perfected an infallible system at roulette.

These stories were told of him, with many others which reflect the credulity rather than the good nature of the tellers; and it is not likely that he contradicted any of them. He may have thought that this background of mystery was a favourable screen for a man who wished to achieve a position of importance in society without making the admission that he had no social background; but his love of mystification for its own sake played a part at least equally important in the hints that he dropped about his past. He did not say, like Frederick Rolfe when he heard an item of news about the Kaiser, "So my god-father has been at it again, has he?": but he spoke of the yacht which he had owned, and of the legal action in which he had defended himself successfully; he mentioned vaguely the time when he had been in the Army, and gave

A. J. A. Symons

hints of the extraordinary transaction in typewriters by which he had made a fortune, and of the strange affair of the lease at Lower Regent Street. He had many good tales to tell of his unmasking of forgers of first editions, such as that of the man who came to the First Edition Club one day and offered a copy of a book which he claimed to be both rare and valuable. Cursory examination made A.J. suspicious that it was a made-up first edition: that is, the man had found an imperfect copy of a genuine first edition, dismembered it, and re-made it with the missing parts taken from a later edition. Suspicion became certainty upon discovery of the fact that incorporated at the end of the book, among the necessary dozen pages of publishers' advertisements, was a notice of a work published several years later than the date of the genuine first edition. Before the vendor could guess his purpose A.J. (in his account of the story) threw the book into the fire, told the man it was a forgery, and suggested that if he was dissatisfied he had a remedy in the police court. He knew exactly how to tell such stories, when to stop with an air which invited his companion to ask questions, and when to imply that he had said more than he intended, and had —very nearly—betrayed a family secret.

"An incident at Newmarket", says his friend Ian Black, "Is fresh in my mind.

"In a small hotel Symons extracted from a book-case two volumes which gave the history and pedigrees of race-horses. He turned the pages rapidly to signal to me two names.

" 'My father owned those two horses', he said with an air of such mystery that I hesitated to pursue the subject further."

This story, like most of the others he told, was true; but it seemed to many people who knew him only at this time to bear all the marks of falsehood. They could not believe that this epicure and dandy could ever have sailed a yacht; that a dilettante could be fascinated quite innocently by games of chance; that a self-acknowledged bookworm could possibly enjoy long country walks. And, as A.J. told more of the truth about himself, so his more recent acquaintances became more firmly convinced that he was telling lies.

His collections, too, were part of the legend, for his ambitions as a collector grew as his financial situation improved. He had been content, in the twenties, to collect mother-of-pearl counters and model theatres, and to display, with a flourish, the gleaming swordstick which he had bought, as he said, to defend himself from footpads: but with his financial position, for a time at least, more or less secure, he roved into remoter fields. Remoter, but still inexpensive; for he had the good sense to see that he could not hope to compete with those of his friends who had seventeenth century folios upon their shelves. He turned to the toys and trinkets of the Victorian era, fine examples of which could still be bought in antique shops for a few shillings. He got considerable aesthetic pleasure from contemplation of these objects, for, as a friend remarked, he loved good craftsmanship, particularly craftsmanship of a kind which has fallen into disuse.

He began this second phase of his career as a collector (the first was given almost wholly to the collection of books) with Victorian mother-of-pearl card cases, snuff boxes, Bristol glass paperweights and prismatic glass obelisks. Within a short time he had bought some dozens of all these things at a cost of only a few pounds. He made it a rule, he explained to his family, never to pay more than a certain small sum for any of these objects. If the vendor refused to sell after some bargaining A.J., with a regretful shake of the head, said that he feared the object, much as he would have liked to possess it, was beyond his means: such tactics, he suggested, rarely failed to be effective. This account of his method of collection may not have been exactly true, but it was nearer to truth, I am sure, than the almost directly contrary tales which he told to less sceptical audiences of the schemes, laid and carried out, to foil other collectors, no matter how great the expense involved.

He viewed these memorials of the past ranged upon his shelves with sharp fastidiousness, and, when he had a large number, pruned his collection of inferior items, which he then sold, generally at a price much above that which he had originally given. If this proved difficult, the inferior pieces would be retained, but they would be put away inconspicuously so that they should not offend the eye they had so lately pleased; perhaps, at a later date, they might themselves form a saleable collection.

A.J. collected Victoriana with the fine boisterous eagerness he gave to all games that interested him. He took advantage, as always, of any gaps he could find in the rules when making his own collection: but it should be said by way of redressing the balance that he showed a readiness to help other collectors which charmed many, who had viewed his acquisitiveness with distaste, into becoming his friends. The story of his gift to Doris Langley Moore has already been told; but he was always eager to add to other collections, and many of his friends gained through his vicarious enthusiasm. He expected the compliment to be returned, and would become humorously indignant—and his companion could never be quite sure that the indignation was merely humorous—if a friend saw a desirable card-case, or some agreeable glass obelisks, and failed to notify him by telephone, postcard or telegram. A motor-car journey in his company involved, inevitably, several stops in order to visit antique shops: and he developed also the habit of collecting houses, not to live in but to look at, all over London. A journey from Bloomsbury to Finchingfield by way of Gordon Square and Epping Forest (calling in at Islington to look at Percy Circus) was, as André Simon remarked, a delightful experience.

"He would slow down or stop altogether in front of one house after another and draw your attention to its good points, its perfect proportions, its wrought-iron balconies or its graceful, welcoming porch. He knew who owned them and who had built them originally, what was the rent now being demanded, and roughly how much would have to be spent to remove an ugly Victorian lean-to glass conservatory or to carry out the necessary alterations for housing his many books and other treasures. And if I ventured to enquire where was the money to come from to buy as many houses as there were weeks in the year, he would accelerate and say something about the folly of allowing sordid monetary considerations to spoil the pleasures of anticipation."

His collecting ardour moved from obelisks and card cases to Victorian transformations, or Protean scenes as they were called in their own day—those curious paintings which, when held before a strong light, reveal a second picture concealed beneath the surface of the first; he turned from Protean scenes to ingeniously-constructed concertina-shaped peepshows which, opened to their full extent, gave the illusion of perspective as they revealed a vista of the Crystal Palace or of Windsor Castle; and at last his fancy settled, like a bee resting permanently on a richly-pollinated flower, upon Victorian musical boxes.

A. J. A. Symons

The degree and the permanence of my brother's enthusiasm for musical boxes surprised many of his friends, who thought it the least interesting of his collections. They ignored, or perhaps they were ignorant, of the fact that he had always been oppressed by his own inability to appreciate classical music. Bach and Beethoven, Brahms and Berlioz, were equally uncongenial to him, and indeed, he would have found it difficult to distinguish between them. This fact was always uncomfortably on his conscience, so that for years he heard with little pleasure the sound of a gramophone or a piano. He was delighted to discover in the musical box a form of music which he could not only understand and enjoy, but which offered the joint pleasures of collection and of becoming an authority on at least this offshoot of music.

The musical-box collection began through his interest in mechanical toys, such as a coloured model of Big Ben which played tunes and moved figures at the hours. This was later relegated to a dust-room as an inferior specimen, but he never ceased to be pleased with a musical chair (which played a tune when one got up from it) and a slightly desiccated negro bearing a tray of fruit, each piece of which opened during the course of a tune, to reveal dancing figures. The graduation from musical toys to musical boxes was an easy one; and as soon as A.J. began to listen to musical boxes and to look at their mechanism he saw that they were, at least for him, a collector's dream.

He was delighted, first of all, by the variations in the wood from which the boxes were made—rosewood, walnut and mahogany; and by the range of sizes—the smallest looking like snuffboxes, the largest like coffins, and those in between like tea caddies. He was astonished by their mechanical ingenuity, by the spiky brass cylinder, the steel comb with pointed prongs, the ratchet or key winder, the miracle by which the impingement of the comb on raised points in the cylinder produced sound. But most of all he was fascinated by the music that the boxes played—by the flashing runs and the pure bass, the way in which the key could be changed yet the melody continued, the muting attachment which could produce the effect of zither or guitar. He corresponded for months with curiosity shops in all parts of England, and bought musical boxes of all shapes and sizes. Those in good condition were sent to Finchingfield; others were strewn about the floor at Little Russell Street until they could be removed to the house of a repairer (sometimes referred to a little magniloquently as the only man of his kind in England) who was able to put into good order the many broken and indifferent boxes A.J. bought, and would even undertake the difficult operation of re-tuning the metal combs on which the tunes were produced. With his assistance musical boxes bought for a few shillings were transformed into working models worth several pounds each; and this achievement strengthened A.J. in his often-repeated view that possessions were much more valuable than money at the bank, because "A millionaire may find the tide of finance turn against him, but musical-boxes, mother-of-pearl counters, books— they represent untold wealth." He investigated the history of musical-boxes, and discovered that all the best boxes had been made in Geneva; he made enquiries from the British Consulate there, and succeeded in tracing a report on the Exhibition of Genevan industries in 1828 which contained valuable information; he made a short film in which he played a few of his boxes; he even overcame his detestation of the radio and gave several broadcasts. They brought an avalanche of letters from listeners who had

boxes to sell, or were anxious to know the exact worth of
a box which was a family heirloom, or had simply enjoyed
his broadcast. Another man might have been more disturbed than pleased by the receipt of some two hundred
offers of boxes, requests for information, and letters of
thanks: but not A.J. He had a special form printed with
a number of questions regarding the name of the maker,
length of comb and number of teeth, and this was sent to all
those who asked for information about the worth of their
boxes, or offered them for sale. A long correspondence
often developed through the offers which he made for
boxes. Some of his correspondents told him their life
stories, others deplored his lack of interest in such
curiosa as musical models of the Inchcape Lighthouse,
others still regarded the prices he offered as inadequate:
but in the end, he generally got what he wanted, at his
own price.

He guarded his collection with jealous care, drawing up
forms of agreement between himself and other collectors
with whom he was exchanging boxes, and binding the
invaluable repairer to use a large quantity of Swiss damper
wire exclusively on A.J.'s own work. Those who asked for
the repairer's name were met by a smile and an evasion;
and this mysterious figure was added to the long list of
men who were thought by his friends to be legendary until
on an appropriate occasion, with a conjuror's flourish, he
produced them. When one of his friends wanted a house he
would produce from the recesses of a memory as capacious
as a Gladstone bag one of the many Essex mansions he
had looked at, and would speak of its virtues with all
the enthusiasm of a house agent. Another friend who had a
taste for chocolates, and was visiting Brussels, received
from A.J. (who had been in Brussels only for two or three
days) minute directions telling him how to find a confec-

tioner in that city who made sweetmeats of peculiar delicacy. Vyvyan Holland, who had lost the key of a complicated lock for a jewel-case, and had been assured by the makers of the lock that nothing but a crowbar would open it, appealed in despair to his resourceful friend. "Two days later a furtive-looking person wearing a dark suit and a bowler hat and carrying a small black bag appeared at my house. I could almost fancy I could see a black mask and a jemmy sticking out of his pocket. In two minutes forty-three seconds by stop-watch he had opened the case, charged me a guinea and gone." Many similar stories could be, and were, told, and they added detail to the legend which he cherished and to which he made his own quite conscious additions.

He became known, at last, as an authority on musical boxes, and other Victoriana; and with authority grew assurance in asserting the virtues of his chosen form of music. He loved to quote Rossini's quip to Wagner that the time would come when they both would be remembered only by their recordings on the musical-box: and he had a perversion of the "Ride of the Valkyries" among his possessions, as well as a large box which played the whole of Mozart's Requiem Mass on several large interchangeable cylinders. He would talk, when introducing his collection, with an erudition which, so far as it concerned musical-boxes, was perfectly genuine. Then he would say in a half-deprecating tone, "Of course, for me the musical-box is the only form of music". He would slyly watch the listener's reaction, and if it seemed not altogether hostile would proceed to a positive statement of the superiority of the musical-box to any other musical instrument.

This preoccupation with Victoriana took up a great deal of time, and more time still was absorbed by his meetings

with fellow-collectors of many kinds. He displayed always
the most exquisitely flattering interest in subjects which
they had at heart—and this interest was not at all feigned,
for he found something intrinsically absorbing in oddities.
From several similar stories let me choose that of Sir
Francis Colchester-Wemyss, who tells of a visit my brother
paid him, when after a worthy meal, "A.J. sat up till after
3 a.m. looking at various odds and ends of bibelots, and was
rather especially interested in a collection of Eighteenth-
Century babies' caps". The letter of thanks that he wrote
after his visit is perfect in its kind: the touch of perfection
being achieved by the beauty of the script in which his
thanks were conveyed:

My dear Colchester-Wemyss,

I have waited until I reached the security of my own
fireside before writing to thank you for the delicious
entertainment with which you so kindly provided me on
Wednesday. At intervals ever since, my mind has dwelt
gratefully on the duck, the Corton Charlemagne, the antique
Port, the Swinburne shelf, and the surprising contents of
the Italian chest. They stand equal; each has its turn in my
affections. I expected a pleasant delectable evening; but not
the feast of treasures as well as table which you provided. A
thousand thanks, indeed, for an evening memorable for
more than wine and food.

This is so remote a corner that I can hardly hope that your
feet, or your tyres, will turn this way. But if they do; if ever
you are prompted to revisit Cambridge, or follow the
horses at Newmarket, or compete for the Dunmow Flitch,
or wonder at Saffron Walden, or even visit Essex—THEN,
I hope, you will allow me to offer you a return of curiosities and vintages, with Spooner transformations in place of
babies' caps, glass obelisks for Swinburne, and musical
boxes as a make-weight for the rest.

Please give my compliments to our two amiable table-
companions, and write me down in your secret books as
Very gratefully yours,
A. J. A. Symons.

Musical Boxes and Protean Scenes

He suggested to James Agate also that they should carry out an exchange of visits, but the dramatic critic replied cautiously that "Loving you doubtless means loving your musical boxes, as loving me certainly means loving my horses, and one of us might not stand the test". In reply A.J. made a specious defence of his own musical ignorance.

Dear Egomet,

As to visiting you and being visited by you, let us sign a treaty in advance setting off (as the bankers say) musical-boxes against horse-boxes. It is quite clear from *Ego* and other sources that you possess an instructed musical sensibility. I do not. My knowledge of music is confined to these Victorian curiosities and their repertory of operatic hackneys (if you will allow the jest) and popular (or once-popular) airs; *Libiame* will do as an example of the first kind, *The Plough Boy* represents the second. I claim this much for the *boite a musique*, that it is an instrument, as is the violin or the piano or the flute, and not a reproducer, as is the gramophone, the telephone, or the radio. A musical-box plays a special, peculiar-to-itself rendering of the tunes in its programme (by means of its specially tuned steel comb); and it makes an "intriguing" (there; I've written it for you!) contribution to the range of musical sounds. But I promise in advance not to show you more than eighty when you come (I have a hundred and eighteen); and even that number shall be reduced to eight if I observe any sign of you being reduced to . . . you know.

As for horses; or, rather, HORSES, you will be intrxgxxd [*Note:* The word is "intrigued" which—see earlier in the letter—my brother did not much approve, and wrote unwillingly] to learn that were it not for them

> I should not now be sorrow's heritor,
> Nor stand a lackey in the house of pain;

that is to say, I should not now be broke. But all this, and the story of John Gielgud's tennis court, and countless trifles of the kind, will vouchsafe themselves more naturally when wine, not ink, is the vehicle of our communication.

A. J. A. Symons

His appetite for letter-writing was exerted also on a Victorian scale. His volume of correspondence, public and private, was very considerable: but more notable than the twenty letters which he boasted of writing every day was the care with which these letters were composed. He regarded dictation to a secretary, and her transmutation of the spoken word into unfeeling type, as a distasteful necessity for business letters, but by preference his communications were always calligraphic, and any that seemed important, either to him or to their recipient, had the benefit of careful drafting before being committed in final form to his writing paper, on which the florid calligraphic name and address occupied almost a quarter of the page. He strove over his phrases until each one was as smooth as glass; and although he knew that some of his friends regarded his method of composition as a strained one, he felt that it accorded too well with the personality he had created for him ever to abandon it. In his correspondence, as in his manner, he became more formal, and the process of "thawing" which Desmond Flower had noticed at their first meeting became a more awe-inspiring one with the years. He accepted readily the charge of pomposity made against him by those who disliked him, and even by some of his friends; it was, he said, a necessary corollary of the regard for human dignity which has been almost forgotten in our time. He obtained a quite remarkable control over his temper, and his conversation grew increasingly urbane and elaborate. He recognized reluctantly that this self-control might indicate a failure of sensibility, and the idea distressed him, but as usual he was able to rationalize his self-distrust.

"This matter of *feeling*", he wrote to a friend, "is one which I shall enjoy discussing with you. I don't believe that people like myself *can* feel at the pitch of intensity

My dear Percy,

your request for an alphabet flatters me, but alas, I have no right to appear among the real scribes who will make up the rest of your record.

I never received any instruction in calligraphy beyond the ordinary school writing lessons, I use the wrong pens and the wrong ink; I am wholly an amateur. But I have loved and practised penmanship ever since I was a schoolboy; perhaps that, and your own indulgent friendship are the real reason for this place among my betters — for which I thank you.

Ever gratefully yours

From 6 Little Russell Street Bloomsbury, W.C.

Holborn 8626

A. Symons

Sept. 7 1935

which Corvo and Z. sometimes reach. That is *our* loss. But feeling isn't thought, though in those who feel so intensely and subjectively it tends to take its place. That is *their* loss. You may not agree to that proposition, but I think I can make it good. It is one of my psychological anchors."

He was on lunching, dining, and visiting terms with an enormous number of people: but an emotional barrier, which he found it increasingly difficult to raise, existed between himself and the rest of the world. He would sometimes boast that he cultivated the society of men and women only so far as they were useful to him, and that every luncheon and every conversation had its potential meaning or actual purpose. In this small piece of self-dramatization he did himself a characteristic injustice, for he charmed his friends more frequently by acts of calculated but unaffected generosity than he annoyed them by the exhibition of touches of financial jugglery, and he often took great trouble to help friends in monetary difficulties. On one occasion he dunned almost every publisher in London, and several of his personal friends, on behalf of an old and forgotten Nineties writer who was living, crippled and penniless, in France; on another he raised a subscription, by one of his famous circular letters, for a friend who had suffered heavy loss through a legal action; on another still he helped to find a new publisher, and a settled income, for a talented artist who had just recovered from a serious illness. This good, however, was done by stealth, and in cold blood. He was incapable of a spontaneous reaction to people, and was inclined to try to form intimate friendships on a basis of reciprocal self-interest. He would make proposals for treaties, such as might be conducted between sovereign states, which were to precede collaboration with friends upon unspecified masterpieces. To one such friend, who had the academic

background which my brother was painfully conscious
of lacking, he wrote:

> It seemed to me, when I came to know you, that I might
> derive vast benefits from your intelligence, trained so differ-
> ently from mine, with such other awarenesses and aptitudes.
> Equally it seemed to me that (in that way) I had something
> to give you; that my instinctive understanding of practical
> affairs, my sense of the dramatic and effective, my vitality
> and imagination (if I may so sound my own trumpet) might
> react, might stimulate, you into manifestations impossible
> to you unaided, unprompted by something outside of your-
> self. You may not think this; I still do. I should like, even,
> to say I *know*, by a subconscious or anything you like, pro-
> cess, that it is so. There are a hundred ways in which, to-
> gether, we should be more effective. You will say that that
> is what you wish for. It is what I wish too; only, alas, I see,
> or find, that the magnetic current cannot, as things are,
> flow: it is, as I said above, impossible for me to be myself,
> and therefore benefit you, while I stand outside your
> barriers. . . .
>
> I no longer ask to be allowed to dominate; but I must
> share. I'm sorry, and in a way a little disappointed in myself.
> Do I still seem to you too greedy? I'd give all I can uncon-
> ditionally to you if I could; I've been trying to; but the
> thing isn't possible.
>
> That, briefly, is the problem for your treaty. I see no
> possible basis for a treaty, alas.

My brother went on to say that he was not questioning
his friend's wisdom in refusing the treaty; and, having said
this, went on to castigate his way of life in terms which
show the indignation he always felt against those who
adhered to a moral determinism, and denied the power
of individuals to control events, or even the course of
their own lives:

> At least call things by their proper names. You have not
> refused a bribe; you have declined a treaty; you did so not

from principle, but from lack of energy; and you lack energy, not because of an obscure medical reason but because you allow yourself, or have chosen to be, dominated by mental attitudes which, though charming as poses, or subjects for novels, the scene Russian and the theme tragic, necessarily act as a brake on personality. What can you expect save an ineffective negativeness when you think that Taste, or Beauty, are simply the higher snobbishness; and proclaim the Inevitability of Everything? All the beauty in the world, you imply, must wait on the approbation of some unknown clique; and all the manifold acts of heroism in history occurred because, the characters of the heroes having been formed by circumstance, such heroisms were inevitable from such men. Truly it is not your ears alone that are deaf; and while you hold such views ineffectiveness may well be "inevitable". . . .

Your defeat of me was (is) a wilful stupidity. Possessing, almost abundantly, just those qualities which are so sadly lacking in you, I was your natural corrective; and a fortunate accident created in me the liking necessary to guide you, a liking from which I could myself have drawn inspiration and pleasure.

What you have made of the situation, we both know. Instead of granting from goodwill that treaty to which I could not force you, you have chosen to defeat me. For my letters you have returned silence, for my attention neglect, for my liking indifference. You set yourself to cure me, when you should have cured yourself. Well; it is not a triumph by which you gain. Before your victory is absolute, have you anything to say?

No treaty was signed as the result of this attempt (which he was anxious to deny, even to himself) to organize emotion. He was exceedingly sensitive to failure on the part of others to conform to a high emotional standard: and just as he had quarrelled with a friend in his early twenties over the quality of the champagne served to him at dinner, so now a trivial disagreement with another

friend who had resigned from the Wine and Food Society
was developed by A.J. into a serious breach:

> You have perhaps understood that I give my friendship
> freely, basing the gift on the instinctive sympathy which I
> am able to feel for those to whom I give it. In return I
> expect, if not an equal response, at least sufficient indulgence
> to cover any slip of business, or accidental omission of
> formality, or seeming error, or unintentional slight. And
> this expectation has never been disappointed, in the course
> of all the friendships I have formed, until now.

This magisterial, carefully-composed reproof ended
with the reflection that it was well to know the narrow
limits to which their friendship stretched, and was signed
"Yours regretfully A.J." The sympathy and understanding
of the recipient were sufficient for the cause of quarrel to
be forgotten, and good relations re-established: but such
was not always the case, and many of his early friends
dropped out of his life, deciding that they were unable to
conform to the exigent emotional standards of one who
revealed sometimes so disturbing a practicality in everyday
affairs.

"He had so many friends!" said André Simon. "He did
not think there was one too many; he loved them all, and
I doubt whether he would have wished for any better
epitaph." The statement is, in the sense in which friendship
implies emotional intimacy, wholly incorrect, for in this
sense probably the only friend A.J. ever had was Harold
Fisher. "Charlie never loved anyone", says Jed Leland in
the film *Citizen Kane*, "he just wanted to be loved.
Except Charlie Kane, of course—he always loved Charlie
Kane." Like Charles Foster Kane, A.J. demanded an
unrestrained affection which he was unable to return.

The legend about him fed, also, on his limitations as a

gourmet. He had never made any attempt to learn a foreign language, and he had not been out of England for more than a few weeks during his whole life: it was inevitable that these facts should become known. Ignorance, however, appears shameful only when concealed. When A.J. announced with all the weight of his rich voice that it is impossible to learn more than one language thoroughly in one lifetime, and that only those of incurably trivial mind could permit themselves to be hampered by an imperfect knowledge of several, when he suggested that those who went abroad for holidays showed themselves profoundly insensitive to the beauties of their own country, he spoke, in his own view, with only a little less than Johnsonian authority. What did it matter that many who did not care to involve themselves in verbal argument with such a formidable figure commented behind his back that one whose limitations were so marked must be indulging a pose in his gastronomic pretensions? Their remarks were sound in theory, but incorrect in practice, for his intelligence and adaptability carried him through triumphantly in a subject where knowledge is more instinctive than factual.

He educated himself in gastronomy with his usual care, and publicized himself upon every possible occasion as a gourmet. Eating, he remarked to a newspaper who sought his views, was one of his hobbies; and he announced some time before the Coronation of Edward VIII that he was preparing a gastronomic guide to London for visitors. "I am familiar with 150 restaurants in London", he said. "Now I am visiting 150 others." He expressed himself undeterred by the months of continual dining-out that lay ahead of him, and promised to reveal the secrets of the kitchens and cellars that were worth inclusion in the guide. The secrets stayed unrevealed, the guide unpublished: but

he continued to dine out almost nightly and eating continued to be his hobby. His advice was often asked on the
finer points of this occupation, and he gave it very readily,
saying that wine should ideally be kept in a room for
twenty-four hours before being drunk and, if served too
cold, should be nursed to warmth in the palms of the
hands; that most continental epicures tucked their napkins
under the collars, but that this was not a point of first
importance; and that the hands should be washed in
unscented soap before dinner, "otherwise one perceives
the aroma of the soap instead of the bouquet of the wine."

He still attended almost every Wine and Food Society
function: the Covent Garden luncheon at which sixteen
fresh vegetables obtainable in England in November were
on the menu, the dinner at Whipsnade Zoo when red deer
and penguins' eggs were eaten, the Bordeaux dinner
presided over by Alice Delysia, and the Cornish luncheon
over which he presided himself; he went down to Bristol
and took the chair at the opening of a Bristol Branch of the
Society, and he talked about musical boxes at a reproduction in 1937 of a dinner held at Windsor Castle a hundred
years before. He was present also at the meetings of the
Lucullus Group, the Society's inner circle of diners who
consumed meals costing up to £5 a head, and at the meetings which were interrupted by unemployed demonstra-
tors a few months before the war. He tried to dispel, in a
newspaper interview, the idea that the Society was composed of "banqueting plutocrats" by saying that "Our
dinners, for which we charge a guinea a head, are less
expensive and less luxurious than those held in most West
End restaurants". From the many memorable meals that
he ate at private parties, and later recorded in the pages of
Wine and Food, one is sufficiently remarkable to be rescued
intact from its resting-place in that magazine:

A. J. A. Symons

The place: The Savoy Hotel.
The date: 2 September, 1936.
The host: Richard Wyndham.
The guests: Tom Driberg, Montague Shearman, Hon. David Tennant, R. J. Brock, Arden Hilliard, E. A. Boyce, St. John Hutchinson, K.C., Ralph Keene, Peter Quennell, John Heygate, Sacheverell Sitwell, Curtis Moffat, Freddy Mayor, Desmond Flower, Hon. Patrick Balfour, Major W. R. Barker, Capt. J. S. Poole, Capt. F. O. Cave, and A. J. A. Symons.
The fare: Paw-paws.
Peanut soup.
Turtle fins.
Roast partridge; Egg plant and pimentos.
Mango fool.
Corn on Cob.
The wines: Tio Pepe.
Piesporter Goldtropfchen 1925.
G. H. Mumm, Cordon Rouge 1923.
Martell 1906.
Mead.

The invitations for this remarkable dinner had read:

To Welcome Home Aginejok.
Richard Wyndham invites you to a Dinka Dinner to be held in the Bahr-el-Ghazal Room, Savoy Hotel, at 8.0 p.m. on September 2nd.
It is hoped that after-dinner speakers will stand on one leg.

Readers of Wyndham's excellent book, *The Gentle Savage*, will remember that "Aginejok" was the native name for the friendly district commissioner who had been his host in the Sudan. "Aginejok" (Captain J. S. Poole) completed his term of service this year, and his former guest conceived the pleasant idea of welcoming him back by an African Dinner in London.

Expectation was high when the guests arrived, and it was not disappointed. The dining-room door opened to disclose

Musical Boxes and Protean Scenes

a tropical scene. Walls and ceilings had been shrouded in thin gauze, from behind which gentle lights diffused the blue glow of Eastern twilight. Fifteen-foot palms hid the corners. At one end of the room a camp bed, protected by mosquito nets, awaited use. The long dining table was lit by candles standing in empty wine bottles. Two impassive Africans, at least six feet six high, naked save for leopard-skin loin cloths, with painted faces and huge spears, stood at the head of the table; and invisible drums sounded the tom-tom invitation to the feast.

The fare consisted of native dishes or their equivalents. The paw-paws were fresh, and may be compared to a mixture of melon and pumpkin—tender, and much to be preferred to the watery Canteloupe. The peanuts had yielded their essence to make a savoury soup, oily, luscious, and extremely good. Both these courses were new to me. So were the turtle fins, though I had heard them praised more than once by our President. Even so, his praises had not fully prepared me for their excellence. When cooked, they are neither fishy nor finny, but resemble sweetbreads for texture, and calf's head for flavour. Agreeably glutinous, they formed a perfect background for the cool champagne which accompanied them and the rich madeira sauce in which they were served. I began to revise my ideas of the hardships of African life.

The Dinkas eat many partridges, roasted in various ways; but they can have no birds more tender than the young ones to which we turned after the disappearance of the delicious turtle fins. It was surprising to learn that the aubergine is a native African vegetable, and the discovery added to my growing envy of those who travel to Africa in the flesh.

The mango fool was a delicious mixture of ice and fruit, suggesting both the tropics and civilisation. We finished the meal, which might well make any Dinka or gourmet envious, with fresh corn-on-the-cob, with which we quaffed mead (the ancient British Metheglin), a fermented drink distilled from honey—though without the live grubs which our host told us were the proper Dinka accompaniment.

After dinner and two brief (but not too brief) speeches,

made by orators standing on one leg (an excellent prece-
dent), the fortunate company was entertained with a film
that will never be released for general circulation—a personal record by Wyndham's cine-camera, of the background, beasts and inhabitants of the Bahr-el-Ghazel. Those
who saw will not easily forget the gleaming limbs of the
strange, handsome, dark dancers, still untamed, who remember still the ritual observances handed down by their
tribe for hundreds, perhaps thousands, of years. Intricate
and beautiful, their convolutions were as natural and graceful as the shy gallop of the giraffe, which we were also
privileged to witness. A memorable meal, superbly arranged
by a man whose talents include painting, writing, and
hospitality.

A. J. A. S.

The First Edition Club, surprisingly, survived its
Secretary's neglect, and the disappearance of the Quarterly.
Rather shakily, with periods of dormancy hardly distinguishable from death, it lived through the thirties.
Sometimes the members grumbled, but many of them
remained faithful, and if they heard no more of the
Nineties Bibliography, they received occasionally bulletins
promising great things for the future. One such was the
announcement, after a long period of quiescence, of
"Some Good Books" to be published by the Club during
1936 and 1937. These books, more than most of those
published in the past, reflected A.J.'s own taste. Aubrey
Beardsley's Letters to Leonard Smithers and Baron
Corvo's translation of the Songs of Meleager (which, it
will be remembered, had been found by Maundy Gregory)
were promised again, together with a Bibliography of the
Works of Somerville and Ross and another (made by
A.J.) of the writings of George Moore: other books mentioned were *Rolfe at Holywell*, "a further venture in
experimental biography", the greater part of which was
to be composed of the letters written by Corvo when he

was starving and quarrelling in North Wales, new
editions of George Meredith's *Modern Love*, Poe's *Tales of
Mystery and Imagination* (with A.J.'s essay on Poe) and
Fitzgerald's translation of the *Rubaiyat*; and Ambrose
Bierce's *Selected Essays*. The first two of these books
actually appeared; and they were both admirable productions, beautifully printed and bound. A drawing by
Beardsley was ingeniously incorporated into the title page
of *Letters to Smithers*, the end-papers were collotype fac-
similes of letters and envelopes and the black cloth binding
with its gold rules was at once substantial and charmingly
decorative. (This view, however, was not held by Mr.
R. A. Walker, editor of the letters, who became increasingly dissatisfied with the form of the book's production
and at one time wanted to take it away from the Club
altogether). It is appropriate that these books, both published in 1937, should have been so finely produced and
printed, for they were the last publications of the First
Edition Club.

Publication of the books was a minor miracle, since the
Club now had no financial support of any kind. It came
about because A.J. was able to bring to fruition one of the
many publishing schemes which he had nursed for several
years. He arranged with a printer, a bookbinder and a
paper-maker (the Chiswick Press, the Leighton-Straker
Bookbinding Company and Arnold & Foster) that they
should extend him three years' credit at 5 per cent interest.
A.J. agreed on his side that all of the Club's publications,
up to £350 a year, should be placed with these firms.
Such an agreement was, of course, an extraordinarily
favourable one for him, and ten years earlier it might have
resulted in a considerable expansion of the Club's activities.
But this extended credit came too late, when he had lost
interest in the Club except so far as it brought a yearly

A. J. A. Symons

income. He realized that the books published through this scheme, to be successful, must have a wider appeal than the other Club publications: but his handling of review copies, and of booksellers, was not such as to press the books' sales. Both books fell almost still-born. The sales, outside the circle of Club members, were so small that he was reluctant to go ahead with any of the other books on his list, even though he had no financial responsibility for three years. The scheme which had seemed to hold so many hopes and such a small risk ended abruptly, and left him owing considerable sums of money to the three firms who had backed him so generously—sums which he had little prospect of paying and which, in fact, were outstanding at the time of his death.

Apart from these publications the Club exhibited each year the fifty books to which they had awarded "The Blue Riband of Book Production", as one admiring reviewer called it. Other exhibitions were infrequent, but interesting. One, showing books produced in the Soviet Union, was opened by the Soviet Ambassador, M. Maisky, with Francis Meynell in the chair; it was supplemented a few months later by an exhibition of books printed in Nazi Germany. Two exhibitions honoured the work of Eric Gill and Percy Smith, and the wood engravings of a young French artist named Valentin le Campion were displayed. This young artist's English was restricted to one or two phrases, and A.J.'s knowledge of French was confined to technical terms touching wine and food. Their conversation, therefore, was almost wholly confined to the words spoken when le Campion produced a series of pictures on amatory subjects which he thought might not be tolerated in London. "Shocking?" he would enquire, as he presented each subject, and A.J. would reply soothingly, "No, no, *charming*".

Musical Boxes and Protean Scenes

In 1935 the Club held a reunion dinner at the Savoy Hotel, with A.J. in the chair, at which every member and guest brought and exhibited one valuable book or manuscript. The books shown included pages from the original MS. of the *Ingoldsby Legends*, first editions of the Brontes' poems, and of *Gil Blas*. The chairman in the course of his speech said, with a slight infringement of truth, that the year had been a successful one for the Club. He observed also that, although he had other occupations by which he had gained a small reputation, the one which he valued most was that of a man of letters. "This year", he wrote serenely to a friend, "May be the last of my non-literary labours".

It might have been: but it was not. He was caught in a toil from which he had no strong wish to escape. Dinner succeeded lunch, and lunch succeeded dinner; his distaste for privacy increased, any social engagement seemed preferable to a lonely meal, and half-deliberately he deprived himself of the opportunity for working. In the five years between publication of *The Quest For Corvo* and the outbreak of war he wrote many engaging but ephemeral articles on subjects ranging from bookplates to interior decoration: but his single serious piece of work was the appraisal of the first hundred books published by the Nonesuch Press which he contributed to *The Nonesuch Century*. He must have composed this tribute with a certain small melancholy: for the first book to appear under the Nonesuch Press imprint was dated 1923, while the First Edition Club had been founded a year earlier. The Club had done something for English book production, but the Nonesuch Press had done a great deal more—had done much that, in the enthusiasm of his early twenties, he had hoped to do himself. Such reflections must have moved in him when he arranged, through the Club, an exhibition to commemorate the Nonesuch Press's tenth anniversary, and when he wrote in his appraisal that "It is due to him (Francis Meynell), more than to any other man, that, in printing at least, the nettle of the machine has been grasped in our time".

Good living had no visible effect upon him. His carriage remained perfectly erect, he put on no weight and he never, in my recollection, became drunk. Nevertheless his friends, even those who were his most ardent table-companions, became alarmed for his health and his future. André Simon urged him to abandon active participation in the Society's affairs for a year or two, and give his time to writing, and another friend observed with distaste his interest in those who had titles and money, and wrote to him: "During the past year I have seen signs of deterioration of character almost amounting to snobbery in you and I was very grieved. I have seen you apparently intimate with people of whom the only thing that could be said of them, good or bad, was that they had money, and I have known you to put up with vulgar impertinence of an almost intolerable nature, on many occasions, in the hope of being invited to yet one more dreary festivity not twenty miles up the river". A doctor who knew him told him that if he did not give up his present way of life he would not reach the age of forty. He listened to them all politely, he agreed with what they said, and at the end of each year he made splendid resolutions which fluttered away with the New Year's calendar leaves. The friend to whom he expressed himself most openly was, characteristically, Harold Fisher, to whom he wrote, after some years of silence:

My dear Harold,
    When I quarrelled with Gladys I knew that a number of

friends would take her side, and discontinue their relations
with me; but I did not expect that our difference would
involve you. Or am I wrong in associating your long silence
with my marital disturbance? Whatever the reason for *our*
difference, it grieves me to lose the countenance of the
oldest friend whose regard I still value; and though I have
felt great reluctance to eat humble-pie, I have at last brought
myself to that stony diet, and now wave you this probably
unexpected, but not, I hope, unwelcome greeting from the
shoaly waters in which my ship steers her difficult course.
Hail, then: my ear will be strained for an answering salute.

Yours ever,

A.J.

Fisher answered laconically by cable from Montreal:
*No differences just thought you were happier with your newer
friends see you November on my return.* He followed the
cable with a letter, and their old relation was re-established.
A.J. told him as much of his story as he cared to tell by
letter:

As I think I said in my last letter, yours was the most
potent of all the influences of my early life; I owe you a
mental debt which I cherish even though I cannot repay it;
and I am deeply relieved that the changes and distances of
recent years have left our old relation undisturbed. It will
be a great pleasure to see you again, and hear the news of your
journeys and successes. Mine can be briefly told. I have
sacrificed too lengthily to mammon and bacchus, and am
striving to use my time more profitably than heretofore. I
find that the one thing worse than failure in business is
success. The Wine and Food Society flourishes and expands,
and carries me with it, a well-fed, more or less voluntary
victim. But I have come to realize in recent months that I
have been accepting as an end what is merely a means.
Behold me now, struggling to escape from my own toils,
and hasten to help me from myself.

The quarrel with his wife Gladys, which is referred

to in the first of these letters, ended, in 1936, in divorce. For some years their life together had been much less than ideally happy, although it had been untouched by any serious infidelity on his part. The gap in sympathy between them widened when, after the collapse of the First Edition Club at Bedford Square, rigid economies in expenditure became necessary. They were effected by A.J.'s occupation during the week of a room at Cedars Road, while Gladys retired to Finchingfield, to be joined by her husband at weekends. Equality of sacrifice was hardly achieved by this arrangement, for it must have become plain after a few weeks to Gladys that while she was economizing in this delightful but isolated house in Essex, her husband was enjoying himself—no doubt apologetically, perhaps with a faintly guilty conscience, but still enjoying himself—in London. He would have enjoyed himself, I think, in whatever path life had cast him: but the fact that he emerged so little scathed from the disastrous campaign of Bedford Square, proved at last a mixed blessing for him.

She had soon another, and more tangible, cause for distress in the suspicion that her husband had a mistress. He was characteristically secretive to his friends about this fact: for he did not take such matters lightly. He never discussed sexual subjects except in an abstract way, and several of his friends have confirmed my own view that he never told a story which had as its basis a joke about sexual acts, and never used other than the mildest expletives. The acquisition of a mistress was not, to him, the simple and casual affair that it seems to many people to-day: before he could accept such an entanglement he had to be sure that a mistress could be made part of the organized pattern of his life. In this case there were many difficulties in the way of direct and unequivocal action: for the woman with whom he had fallen in love was already married and her husband, although he knew of her unfaithfulness, did not wish to divorce her. She was young and beautiful, and he was strongly attracted to her sexually: but she had two children, and a ménage shared with her would entail provision for them also. It is certain that he considered all these things, for he was not a man in whose life sexual passion ever played more than a subsidiary part. When he had considered them he decided, perhaps unwillingly, to carry on an intrigue which would, as far as possible, leave the rest of his life undisturbed.

There is a limit, however, to the period of time over which such an affair can be carried on without discovery: and when his wife obtained proof of her suspicions she felt bitterly towards him. It is easy to understand and sympathize with this bitterness for she felt, with justice, that she had played a large part in building his social and literary success. He was a man who played out his life, by choice, in public, and private affairs were much less important to him than public actions: but the private life existed, and she was a vital part of it. She had seen a gauche boy change into an accomplished and witty man; she knew how strongly he was influenced by the family life of which he rarely spoke to friends; she had helped to inform a taste in clothes and furnishings that was in his youth crude and flamboyant; she had disciplined him—as far as he could be disciplined—to literary work. Now her handiwork was complete, and he was moving, quite deliberately, away from her. At last, both husband and wife realized that they must part.

It is always difficult to view a quarrel impartially, particularly when one knows both the participants. I should be tipping the scales unfairly if I did not say that my brother realized the debt he owed to his wife, and the light in which she must regard their separation. He was well aware that he had done her an injury, and he felt a sympathy for her which never wavered, although the bitterness which she felt towards him did not noticeably decrease with the passing of time. The prudential considerations which had checked him from living openly with his mistress still operated even after his divorce. He did not wish to cause scandal, either in his Essex village (where a number of the local gentry signified their disapproval of him), or among his friends in London (several of whom took his wife's part), and he was not prepared to involve himself financially in providing for a family that was not his own. His love-affair remained simply a love-affair, and he lived alone in London or at Finchingfield. He missed his wife increasingly. There was no hostess at Brick House, no companion to greet him when he arrived there at weekends; and the loss of the firm foundation for success which marriage had provided took away his last incentive to write. The recurrent waves of distaste which he felt for the life he was leading were, however, checked by fresh immersions in the healing waters of gastronomy and conversation; the will to write was easily dispelled for a week or two by each fresh triumph of table talk; until at last the change in his affairs which he had frequently desired was brought about by external forces when, on September 3rd, 1939, England declared war on Germany.

CHAPTER XIII

"I HAVE BUILT MY LIFE FOR PEACE"

———————

A FEW days after war had been declared, A.J. leaned with his back against the marble mantelpiece of the sitting room at Cedars Road and said, with a kind of gloomy complacency, "I am a ruined man." I was not much disposed to believe him, and I felt the mixture of irritation and envy that is always experienced by emotional puritans in the presence of ardours or depressions extravagantly expressed. *Ruin*, I pointed out, was surely a relative term. Those who were likely to be called up for armed service might well regard themselves as likely to be ruined, both physically and financially: but for him there would be, as somehow there always had been, even in the extremities of overdraft, lunches and dinners and wine-tastings; there would be the literary life, which had little to do with the creation of literature; there would be, surely, a comfortable and well-paid job as adviser on food to a Ministry. His self-absorbed melancholy remained untouched by this churlishness, but he brightened momentarily into his Punch-like smile, and proceeded further to outrage my puritanism. "You may be perfectly right", he said. "I hope you are. Acting upon the basis of what you say, I have just ordered three new suits."

"Really", I said, "it does seem ridiculous to order new suits at a time like this."

A. J. A. Symons

"That, my dear Julian, is where you are wrong. We are entering upon a period of restriction, a period perhaps even of barter. Money will become of comparatively little importance. Property, whether it is in the form of suits or musical boxes, may be the current means of exchange. Whether all goes as well for me as you suggest, or whether, as I fear myself, membership of the Club and the Society drops to vanishing point and leaves me without an income, the purchase of three new suits is a sound economy. In twelve months' time they would probably cost me twice as much."

"And supposing England is bombed to bits?"

He shrugged elegant shoulders. "Then what possible difference can be made by my three suits? But we shall not be bombed to bits." And, with the zeal of one who had been in the past a master-strategist at the War Game, he told me of England's tactical advantages in the world struggle. The recital cheered him greatly, and at last he said, "I may be a ruined man, but I have always been on the threshold of fortune, and a new scheme I have in mind should enable me to cross it". What was the scheme? I asked, but he shook his head, still smiling mischievously, and would say no more than that it was a little book which might sell a million copies.

The scheme, which did not make his fortune, was the "Unration Book", a parody in form and content of the original Ration Book, designed to show that even if restrictions became rigorous there would still be (in the words of a circular sent out at the time) "a plenitude of good things." Both A.J. and Simon were, of course, aware that the publication of such a parody might not be viewed favourably by the Ministry of Food, and they were concerned to assure the Ministry that no confusion could arise between original and parody. "We have given it a marked blue cover, altered the front, and put a bold notice on the back", they said. The notice on the front read

> THE UNRATION BOOK
> which has nothing whatsoever
> to do with any Government,
> and is based solely
> on common
> sense.

and was not, perhaps, likely to endear the Society to Ministry officials. The instructions inside were generally rather laboriously facetious, but some of them parodied phrases in the Ration Book very sharply:

SPARE COUNTERFOILS.
15. Do nothing with the counterfoils which are not on page 10 until told what to do.

Two of the "Notes on Beer, Wines and Spirits" are pleasantly nonsensical:

Times and Places of Consumption.
It is not in any way an offence to consume beer, wines or spirits save on premises licensed for the purpose. The hours at which this offence can be committed are ascertainable at the nearest Post-Office, prohibition centre, Food Office, hotel or inn. They vary, naturally, from district to district. Persons under 16 are able to commit the offence even during permitted hours.

Sizes of bottles.
Owing to war-time restrictions, wines are now available only in bottles of the following sizes: the nip, or quarter bottle; the half-bottle; the imperial pint; the bottle; the magnum, or double bottle; the tregnum, or triple bottle; the jeroboam or double magnum; and the tuppit-hen, which equals half a cock. Consumers requiring wines in other sizes should apply

to the nearest Food Restriction office, stating the purpose to which they propose putting the wine when obtained.

The interior of the book contained coupons which described various ways of preparing dishes; and at the end of it was a long list of unrationed foods, which makes sad reading to-day. The book omitted, however, any recipes or suggestions for methods of cooking and in this its sponsors erred fatally, from a sales point of view. The Unration Book had no practical use in a kitchen. When it had been bought for sixpence it might afford ten minutes' amusement, but after that it would be discarded. Its publication revealed also an error in the assessment of public feeling, for the disclosure that plover, doe venison, braised duck and roast blackcock were still unrationed, acted merely as an irritant for those to whom rationing was a serious, and even a depressing, subject. The Unration Book was suitably embalmed in the deadly praise of a *Times* fourth leader: its sale, so far from being a million copies, did not recover the costs of production. Its sponsors had erred again through their inability to realize that what pleases thousands is generally distasteful to a million people.

In some part, the failure of the Unration Book may also have been due to the fact that A.J., who always handled the business affairs of the Society, had nothing to do with publicising it. Simon had complained for some time, although intermittently, that he was being dexterously steered away from the handling of any business except signing cheques, and had pointed out that although the time must doubtless come when the Society would belong solely to A.J., that time had not yet arrived. From the time of the Unration Book's publication, however, the business affairs of the Society passed into Simon's hands, for his partner had been attacked by a sudden and mysterious illness.

One day in November A.J. was brought home to Cedars Road in a cab. It was obvious that he was alarmingly ill. He was unable to walk without assistance, he was hardly able to articulate, and he was afflicted by a paralysis which made it impossible for him to hold a cup in his hands without spilling its contents. He lay for two weeks in his great bedroom at Clapham, unable to bear light or warmth, or to take any food other than soup and gruel. Then, nursed devotedly by my mother, his condition slowly improved, although he did not recover fully. He hardly moved out of bed for weeks, and when he did get up his power of locomotion was uncertain. This distressed him less, however, than his inability to articulate clearly, and the need to rely on others to sign the letters which he dictated in a blurred and feeble voice.

He attributed the illness at first to eating a bad oyster; then he thought that he had suffered a paralytic stroke. He consulted several specialists. Their views of the cause of his condition varied: some thought that he had suffered a brain hemorrhage which might, or might not, recur; others told him that his illness had probably been encephalitis, or sleeping sickness, and this view cheered him considerably because it implied that his hesitation of hand and voice would probably pass away. Neither at this nor at any other time did the specialists whom he consulted tell him the real nature of his illness: nor did any member of his family know it.

For the first two weeks of his illness, A.J. was hardly conscious of anything but pain: but then his mind worked again with its usual agility. He fretted about his illness, about the progress of the Unration Book, about the need to continue a book on which he had started work. He was impatient, also, to be able to read again, so that he could consult medical books and discover the exact nature of his complaint. For a long time, however, he could not read, or bear a bright light near him; and he did not go outside the house for two months. To amuse him during these long days I read him many stories from those modern writers whose works he had condemned in mass, without reading them. "I am at your mercy", he muttered thickly, and with the ghost of a smile. "Read what you will." He enjoyed, I remember, Conrad Aiken's story, "The Disciple", and two of William Saroyan's least sentimental tales, "Little Miss Universe" and "Our Little Brown Brothers the Filipinos", although he felt bound to make a gesture of deprecation regarding them. "Rather reminiscent of Kipling—a minor Kipling", he said of Saroyan, and of Aiken—whose best work, as he well knew, I greatly admired—he said wickedly, "He writes almost as well as one of the lesser Nineties figures". We talked also about politics, and he discovered for the first time, and with horror, the rigidities of the Communist viewpoint. "My dear fellow, I'm appalled by the Philistinism shown by you and my friend X." ("X" was a well-known writer on a daily newspaper). "*You* seem to have a bloodthirsty desire to see the heads of established literary figures roll in the dust, which is only equalled by your enthusiasm for the obscurer works of modern writers. And as for 'X' do you know what he said to me not long ago? 'When we come to power, my dear A.J., *you* are one of the first people we shall have to bump off. Regretfully, of course, but it will have to be done'."

I suggested that "X" had not been altogether serious, but A.J. would not believe me. "I have always been a Socialist", he said—and then, seeing my basilisk eye upon him, added "even if I have not always avowed my faith publicly—I have always been a Socialist because I have always believed that Socialists were trying to ensure a freer, fuller life for mankind. But if they are going to imprison men of good will, harmless collectors of musical boxes and first editions, then I shall have to think again." He did not, however, carry his investigation of Communism and Socialism very far. The conclusions to be drawn from it regarding his own life and likely future were too discouraging.

His bedroom was crowded with musical boxes of varied kinds and sizes, and two or three friends and fellow-collectors augmented the collection from time to time. There were few evenings on which my mother, my sister or I were not called on to play a dozen tunes from half-a-dozen different boxes. We would stand shivering there (the winter of 1939 was a cold one, yet he could not bear a fire in the room) playing tune after tune while the invalid, from the obscurity of the corner in which his bed stood, out of the light, would murmur, "Just another two or three tunes. That forte-piano box with the rose-wood top, now—can we have that, do you think? . . ."

At this time, also, he made a last attempt to master his failure to appreciate classical music. He was aware that although he might suggest, within a narrow circle, that the purest and most perfect music was played by musical boxes, this was not a view that could be maintained successfully in public. Now, by two happy chances, one friend lent him an E.M.G. hand-made gramophone, and another lent him two thousand gramophone records; and gramophone and records were added to the confusion of musical boxes, books and papers in the bedroom. The gramophone was certainly a remarkable machine, both in appearance and performance, and A.J. viewed it with the warm affection which he felt always for anything novel, and good in its kind, which had come into his possession. He sent for descriptive material regarding the machine's performance, was very particular in the choice of needles, and told his visitors solemnly, "This is a superlatively good machine of its kind, because it has a horn thirty feet in length—convected, as you can see, to a mere eight feet." With the aid of this machine and of the records, which ranged from Bach and Beethoven to Güngl and Waldteufel, he hoped to obtain a fuller appreciation of music. His family was employed in the capacity of record-changers, and they were assisted by a friend of mine who had a wide knowledge of music, and was amused by A.J.'s project of musical self-education. My friend's visits were paid two or three times a week, and they were eagerly awaited: but, alas, the attempt failed. The unfamiliar and complicated harmonies did not please A.J.'s ear, and he never passed beyond appreciation of a few simple pieces which had an easily recognizable rhythm, and repetition of an original motive—that bore, in fact, some relation to a musical box rendering. After my friend had paid half-a-dozen visits, the two musical enthusiasts reached agreement; they selected records alternately, so that a programme combining Ravel and Rossini, Wagner and Waldteufel, could be heard through the bedroom door. As, slowly A.J.'s power of movement increased, the gramophone was played less often, and at last was altogether silent. He abandoned the attempt to become a musical scholar, and contented himself with evolving more, and more ingenious, theories about the peculiar virtues inherent in the sounds produced by the impingement of comb on cylinder.

In January he had so far recovered that he was able to walk two miles without feeling unduly tired, although a thickness, and hesitation, of speech remained with him, and he was able to execute his elaborate signature only by an effort of concentration which was painful to witness. He wrote to Harold Fisher, referring to his illness as a severe nervous breakdown, and saying that he was still unwell. He went on to speak of his plans for a new book. "The weather keeps me from convalescence, and I am tied here in this house of many memories. If you come to London while it is still cold, you will probably find me reluctantly detained here, and very glad to see you, and to read to you, in the customary manner, my opening chapters." But although he told Fisher that he was writing with more fluency, and more success, than ever before, his book moved slowly. When he had sufficiently recovered, and the weather grew warmer, he went down to Brick House: but the acuteness with which he felt the limitations imposed on him by illness is shown by his humorous description of them in a letter to Edward Wadsworth:

When I was about to move down here from my sickbed in London, my neighbour John Aldrich (sic) was having a show at the Leicester Galleries. (Do you know A's work)? I wanted to see it, but not to be seen myself, dumb as I was. So on the last day, a Saturday morning, I was painfully dragged to Leicester Square, where, as I hoped, I could look at the pictures in peace. Alas! I had miscalculated. It was not the last day of the Aldrich show, but the day after; not the last day of the Aldrich show, but the first of the Sickert! And instead of the Gallery being empty, a smart and familiar crowd observed my haggard entry, unshaved, in an old and shabby suit, still suffering from the paralysis of voice and hand and foot. These affections, particularly the voice, took an odd form; they all resembled intoxication. My voice was not completely mute; it was blurred in all its sounds, and I involuntarily elided syllables; instead of "us-u-al", I would say "u-shal". Some words I could not

articulate at all. The unsteadiness of my hand was not, of
course, perceptible; but the halting drag of my gait was. It
was a *wet* morning; and over my shabby suit I had an even
shabbier raincoat. Picture me, then, in this condition, seeming to be both tight and down at heel, confronted, and
at once saluted, by Eddie and Cecil Phillips. I could
not withdraw; and I could hardly speak. They both, very
creditably, hid completely the surprise they must have felt
at my appearing, so, at a smart private view. I muttered
some gloomy words about Aldrich, looked in despair at
some Sickerts, shrank in hostile silence from two other
friends who were bearing down on me, and left in spleen.

His hesitation of voice was not as noticeable as he
feared: but like all men who have enjoyed good health
for most of their lives he was much distressed by his own
illness, and indeed the varying views expressed by his
doctors gave small ground for confidence. In the presence
of friends, however, he was capable of forgetting his
perturbation about the present and future; and when, after
his return to Brick House, he went down to stay with
Doris Langley Moore at Harrogate, she found him as
amiable, and full of enthusiasm for other people's collections, as ever. He was surprised that she had not realized
the possibilities opened by the war of extending her
collection of past clothes and costumes, and pointed out
that people were dispersing superfluous possessions and
clearing out attics—were, in short, entirely in the frame
of mind to dispose of clothes which had been worn by
their ancestors. He drafted an advertisement for her, which
was sent to *The Times* and the *Daily Telegraph*. "And
now", A.J. said on departure, "I shall wait to hear how
you fare under the *avalanche* of replies." His forecast was
perfectly correct. As the result of his intervention (Mrs.
Moore has recorded), the collection was doubled, and

"I Have Built My Life for Peace"

"A.J. could hardly have been more pleased and attentive if it had been his own".

At the same visit he discussed with her his lack of facility in writing, a reluctance to set pen to paper which she also experienced. He gave his own verbal explanation, in words which much impressed her:

"I suppose we feel that writing is the thing by which we stand or fall, and subconsciously our minds try to defer the awful moment when we must produce proof of our merit, our one real claim to consideration. We know that our social life, however successful, and our hobbies, however agreeable, are side issues. We have undertaken to be writers, and so we weigh every word and pause and hold back, dreading to see the work materialize in case it should fall short."

Soon after his return he discussed the problem again, by letter, and at the same time sent her one of those bulletins about his physical situation which went to some friends almost weekly:

My dear Doris,

I came, I was seen, I was re-diagnosed. And I am re-prieved! Horder and Holmes are agreed on a new theory. It seems that I may not have had a hemorrhage. Instead, they assert an *inflammation* of the brain—of the part of the brain in question. In fact, an encephalitis, the famous "sleeping sickness". I did not dare to ask Horder if, in the absence of any tsetse fly, he presumed my attack to have been caught from *writing* about Africa—but there you are. The advantage of this new theory (which is like the old one, alas, in not fitting *all* the facts) is that the virus has passed, and there are now only after effects to deal with, which are all virtually certain to pass away. Also it imposes a less anchoritic life on me, since there is no longer the fear that lifting the slightest weight, experiencing excitement, or worrying overmuch, will restart the hemorrhage, and so

A. J. A. Symons

kill me. Hence I am a happier man than when I left Harrogate. Our complexes, however—or shall I say our complex?—is left in possession of the field, unexplained, unanointed, disannealed. That it exists is certain: an aversion from work that we both know that we can do. I suppose that the obvious answer is the right one: timidity, from lack of confidence in oneself. Hence the bolstering-up of the personality by antique-collecting's artful aid, and all those easy excuses for dallying which we have both invented for ourselves. It will remedy itself, I suspect, as we grow older. I am consulting Ogden.

Have you considered Adlerian theories at all? The "organic inferiority" notion explains a great deal, when it applies. I can see many ways in which it might be the key to my own problems. Perhaps even yours?

The sun here is much hotter than with you, but I am in every other way less comfortable. It was most noble of you both to cherish me so closely, and I am very grateful for a very enjoyable break—which, taking you at your word, I shall ask to be allowed to repeat as soon as the fine spell goes. . . .

She (character in book) must have developed great powers of self-resistance—the mark of the true egoist. Alas! mine too are vast. In the egoist, all things are transformed by the personal prejudice. Fraud in any one else is fraud: but in oneself it is not. It is this which enables burglars to retain a conviction of their honesty, even after they have been caught red-handed, tried and convicted. Et tu, Brute?

This letter is long enough: yet more follows. I am writing in a garden lit by the westering sun; and "the last pale beam of even" is not enough to justify my seat. You shall hear more from a more sheltered spot. And so, God bless you and goodbye, for the moment, from

Your accomplex,

A.J.

He was mentally, as well as physically, changed by his illness. At about this time the love-affair that had occupied his whole emotional life for five years finished. Its ending was not chosen, or desired, by him, and he felt the blow of parting very heavily. He had been circumspect in this affair at a time when the woman he loved was prepared to act impetuously and now, at the end of five years in which they had never made a home together, she told him that she was no longer in love with him. His nature was too generous for him to feel much bitterness: but he returned to Finchingfield a lonely man. The ending of this love-affair induced in him a tendency to look back over all the performances of his life. He saw much with which he was dissatisfied: and he was particularly concerned by his failure to become, completely, a writer. He showed at this time a capacity for self-analysis that he had not possessed, or desired, earlier in life. He would discuss with me, coolly and logically, the things that had turned him away from writing; he would show that such influences no longer had force. Why, then, did he suffer from this constriction of the pen, why did his mind move like a butterfly from subject to subject? The answer to this question was to be found at least partially in the nature of his illness, which did not permit him to concentrate for lengthy periods: but he did not know this, now or at any later time, and, unaware of it, would sometimes suggest, only half-jokingly, that he might be going mad.

In the meantime André Simon was doing the whole work of the Wine and Food Society. This work was reduced by the drop in the Society's membership to little more than half the pre-war figure, but it was still quite considerable in volume. In these early days of the war the partners tried to make an adaptation which finally proved impossible, and to hold functions which should not be too remote from those of the lost world in which we lived before September, 1939. A.J., from the fastness of Finchingfield, offered a variety of useful suggestions,

A. J. A. Symons

like his hint that, in order to provide a sop for members' consciences, the phrase Oyster *Tasting* should replace Oyster *Feast*: but the actual work of organizing the Oyster Tasting, of editing, arranging and despatching the quarterly *Wine and Food*, and of dealing with the complaints, resignations and enquiries of members was necessarily handled by André Simon. Although he performed these tasks willingly, he did not find them altogether congenial, and he discovered with some alarm A.J.'s habit of leaving accounts unpaid as long as possible in order to obtain the maximum length of credit. He was seriously annoyed, also, when he found that, as usual, A.J. had overdrawn his share of the Society's profits. This was usually balanced by Simon drawing a cheque to balance the amount but this year, as he pointed out, there was no money available on which to draw.

A prolonged squabble about money matters ensued. Simon felt, quite rightly, that A.J. was doing little to help the Society, and he did not spare his partner severe reproaches. With the fall of France his volatile temperament touched a nadir of low spirits. Much disturbed about his own position, and the possibility of internment (for he was a French citizen) he despaired of continuing the Society at all in any active form, and suggested that their troubles would be solved most simply by a bomb sending them all to Heaven—"the sooner the better". A stream of letters from his home at East Grinstead attacked the recovering invalid who, infuriatingly, was taking a late summer holiday in Cornwall. A little illogically Simon complained both that his partner did nothing for the Society, and also that he interfered too much in its affairs. The arrangement by which cheques were signed by both partners he found an intolerable nuisance, and he was annoyed also by the fact that some of the Society's stock

of books and pamphlets had been delivered to Finchingfield, instead of his home at East Grinstead (although at
the same time it was troublesome to have the stock at
East Grinstead). Simon was at this time dealing with
many petty items that had formerly been handled by a
secretary; he had no idea of the severity of his partner's
illness, and felt it unjust that he should bear the burden of
all the Society's work. It is easy to sympathize with him.
But it is possible also to admire the moderation and logic
with which this stream of complaints was answered in
the letters which A.J. addressed to "My dear Vintner":

> Parts of your letter mystify me. "This dual business—not
> only cheques but stock and books—is bound to lead to
> delay, trouble and irritation." Delay. What delay is there
> likely to be that could possibly matter? During the last
> three months we have issued fifteen cheques; there will in
> all probability be fewer in the next three. None of them
> was urgent; none was kept by me more than three days.
> Stock and books. I do not know what stock I have or shall
> have here, but in any event I understand that you have sup-
> plies of everything. How can my possessing a reserve stock
> cause you either trouble or irritation? I do not particularly
> want to keep W. and F. stock here, save on the principle
> that of two reserve places one is more likely to survive than
> a single reserve place. Books. So far as I know, you have
> them all. If not, they are in all probability still at Little
> Russell Street. If they come down here (my van has
> deserted, and all save chairs and tables are in situ, and in
> peril, still) you shall have them. I fail to see any reason
> deriving from the grounds you name which need make you
> fear "delay, trouble and irritation".
> You continue, "I would have thought that it was more
> sensible to let me run what there is of the W. and F.S. from
> here, for the duration, and put the whole of your mind to
> your books, etc." It is not clear to me whether the implied
> complaint in this sentence refers to the past or anticipates the
> future. If to the past, I can only retort that you are hard to

A. J. A. Symons

please. Surely you will not suggest that I have interfered overmuch, or indeed at all, since last November, when I fell ill? For the greater part of that time you signed cheques, engaged staff, and did whatever you wished without reference to me. My few interventions since have been mainly taken at your own suggestion, and looking back I do not see why you should regret them. But for me, as you agreed in your last letter, the whole show would have been impulsively wound up in July. But for me, your last Editorial would have been far more open to criticism than was in fact the case. And so on. . . .

In one of your recent letters you referred to the "show of temper" in my communications. I did not controvert the phrase then, and do so now only to assure you that no word in this present epistle is written in temper. I still have too lively a remembrance of your kindness to me in the early days of our acquaintance to do more than regret, a little resentfully, your "delay, trouble and irritation" now. I see clearly that you have many causes for quarrelling with life; and I do my best to play the role of whipping boy, which you have clearly allotted to me, with a good grace. If I seem sometimes to flinch, you must remember that I am still very far from well, and often very worried.

This letter brought a lull: but not for long. The air raids on London emphasized the fact that the world in which the Wine and Food Society had flourished was dying, and with it the hope of future income. Within a week or two the overwrought Simon was again reproaching the partner whose mysterious, and as it may have appeared convenient, illness prevented him from doing any work, but permitted him to go for long holidays in Cornwall, and to walk several miles a day. A.J. was accused of being a spoilt child who believed that whatever he received was no more than his due; who was past help because he took whatever he wanted, regardless of whether he had any right to it; who had been responsible for the failure of the First Edition Club years ago, and was now largely responsible for the unprofitable nature of the Society. All this, Simon observed, was not said in anger, but simply that his young friend might still obtain some profit from it, and learn a lesson from the truth. To these and similar observations the sinner bowed his head, as he would not have bowed it twelve months before, and acknowledged that "There is too much truth in what you say for me to take offence at it. You must take my word for it that I do see the error of my ways, more clearly than may seem to be the case". He offered Simon one of the several ironical epitaphs that he composed upon himself:

IN
GRACIOUS MEMORY
OF
A.J.A.S.
WHO
OVERDREW TWO HUNDRED POUNDS
AND SO
FORFEITED
ALL CLAIM TO
ADMIRATION, TOLERATION
OR
CONSIDERATION

Simon was wrong, however, he observed, in thinking that his illness had left no damaging traces. He had now investigated the supposed encephalitis in some detail:

> I have very little hope of escaping without physical impairment. . . . Apparently every case of encephalitis differs in degree and consequence from every other, though the main outlines are not varied. It is an inflammation of the brain, caused (it is presumed) by a virus—a germ not identified. This inflammation causes hemorrhage, which in turn causes damage to nervous tissues in the brain—usually those

which control motor activities, and very frequently those which suffered in my case, the nerves which govern the larynx, right hand and right foot. The nervous tissue which is damaged cannot be restored, but it is possible, by a process of re-education, for spare tissues to be trained to do the work formerly executed by the damaged parts; though the work is never done as well by the substitute as it was originally. My present situation is that I am making good progress with the re-education. I cannot swallow perfectly, but I can do so sufficiently. I cannot speak eloquently; but I am not inarticulate. And, day by day, my general nervous system is recovering strength after the all but knock-down blow to which it was subjected.

The relations between the partners became amiable again: and indeed it would be true to say that on my brother's side they were never other than friendly. Both realized that while the war lasted the Society could be only a very small source of income. During 1940 A.J. drew £10 from it. It is true that this was partly because he had overdrawn in the previous year, but it is a fact that in the twenty-one months from the outbreak of war to his death, he had practically no income.

"I have built my life for peace, and not for war", my brother said sadly. He realized clearly that there must be a great difference between our personal, and social, economy in peace and in war. Such a belief prompted his remarks to his friend Ian Black, when Black came down to see him at Brick House:

"My dear fellow", he said, "you must re-condition your life. It is no use being someone who was something in the City. You need a background. You must write a book. Every man of reasonable character and persistence can write one book. It does not matter whether your book is a success. The important thing is that it should be published. I can then introduce you to my influential friends with confidence." At the same time he observed that there was always a room for his friend Ian at Brick House. "My cellar is full. Kitty is a good cook. We have nearly a hundred musical boxes and ten thousand books to console us."

Black remembered the advice and wrote the book. It was called *A Friend of France*; and it was published, although not with conspicuous success. He remembered also, in the autumn of 1940, A.J.'s offer of a room at Brick House, and he has left a pleasant picture of the weeks he spent there:

"I shall always remember those weeks in Essex. The air attack on London had heightened our appreciation of the smallest comfort, and pleasures, hitherto taken for granted, assumed now roles of unusual significance.

"The log fires at Brick House, the long evenings spent in discussion, listening to Lord Haw-Haw—an attractive novelty—writing songs for Victorian airs played on the latest musical box, or being consistently defeated by A.J. at innumerable games of chance, of which he had an endless repertoire, were a welcome joy.

" 'It is clear', said Symons to me one evening at dinner, 'It is quite clear that we shall have inflation. Whatever you do, keep all you own. This is a time to buy and not to sell. I am a rich man. My books, my wine, my house, my mother-of-pearl counters, are each day rising in value. I am instructing my agents to buy more, I am acquiring new property in the village. This is a time to owe money, and not to lend it. The banks are in a dangerous position. In a few years, we shall pay off our overdraft with a pittance.'

"I could not resist reminding my friend that at this moment he owed me a sum of relative importance.

" 'My dear fellow', he said with sincere distress, 'I must deal with that matter. But you do agree with me that inflation is certain?'

"We talked till the early hours, when, between two final

glasses of claret, A.J., to conclude our discussion, wrote this poem, which he handed to me with suitable gravity:

> 'There is not an inflation', cried
>   The prudent Ian Black;
> 'Prices are mounting daily, but
>   We need not put them back.
> 'What matters is the *volume*
>   Providing that be right,
> 'Then simple regulation
>   Can hold the pound in sight.
> 'Who cares a hang that butter
>   Is one and seven a pound,
> 'Or cares a curse that onions
>   Now simply can't be found,
> 'When bullets, tanks and rifles
>   And Bren guns, too, abound?
> 'Consider how the cost is
>   Made up from income tax;
> 'You can't call *that* inflation,
>   Or if you do you're lax.'
>
> He ceased; but all was silence,
>   For only tears are cheap,
> And those who had to foot the bill
>   Had crept away to weep.

To Black, and to many other friends who came to see him, A.J. expounded his new idea for making money, an idea which seemed to me, as it seemed to him, to have vast possibilities. Many of his series of Victorian protean scenes pointed a serious and inescapable Victorian moral. Why should not a series of modern scenes be produced, with a direct propagandist value? Perhaps his suggestion that millions of them might be dropped on occupied countries, "Printed with the faces of collaborating villains which before the light will change into a portrait of Hitler", might not be absolutely practical; but there seemed no flaw in his idea that there would be a huge demand in this country for a series which embodied such themes as "Hitler as he imagines himself" (a triumphant figure straddling the world) transformed on being held before the light to "Hitler as he really is" (a shambling, bloody, ape-like figure worthy of a Soviet cartoonist). What was lacking to make such a series enormously successful? Merely a little money. But the friends and publishers he approached were less enthusiastic. A great deal of money would be needed: and perhaps some of the people he approached thought the propounder of the scheme a little over-ingenious and over-resourceful. Moreover, the technical process of production presented considerable difficulties. Two or three attempts had already been made to reproduce the effect of Victorian transformations (one was a publicity scheme of the Shell Company), and they had been conspicuously unsuccessful in capturing the flat, effective realism of Victorian hack artists. Without a backer the scheme could not be carried through: and A.J.'s own enthusiasm was easily quenched. He had indeed little ground for optimism at this time. He made attempts to find suitable and congenial work: but the letters he wrote to the acquaintances and friends of pre-war days were ignored, or answered by polite and formal gestures of refusal.

Apart from his holiday in Cornwall, he hardly stirred from Brick House during the summer and autumn months of 1940: and strangely enough, in spite of the fact that he had no income, the sum of his possessions seemed to increase rather than to diminish. He was, I think, secretly not displeased by that opportunity of storing part of the Wine and Food reserve stock of pamphlets and magazines; he very readily accepted responsibility for some of Desmond Flower's wine, and many of

A. J. A. Symons

Vyvyan Holland's books; and he was delighted by the chance of transferring sixty cases of books and two large bookcases from Little Russell Street to the great barn that had been the Games Room. "Five thousand books have just arrived", he wrote to me, "The barn is now a library. God help you when you come." When I arrived I found a rich Turkey carpet on the floor of the barn, Bristol glass paper-weights carefully arranged in the alcove that had contained table tennis racquets, and A.J. sitting happily in the midst of confusion, sorting great piles of books. At such times he was still boyishly gay and at weekends, when he was entertaining friends, he talked as brilliantly as ever; but after they had gone away he was touched frequently by a deep melancholy which had never marked him before his illness. He was now, for the second time in his life, moved to try to write for his living, and he found himself unable to do it. My mother, who stayed at Brick House during the summer, would enter the study where he had gone to work, and find him reading a book or looking out of the window into the garden. "Don't go away", he would say. "Sit on the sofa there. I can't work when I'm alone." And then, instead of working he would talk to her, or read her a story, breaking off to ask: "What do you think of my voice? Is it improving at all?" The hesitation and thickness of speech had now almost disappeared, except when he had to deal with certain unfortunate conjunctions of consonants, but they still worried him. When he was asked to broadcast again with his musical boxes he feared that he would not be allowed to speak in person, and was delighted when he passed a test. The thickening of his speech was more noticeable through the radio medium than in ordinary speech, but that fact remained unknown to him. As usual he received dozens of appreciative letters, and offers of

238

musical boxes for sale. These started him off again on a search for good boxes, and he even contemplated the construction of a Victorian Museum, containing examples from all the many knick-knacks of that age.

"IF I live down this illness", he wrote to a friend, "IF I survive the war, IF circumstances permit, I have it in mind to start a Victorian society: to get a fine Victorian house, and use it as a new-model museum to hold my own curiosities, and all the other interesting Victoriana, of no particular financial value, but of enormous interest to the social historian and student of the future—and, indeed, to any right-minded citizen of the future, if the future produces any such, as I suppose it will."

Much of his time was spent in the garden, where he constructed a remarkable and disturbing croquet course on the small, sloping, bumpy lawn. This croquet course bore a certain resemblance to that in *Alice's Adventures in Wonderland*, for although the balls were not hedgehogs nor the mallets flamingoes, the difficulties of the course were not easily overcome. The local rules varied from hoop to hoop, and were never revealed before they had been infringed. One of the deadliest hoops was placed on the edge of a sharp dip in the lawn, and when his visitor's ball was on the wrong side of the dip A.J. would say casually, "I should have mentioned—you go through from *this* side." Few people played on that croquet course more than once.

Such were his diversions. They soothed his troubled spirit less than the good reception given to an article which he wrote on Theodore Hook in a book called *English Wits*, edited by Leonard Russell. He was always afraid, now, of a weakening in mental power, and because of this he was immensely pleased when several reviewers picked out his article for special praise. He had chosen once again a story that attracted him in its relation to the problems of his own life. In the career of the unthrifty, witty, good-looking man who was a successful dramatist in his teens and had always a consciousness of great gifts unfulfilled, he saw a ghastly *memento mori* for himself. He was fascinated by the details of country house parties at which Hook was the only untitled guest, by dinners he attended where "The long mahogany tables were set with their sparkling crested silver under the Waterford chandeliers", and where "the liveried servants, removing the first, placed the second service before the critical Tory grandees of the fourth George or William"; and the fact that Hook returned from these feasts to semi-rural retirement and little-known domesticity with his mistress and four illegitimate children, there to lament the hours and days wasted in foolish idleness, made the picture a perfect one. My brother propounded, without answering, the question which absorbed him indirectly in relation to his own life, as well as directly in relation to Hook's: what led this man, "so attractive, so capable, so young", to make a farce of his life, by practising more and more outrageous practical jokes? While he regarded Hook's love of practical jokes as pathological, his own love of social position seemed to A.J. quite natural, and in a skilful piece of pleading he rebelled against the general view of Hook as a snob, since "Poor men as well as rich may like fine porticoes, grand façades, and all the panoply of magnificence". The last phrase in his essay is one of the most successful of his purple passages:

"The legend will long remain of the queer fish who all his life swam so desperately in the shallow waters of his own laughter."

The praise of critics was pleasant: but he was conscious that one essay, and a few odd chapters of a book, were not much to show for nearly a year spent at Brick House. "A new life", he wrote to Desmond Flower, "with new habits and a new routine. But most of the old defects, I fear." In the winter he was quite alone there for days, and sometimes weeks at a time: alone with his "Lamb-like" slur of speech and the cellar of wine which, on the advice of his doctors, he drank sparingly; with his Victoriana, his bank overdraft and his unpaid bills; with the sets of standard authors on his shelves and all the ideas for books that remained, unwritten or uncompleted, in his head.

Year	Port	Claret	Burgundy	White Burgundy	Rhenish	Sauternes	Champagne
1919	2	4	5	5	3	4	4
1920	6	7	3	4	6	3	5
1921	2	5	5	5	7	7	7
1922	6	3	1	5	2	3	0
1923	4	6	7	6	3	4	4
1924	6	6	4	4	3	6	2
1925	3	3	2	3	4	2	0
1926	3	5	6	6	3	3	6
1927	7	1	0	1	4	3	0
1928	2	6	5	7	1	4	7
1929	3	7	7	7	5	7	6
1930	2	0	1	3	3	0	0
1931	6	2	0	1	2	2	1
1932	0	0	2	3	3	0	3
1933	4	5	5	6	6	3	6
1934	6	6	6	5	7	4	6
1935	6	3	4	6	5	3	2
1936	3	4	2	4	1	4	2
1937		5	5	6	6	6	6

Revised for the year 1939
0 = no good   7 = the best

CHAPTER XIV

ALL THE UNWRITTEN BOOKS

THE bombs fell in London; the papers told stories of the struggle of Spitfire pilots against the Luftwaffe; and from his enforced seclusion in Essex the sick man watched it all, and thought restlessly of the active part which he might have taken in the war. He noted with detached interest that, on the first day after his return from Cornwall, there was an air-battle over the house, and the air was thick with parachutes, one of which seemed to be coming straight into his garden; three German airmen baled out, one on Finchingfield green, and were rounded up and taken to an empty house. Physical fear had little part in his nature, although one of his friends has told how he waited, when about to cross the road in Holborn, until there was no traffic within a hundred yards, and then set out, observing: "It would be a thousand pities if a piece of carelessness on my part should result in the curtailing of my otherwise unendable life." The same friend remarked that his energy and love of life were so great that he did not in his heart admit that he would ever die at all. He felt (and often felt rightly) that he could have done any work that interested him better than those to whom it had been allotted as their portion.

Sometimes he would embroider this theme, only half-humorously, and it was plain to all who knew him well that he could have been a remarkable and successful politician, a brilliant speaker in the House of Commons

and more successful still, perhaps, in that dexterous deploy-
ment of political forces by which power is won and kept;
or a skilful promoter of companies, which he would have
played with as a juggler plays with moving multi-coloured
balls; or an earnest and eloquent advocate, an actor of
many character parts, or a diplomat. He could have played
excellently, with that deceptive urbanity which hid a
disarming gusto, any part in which an element of speculation was mingled with an element of personal power;
in which a character was a series of masks, each worn for
its appropriate occasion, until at last masks and character
were indistinguishable. He must have thought of all these
things as he read the newspapers, and listened to the radio
during the long months of air raids and of rationing's
first severities, and wrote hopefully to his former wife:
"Thank God I am free of the fear that haunted me so
long, that I never should be my normal self again. Traces
remain all round, of course, but I am oh, so much better,
so much, much better, that I don't grudge the last few
symptoms." But optimism cannot have been his prevail-
ing mood as he remembered how, ten years earlier, he had
leaned against the mantelpiece in his study at Bedford
Square, and said to Desmond Flower: "This is a very
serious day. It is my thirtieth birthday. To-day I leave the
decade of promise and enter the age of accomplishment.
I do not know that I shall succeed." Now that he looked
back (a thing that only illness and isolation provoked him
to do) he was less than satisfied with what he had done;
and since, as he said to Doris Langley Moore, he regarded
himself, first of all, as a writer, the thing that distressed
him most was the shelf on which stood the slender
achievement of forty years.

He had believed from early youth that he had an

extraordinary talent for writing; and he was not wrong: but from youth he had always found it difficult to concentrate on any literary work, a difficulty plainly shown in his early attempts to write, as well as in such evidence as his remark in an eight-page letter to one of the many doctors whom he consulted about his illness, that "I have always been a careful, but also costive writer, to whom the act of composition has always been accompanied by more pain than pleasure". The few stories which he essayed in his teens are remarkable in the care of their construction, in their imitation of the manner of Edgar Allan Poe and in the fact that, without exception, they were left unfinished. The opening lines of a tale called *A Bottomless Grave* are typical:

> My name is John Brenwalter. My father, a drunkard, had a patent for making coffee-berries out of clay; but he was an honest man and would not engage himself in the manufacture. He was, therefore, only moderately wealthy, his royalties from his really valuable invention bringing him hardly enough to pay his expenses of litigation with rogues guilty of infringement. So I lacked many advantages enjoyed by the children of unscrupulous and dishonest parents, and had it not been for a noble and devoted mother, who neglected all my brothers and sisters and personally supervised my education, should have grown up in ignorance and been compelled to teach school. To be the favourite child of a good woman is better than gold.

Such a style lacks little of maturity, even though the material upon which it is employed is not original; but neither at this nor at any later time did he ever finish any fictional work, with the exception of the little squib about the Queen of Sheba.

When, in his maturity, he began to consider seriously the art of biography, and decided that English biography "has failed in beauty as it has in truth", he contracted to produce a definitive biography of Oscar Wilde. The problems of Wilde's career and character had fascinated him from an early age, and they continued to occupy his mind, at intervals, for the rest of his life; but when he died only five chapters of the book had been completed.

There were many reasons for his failure to complete the work which had been for years so near his heart; and idleness and financial difficulties were almost the least of them. It is true that his deep-rooted aversion from the act of writing was encouraged by the many immediately amusing prospects that offered themselves every day to his attention; true also that the generous advance he received from his publisher was rather a deterrent than an incentive to his mind. But still, as he observed to his publisher, he was in an exceedingly favourable position to write this biography. Oscar Wilde's only surviving son was one of his greatest friends, and gave him much help; and he was also one of the comparatively few people to remain consistently friendly through a period of years with that turbulent and incalculable actor in the story of Wilde's life, Lord Alfred Douglas. The friendship of these two men and of many others, including Christopher Millard (who had been secretary to Wilde's friend Robert Ross), placed in his hands many original documents which had not been at the disposal of any previous biographer (and most of them, it may be said, remain still unpublished). Thus he planned to include in the book many of Wilde's letters written from prison, the love-letters that he wrote to Lord Alfred Douglas after he left prison but before they stayed together in Naples, and many of the letters that Wilde wrote in his last months to Robert Ross. The book was to tell also the full story of the famous *De Profundis* manuscript, that letter of many thousand words written to Douglas which is locked up in the British Museum until 1960, and of which only part has ever been made available to the public. The political influences concealed behind Wilde's trial were to be brought into the open. The tale of the strange feud between Douglas and Robert Ross after Wilde's death, and the way in which Douglas forced Ross to take action for libel against him by proclaiming that Ross was a sodomite, was to be told in full, together with the part played in that action by the talented, morose journalist T. W. H. Crosland. Long accounts by Robert Ross and Reginald Turner, which had never seen print, of Wilde's sufferings in his last days, and of his death, were to be used. And as a background to all this he planned to show the distant world of the nineties in which Wilde achieved his successes of conversation, drama and self-advertisement, and which he shocked by his homosexuality—that world in which "three-volume novels were still read in rectories, and had not quite disappeared from the publishers' lists", in which loo and whist were the popular card-games, and "A cobweb of conventions imposed the duty of appearing respectable upon every class except the criminal".

He gathered into his hands over the years an immense quantity of material, he wrote hundreds of letters, and bought and sold a great deal of Wildeana. All that remained was the writing of the book and that, as he said, should come easily. But somehow it did not come easily. There were always reasons, if not always good ones, for his procrastination. He had discovered many little-known facts about his hero, and was intent to correct the mis-understandings and mis-statements of some other biographers, and to weigh influences more nicely than they had done. Such a finely-spun piece of work involved also of necessity many hesitations and retractions: it could not be completed in a day, nor in a year. In the early thirties he was too much disturbed by the collapse of the First Edition Club to settle to writing. Later he was occupied by Corvo, and then by the Wine and Food Society. And Lord Alfred Douglas, although he remained on terms of friendship with my brother, was not pleased when he discovered that his friend wished to print unpublished letters, and to revive forgotten stories, about Douglas's early career. All these things delayed him, as well as the persistent publication of routine biographies of Wilde by men who had only a fraction of his own insight into Wilde's character, and merely rehearsed well-worn facts over and over without making independent researches. But the chief barrier to his completion of the book lay in his own mind.

I have mentioned already his fragmentary method of composition. In working on this biography he filled book after book with notes, he began chapters and left them after writing a page or two, he rewrote again and again the account of Wilde's first meeting with Lord Alfred Douglas, he put down sentences, and sometimes even phrases, on separate sheets of paper without making any attempt to link them together. One of these notebooks begins with several witty phrases like "He was an embodied reputation in search of an income", continues with notes on dances named after Wilde such as the "Oscar Wilde galop", the "Oscar Polka Mazurka" and "Oscar's Schottische", moves to a number of notes on Lily Langtry, who played an inconspicuous part in Wilde's life, and on Frank Miles, who shared rooms with Wilde, and has been little mentioned by other biographers, and ends with gnomic remarks like "See *New York Times* Feb. 4, 1882—*important*", "Oscar, if you do, throw up Burne Jones" and "Granville Murray—good subject for article."

The book which he left uncompleted might have been one of the high points in English biography. The character of Wilde was one which he perfectly understood, for in dandyism, love of display, and urbanity, it resembled his own; and in treating it he had decided to use a modified form of one of the methods described in his address on biography, and to "lift the curtain on a hero fully developed and manifesting the idiosyncrasies which make him worth writing about, to follow his career until its end, illustrating meanwhile the changing of his character with the years; and then, at the finish, to retrace the steps by which he has become what, in the first chapter, he was shown as being". The first chapter of his biography, "The Diner-Out", was an account of one of the "half-forgotten dinner-parties of the past", a party given by Frank Harris for the Princess of Monaco which became one of Wilde's triumphs of wit, fantasy and good humour. It was followed by an account of Wilde's life at Oxford, and an examination of the influence upon him of Ruskin, Pater and Matthew Arnold, and also of John Pentland Mahaffy, the Irish professor, cricketer and wit. This was succeeded by chapters, more or less chronological, on Wilde's life in London when he came down from Oxford, his lecture tour in America and his attempt to conquer Paris. There, unfortunately, the book in its completed form ends: but these 30,000 words are written with a masterly freshness and vividness, in a style which has even more than my brother's customary formal urbanity. The story of Wilde's Oxford career has been told by other biographers, but none before him had made adequate use of Wilde's tour in Greece with Mahaffy, nobody else had shown awareness of such entertaining sidelights as the letters written to Wilde in youth by a pained parent ("Dear Oscar, I was very much pained the last time I was at your house when I went into the drawing room and saw Fidelia sitting upon your knee"). Nobody else writing a full-length biography of Wilde had described his American adventure in such detail, and with such care; nobody else had taken pains to investigate the careers of such minor characters in the Wilde canon as Robert Ross and Robert Harborough Sherard, and make them living and interesting figures. The quality of the writing in these chapters is high: the sentences, written again and again, have the simplicity and lustre that conceals a considerable art. When, in 1941, the chapter on "Wilde at Oxford" was published in *Horizon*, it was met with a chorus of praise which warmed A.J.'s cooling optimism about his future. "My Wilde at Oxford has had a strong effect on the critics", he wrote to me. "Nicolson and MacCarthy are the latest converts. Connolly has written for more, on the ground that he will never get anything as good again. I have answered that I have no intention of dying yet, and that his conclusion is therefore premature. . . ."

Three months later he was dead.

At intervals during the thirties, A.J. announced his intention of writing a book, or at least a long article, about a figure who bore as little resemblance as possible to Oscar Wilde: a man named Charles Stokes.

Captain Stokes was one of those Nineteenth Century African adventurers whose lives had an unending interest for my brother. Tall, handsome and loud-voiced, "Stokesi" was for some time the most famous trader, chiefly in ivory, in the Eastern interior of Africa. In the mid-nineties he was arrested by the Belgian authorities

in the Congo State on a charge of supplying arms to the
Arabs with a view to inciting Civil War. After a brisk
trial by court-martial he was executed. This execution led
to representations by the British Ambassador to Belgium,
Sir Francis Plunkett, about irregularities at the trial, and
it is clear from the Blue Paper published in 1896 that an
"international incident" was narrowly avoided.

A.J.'s design was to unravel the web of political intrigue,
personal chicanery, and courage, cowardice and mis-
calculation that led to the death of the brash trader in
ivory. He entered the lists with his usual enthusiasm and
made elaborate, but unsuccessful, attempts to penetrate
the secrets of the Foreign Office. At last, when another
man would have written an inadequate essay, he gave
up the whole idea in despair of obtaining sufficiently
accurate information about the background of Stokes'
career. The actual writing got little further than the first
few pages; even so, it was subjected to his customary
revision. Here are two versions of his opening paragraph:

> One night in Africa Captain Stairs put on the Marquis
> de Bouchamps' boots. The reason for the mistake was haste;
> and the reason for his haste was the sound of violent kicking
> on the door below, accompanied by furious shouting in a
> broad Irish brogue. Alarm was easily taken in Africa in
> 1891, and the Captain, risking nothing from delay, dressed
> hurriedly and donned the wrong boots. But the visitor who
> had aroused him from heavy sleep proved harmless; a tall,
> handsome, loud-voiced Irishman, flushed and half-quarrel-
> some with drink, who refused to depart until he had shaken
> the hand of the leader of the Katanga expedition. So Stairs
> shook him by the hand, and learned that his untimely
> visitor was Charles Stokes.

The first sentence delighted A.J. particularly, and he
repeated it so often to his family, that it became a kind of

joke. His revision (one of several) may seem to many an indication of inability to let good writing alone:

> One July night in Bagamoyo Captain Stairs put on the Marquis de Bouchamps' boots. The reason for his mistake was the insistent desire of a tipsy Irishman to shake the hand of the leader of the Katanga Expedition, a desire which seemed inclined to veer from friendliness to physical violence at a hint of refusal. And so, to quiet his noisy demands, the Captain was summoned from his sleep; and in his haste put on the wrong boots.

When Captain Stokes proved an unrewarding subject he turned to another, of which the motive power was neither the frustration of literary ability through mental aberration, nor the struggle of a man of action against the natural and human forces checking a desired achievement, but another of his favourite themes: the power and operation of money. He would certainly have accepted the view of Emerson that "Money is, in its effects and laws, as beautiful as roses. Property keeps the accounts of the world, and is always moral". His interest in the behaviour and effects of money, in its connection with character, and in its beneficial or harmful effect on its recipients, had been constant, even though frequently dormant, since his youth. It was revived when one day, as he looked casually along a row of once-famous Victorian books, it occurred to him that there were no modern successors to that favoured Victorian *genre*, the personification of some inanimate object—the adventures of a guinea, of a watch, or of a hansom cab. Why not, then, show the vicissitudes, not fictional but factual, of a sum of money, from minimal beginnings into the Danae's shower that can alter, in a fractional degree, the face of history?

The idea fascinated him, and he knew that the best assurance of interesting others is to touch a theme that interests oneself: but for some time he found no family whose story answered all the requirements in his mind. The theme became a favourite, but unrewarding, one in his conversation, until one day his friend David Tennant said: "But why not write the history of *our* family?" The sketch that Tennant gave him of the rise of his family in less than a century and a half convinced the delighted biographer that here was a subject ready to his hand, one which would permit at the same time a restatement in miniature of commercial development in the Nineteenth Century (which he was well equipped to write, by interest and sympathy) and a description of the careers of romantic and exciting individuals. He explained his idea in a letter of thirteen pages to a publisher who was sufficiently impressed, and sufficiently courageous, to support his enthusiasm with a handsome advance; he obtained, partly through the fervent advocacy of David Tennant, a qualified approval of his project from the Tennant family; and two months before the outbreak of war he went to Scotland to stay with Lieutenant-Colonel John Edward Tennant, of Innes, in Morayshire.

His plans were announced, and his friends met them with less than their usual approval. "What is this nonsense I hear", James Agate wrote to him, "about your having laid aside your work on Oscar Wilde to write a life of some people called Tennant? You are justified in breaking off a *magnum opus* only if it is to write letters to me." Other friends expressed the view that a history of the Tennants must obviously be a commissioned book, of the kind generally given to a literary hack, and that his reputation would suffer severely through the publication of such a book with his name attached to it. Their reaction was a natural one, but such fears were unjustified: for the literary integrity that checked him always from producing shabby or unworthy work, was placing in his path difficulties quite unknown to those friends who thought that this must necessarily be an "official" history, backed by Lord Glenconner. "The would-be biographer", as A.J. remarked, "Is seldom welcomed by the descendants of those about whom he wishes to write, unless it is clear that he will disclose no disconcerting truths." He had already experienced difficulties with Rolfe's brother on this score, and Colonel Tennant, once away from the sound of A.J.'s persuasive voice, made it plain that the family would regard with no friendly eye any excursions off the well-known course that they were willing to chart for him. A preliminary note publicizing the book which he sent to Colonel Tennant was returned to him revised very drastically; his intention of linking the history of the Tennant family with a picture of its biographer did not meet with approval; and in an accompanying letter Colonel Tennant expressed his alarm at the prospect of the publication of the kind of book my brother had in mind. The book the family would like to see, he said, would be "a charming medallion of the worth-while things that happened", and an interpretation of the family based on money "must not be the theme of a book".

Perhaps this was not an insuperable obstacle, even to the biographer who observed dryly that "To say nothing but good of the dead is a pious convention which has reduced biography to the level of memorial sculpture": but it may may well have appeared so when, within four months of his journey to Scotland and the start of a quest which he hoped would be as rewarding as *The Quest For Corvo*, he was struck down by illness. The first two chapters of the book were written but when, after a lapse of months, he found himself physically able to return to it, the mental stimulus which prompted them had gone.

A. J. A. Symons

The two chapters completed, however, make it clear that the book would have been received with something less than enthusiasm by some members of the Tennant family. They are a brilliant excursion in the auto-biographical-biographical kind of his earlier book, and it seems likely that this book would have been more directly autobiographical than *The Quest For Corvo*. The first chapter tells how the eager biographer, deeply anxious to impress Colonel Tennant, arrived at the station an hour before his train's departure, and, through his reliance on an incorrect station clock, missed the train. The outline of the reasons which prompted my brother to choose his theme, and the description of his friendly reception by Colonel Tennant in his Scottish home which follows, is admirably done; but neither this, nor the ensuing chapter in which Colonel Tennant tells his interested but (as he represents himself) at once faintly envious and ironically amused visitor some details of his ancestry, was likely to please a family that took itself with a seriousness altogether becoming to its own high place in the world.

Among the personal notes contained in these two chapters, there is one, an acknowledgement of my brother's reaction to the conditions of his early life, which must be noticed by his biographer. In comparing his own fortune in life with that of Colonel Tennant, and in coveting momentarily "his shining motor-cars, his white tower, his avenues, his landscape, his lairdship, his City success, his racing yacht", A.J. brooded also upon his own enforced lack of family pride, that "natural form of egotism from which I was early debarred by chance". He described, in one long, revealing paragraph, his confinement inside a narrow enclave, "with three brothers and a sister as fellow prisoners", our cult of isolation, and our intense, introverted domesticity. For the most part, he says, he liked this life, for he knew no other; but his contentment was joined with periods of misery in which he regretted the restrictions placed on him by his birth. "I remember being deeply envious of a cobbler near our home, the fascia of whose shop bore the noble name of De Launay. If I could thus have claimed relationship with the great, even at so distant a remove, I should, I felt, have been happy." He provided the necessary compensation when he dignified himself with the name of "Alroy"; and the snobbery of the alteration, like that of his remarks about the noble name for which he yearned, is rendered inoffensive by his own calmly amused consciousness of what he was doing.

When illness and family opposition proved, temporarily as he told himself, too much for him, when he saw that *The Tennants of Glenconner* could not be written easily, he put his mind to another African story, a study of the explorations of Lieutenant (later Sir) Richard Burton and John Hanning Speke. He wrote five chapters of this book: they lack the originality of the Tennant biography, but show an undiminished smoothness in style, and perhaps an increased care in choice of epithet. But in the course of writing these chapters his attention wandered frequently and unpleasantly to his wavering hand and still slightly uncertain locomotion; to the curious giddiness which he felt when he looked upward, and which had not disappeared; to the depressing course of the War and the unhappy state of his bank balance; and to the melancholy and lonely future that seemed to confront him. "Writing seems to be the one activity left to me", he wrote to Philip Gosse. "But even that requires more calm than my disorganized circumstances command. I am supposed to avoid all disturbing contacts or situations, but to sit writing seraphically is as difficult, at the present moment, as to take a prolonged pleasure cruise in the North Sea." He was much cast down when the B.B.C., politely but firmly, suggested that he should not read his own script for a new musical box broadcast. He became more and more concerned to discover the cause and nature of his mysterious illness, for he sensed a certain reserve in what doctors told him; and then in the midst of these or other investigations an undispellable vagueness would overcome him and he would sit in his study or in his shagreen and white room, looking at nothing, disinclined even to finish a letter or to take exercise. In these moments of depression he would say, as he said to Tom Driberg, "Don't put off. Don't put off. Do your best work as young as you can". And the thought was with him then that he might have put off too long. But in a few hours his buoyant optimism would reassert itself. He was, after all, only forty years old, and the Biblical span of life is three score years and ten. Nothing was impossible to him, he felt, if he were given another thirty years of active mental and physical life.

CHAPTER XV

THE END

O N a warm spring day early in 1941 Ian Black
came down to spend a weekend at Finchingfield. He arrived before lunch and entered,
without announcement, by the garden. He was not surprised to see the table set for luncheon, because he knew
that Kitty, the village girl who was A.J.'s invaluable maid
and cook, came in only for an hour or two in the morning
and evening: but these signs of preparation made the
apparent absence of his host more marked. The visitor
waited and wondered, and his wonder increased when he
found that, in spite of the warmth of the day, fires had
been lighted in each of the ground floor rooms. He ex-
plored the garden without result, and the barns; then he
visited the first floor, and when he tapped on the door of his
host's bedroom a sepulchral voice told him to come in.

The heavy curtains in the bedroom were closed, and
the room was in complete darkness. In a thick voice the
invalid complained that he could not bear any light, and
said that he was cold: he asked that Black should telephone
to a medical friend in a village nearby who, although not
one of the doctors treating him, was interested in his case.
Black was alarmed and distressed, but his alarm abated
somewhat when A.J. was able to join his friends at tea.
He had obviously experienced a setback of some kind, and
complained that his eyes, which he covered with dark
glasses, gave him pain. After tea Black walked alone in the

garden, and returned to find his friend thinking lugub-
riously of the necessity for making a will. "What would
you like me to leave you?" he asked. "Name what you
want, but remember that the musical boxes are reserved
for the nation." Black returned to London really worried,
for the first time, by his friend's state of health. Very few
of those who knew A.J. well realized that his illness was
serious. He discussed his symptoms so avidly, and with
such ghoulish glee, he was so much concerned in his friends'
presence to maintain the appearance of health, and to
convince them, and through them himself, that his mental
power had suffered no diminution, that some of them half-
believed his whole illness to be a vast self-induced hypnosis,
which had as its end the evasion of payment of his more
pressing debts.

He attributed this second set-back (for in such a light he
determinedly regarded it) to the variation from the simple
routine of his life caused by the visits, on successive days,
of several friends. He sat up late for a week on end, eating
and drinking and talking with much of his pre-war gusto.
"At the end of it", he wrote, "I felt overwhelmingly tired,
and went to bed at 9.30. I didn't rise till 11.30 next day,
and behold, I felt like one for whom a grave is open. So
I went to bed again at 9.30, rose again at 11.30. No use; I
felt like one half-risen from the grave, with a good deal
of mould clinging to hands and face and feet. So I went to
bed at eight, and next day could not rise at all. My complaint came back on me with a triumphant crow." All the
symptoms that had marked the first attack fifteen months
before came back, and although he improved a little after
a few days he was conscious that a thick mist had settled
over his senses, making prolonged physical and mental
effort impossible.

Almost desperately he retained contact with his friends,

sending them long reports of his retrogression; he welcomed my mother's return to Finchingfield, and my own occasional visits from London. "I have almost lost the use of hands", he wrote to me. "I shall have to learn to typewrite with my toes, I suppose." I went down one weekend and found him in the great barn, engaged, as he often was, in sorting and rearranging books on the shelves. He asked me anxiously, as he asked everybody, if his speech was improving, and I said that I thought it was. Then he got up, stared out of the window into the garden, and said "What do you think of Sir James as a name?" I looked, I suppose, a little vacant, for he asked with a touch of impatience: "Does the name Sir James Symons run euphoniously?" A frown corrugated his still remarkably smooth brow. "Somehow Sir A.J. seems a little unsuitably abrupt. I favour Sir James. But the whole thing is a serious problem." I asked rather diffidently if a knighthood had actually been offered to him, but he waved the question aside. "It is serious because, as you realize, if I accept a knighthood, I put an end to my literary career. For a man of letters a knighthood is the seal of fame which is at the same time a kiss of death. But I am beginning to think that my literary life is over, and that I shall never do anything again." He turned to me and said with a kind of horror, "Surely my active life cannot be over when I am only forty years old?"

Such uncomfortable questions (I never learned whether his hints of an offered knighthood had any foundation in fact, or were simply a characteristic piece of self-deceptive camouflage) made him, in some ways, a difficult companion at this time; but in general illness mellowed him in a way that made him, at least for me, a much more charming and sympathetic companion than he had been in the past. There were differences between us which were

rooted in our different ages, and in our relations as eldest and
youngest brother; and I had reacted in several ways, more
or less consciously, from his example. My dress was
conscientiously untidy, I showed an active disinterest in
his extra-literary activities, and derided his civilized
urbanity of speech and writing. This rejection of his own
standards of living did not go unnoticed, nor by implication unreproved. When I told him that I wanted to start a
small verse magazine he asked me how I was going to pay
for it. I said hopefully that if I could sell 800 copies I should
not make a loss, and he laughed and said scornfully:
"What makes you think you can sell eighty?" It is an
indication of his fundamental amiability (when I think
how often I must have irritated him) that, when the
magazine appeared, he bought twenty copies of every
issue, and gave them away to friends.

But all that was in the past, and now we talked of modern
poetry, of Henry James and of Trollope; and he deferred
to my taste with a pleasant irony. I induced him to read
Henry James in bulk, I think for the first time (though that
was a thing he would never admit): "How overwrought
and overwritten *The Death of the Lion* is", he wrote to
me. "What a 'sweet depravity of ear' is needed to enjoy
Our Henry. I am reading O. Henry instead." He was
distressed by the death of his beautiful golden cat Serafino;
but this distress was alleviated by my promise to send down
to him a wonderful blue Persian cat of my own, named
Trotsky. He had envied me the possession of this aristocratic creature from the day he saw it, and wrote:

> I regret to say that Serafino has been translated to the next
> world. A vacancy therefore opens for a hardworking, clean,
> industrious and ferocious cat, who will be prepared to assist
> in writing books, cleaning silver, and eating rats and
> mice. Names and addresses of suitable candidates will be

The End

welcomed. I am prepared to give the job to Trotsky.
Is he clean?

I was conducting at that time a campaign of inter-
mittent gunfire (or perhaps I do myself too much honour,
and should say pea-shooting) against Cyril Connolly's
magazine *Horizon*; and A.J. followed the letters on either
side with an attention which flattered and astonished me.
He wrote to me several times about it, emphasizing gently
and with the most delicate care for my self-esteem, what
seemed to him the tactlessness and needless hostility of my
attack:

My dear Julian,
    The Connolly correspondence entertains and alarms me.
If I were not your brother, how naive, amateur, slack, in-
efficient, misleading and unintentionally comic (to say
nothing of being flippant) might I not seem to you. No
wonder I am subdued to the point of silence, and write only
late at night after blackout and after I have made sure there
are no stamps left for posting with, when such electrically
charged wires as you are stretched out in the dark, first to
trip and then to shock the unwary. It is to Connolly's credit,
I think, that he answered, and in such off-hand style, your
carefully considered bombardment. Before I give you my
report (as a snooping neutral observer) on the damage done,
may I give you a crumb of advice? I may? Thank you (and
I hope you may survive to thank *me*!). This: it is seldom
advisable to be so downright in castigation that your interlocutor can only agree with you at the cost of his own good
opinion of himself. Thus if you tell me that I *may* be
wrong, I shall agree with you. If you tell me that, in any
given instance, I *am* wrong, I shall admit the possibility.
But if you tell me that I *must* be wrong, I shall damn your
eyes. And if you say to me, as you did to C., that a suggestion made by me is "innocent to the point of idiocy", you
will probably rouse a resentment as lasting as the one which
(I am glad to see) you appear to entertain for ———. It was a

mistake (you will remember my contention) to sentence
Hatry to the maximum term for his offence, when he had
mitigated the offence in several ways; by doing so, the law
deprived future offenders of any incentive to confess, not
avoid arrest, not destroy evidence, and all the other things
that Hatry did to help the prosecution. And in the same way
it is a mistake to denounce C.'s dealings in terms which you
might apply to the late James Douglas or the present ———
———, unless you are certain that CC. and company are
certain to play no part in your life. Indeed, if I were Connolly, I could not resist making this point against you. I
should retort your charge of naivety. What! Did Mr.
Symons really think that this was the way to present "constructive" criticism? To put his suggestions forward with
an emphasis and in a fashion which completely precluded
their acceptance? He must indeed be innocent to the point
of (how can I make this machine whisper the word?) to
suppose that advice so tendered could ever be made use of.
But perhaps you seem to yourself to have stopped shorter
this side of insult than you seem to me to have done?

And now for a count of the dead and wounded.

He went on to a detailed criticism in some hundreds
of words, which has no present interest, and concluded:

Alas for letters, or this one. I have been interrupted, and a
day has passed. I cannot recapture the mood in which I set
out to weigh your charges. Snow has fallen; and the village,
always dangerously like a picture-postcard, has become a
Christmas card instead. John Gielgud has paid me a long
visit, leaving an enviable cloud of incense and success behind. I cannot go on. But I have a land-mine in my locker
(so not to speak) for *you*. Are you not (or, as Le Fanu would
say, Are not you) becoming an Art for Arts Sakist, almost
unaware? Me, I welcome the transformation. Imperfectly
though my practice accords with my precept, I have always
held, and supposed that I believed, that the act of creative
writing (in which, yes, I include your excellent explanation
of Ben Jonson) was the final end and interest for my sort of
mind—which I also hold and believe (sometimes) to be the

right sort of mind. Alas! how have I played a traitor to my own code; what dozens of distractions I have invented to persuade me from my own purpose. Wine in its minutiæ, books in *theirs*, musical boxes, gregariousness, collectanea, a vague search for universal knowledge—how many paths for wandering I have preferred to the straight road. And now *you*, who seemed to be set in the mud, duty, effort, glory of politics start up to reproach me, and profess the true faith with all the energy of the convert. Oh, why is my mind minimifidian, even to its own ends?

In retrospect his interest seems less surprising to me. I find in it now a small symbol of his need to hang on, even at second hand, to the literary and social world which had slipped so far away from him. He was pleased by any occupation which kept him from thinking about his own illness and debts, or about the unfavourable course of the war, or about his possible future life in a world which, he saw clearly, would have a very different standard of values from those by which he had lived. He viewed with dis-satisfaction the passing days spent in a fashion which he thought, with a shade of over-emphasis, anchoritic, and an angry knowledge of the life that might have been his if all had gone well, made him write to the partner of his broken love-affair: "Even now I cannot forgive you for the happiness we have lost; the wonderful years we might have had in this beautiful house, the friendships, the discoveries, the enlargements and release of mind. We should have become legendary figures, symbolising a form of life only to be reached by the fortunate few." And then he turned, as he turned in almost every letter he wrote in these days, to speculation about his chances of survival. "Encephalitis is a complaint with a wide field of consequences. Many of them are fatal; many doom their victim to a long withering agony. But then it may be a tumour on the brain, such as killed Oscar, or it may be . . . oh, all kinds of things."

Was his trouble encephalitis? He began to doubt it: and to his restless mind such doubt was an affront. He had formerly read medical books in order to discover his chances of recovery from encephalitis: now he read them in the fear of some fresh, disastrous discovery. An incautious acquaintance put him upon a new track by suggesting that he might be suffering from disseminate sclerosis, and then later (but too late) retracted the suggestion. A.J. discovered that this disease accorded with almost all of his symptoms—the partial paralysis, the slur of speech, the lethargy, and even the inability to look upward. He found out, also, that the disease was incurable.

The possibility, even, that he might be suffering from such a disease depressed him, and in this last summer he made little attempt to write. I remember him, sitting in the garden at the back of the house, stripped above the waist (he thought that the effect of the sunlight on his body might be beneficial). He had taken a dislike to the tiny moles that marked his torso, and pieces of silk were tied round them, an old-fashioned remedy for their dispersal. He walked, uncertainly but still not feebly, down the garden; he played his home-made croquet keenly; he kept up a consistent, though not a calligraphic, flow of correspondence and, since he was now unable to sign his name unwaveringly, invented several new signatures composed of little crosses or circles, which made up his initials. He never ceased to be delighted by the letters he received from those who had read the recently-published Penguin edition of *The Quest For Corvo*; he referred to these letters as his daily tonic, and was scrupulously careful to answer all of them. It was difficult to believe that he was danger-

The End

ously ill, and tempting to think that his trouble might be neurotic as much as physical.

My mother, who was with him daily, was less easy about him, but I did not take her fears as seriously as I should have done and was shocked when I came down for a weekend and saw him, as had Ian Black some weeks before, in a darkened room, obviously in great pain, and hardly able to speak. He whispered to me that he was to go to Colchester Hospital, and that he would like me to see that half a dozen copies of the Penguin edition of the *Quest* were sent with him, so that he could give them to nurses. Dr. Propert, who came from Colchester to see him, shocked my brother by saying (this was the first time that such words had been said, either to him or to his family) that he could offer no hope of any permanent, or full, recovery.

It seemed for a few days that this view might be too pessimistic. In hospital he appeared to recover from this attack, as he had done from others and, again, he persisted in regarding it only as a set-back. He said to Tom Driberg, who went down to see him: "If it is, as may be surmised, the form of encephalitis known as Parkinsonism, I must resign myself to the fact that it is usually (though not invariably) fatal. If, on the other hand—" And then he elaborated, once again, schemes for work during con-valescence, and told of the plan he was making for the housing of the choicest of his musical boxes and polyphons in a museum. This plan was carried out after his death, and the Symons Collection is now a feature of the Pitt-Rivers Museum at Oxford.

He was less cheerful in writing to Simon, which he did, since he had now lost the use of his hands, through the medium of my sister Edith. "I am dictating this letter with great difficulty", he said, "so please forgive any angularity

of expression that my weakness may import into it. . . .
There is a possibility, which I do not welcome, that I may
never be able to work again." But slowly, very slowly,
he improved. He gave the copies of his book to the nurses;
and I have no doubt that, although they were in the
Penguin edition, he gave them with an awful gravity.
He became friendly with Dr. Propert, who admired the
struggle for life that was being made by this strange patient
and the remarkably clear insight into his illness that he
showed, was impressed by his freedom from fear, and
attracted by his interest and curiosity. A.J., on his side,
liked and trusted his doctor. "I have taken my doctor's
cellar in hand", he said, when I went to see him, "I have
told him that it will pay him to keep me alive simply to
look after his wine." The most famous of his several
specialists came down to look at him, and, very feebly, he
was able to totter down the hospital corridor with a
helping arm. The specialist spoke cheering words, and said
that he might go home very soon; my mother made
arrangements for the patient's return to Brick House; and
then a telephone call from the hospital told her that he had
died, quite peacefully, on the night of August 26th, 1941.

An examination of the brain was carried out after his
death and it was found that he did not, after all, suffer from
encephalitis; nor from disseminated sclerosis, although he
had symptoms which are almost indistinguishable from
a certain form of that disease. The cause of his death was a
haemangioma of the brain stem. A haemangioma is a
small collection of capillary blood vessels which are dilated
and fragile. They are quite often seen on the surface of the
body, where they produce the kind of small or large naevus
which is popularly called "a port-wine stain". A haemangioma is not, of necessity, either dangerous or important;
A.J. in fact had one on his leg, which gave him no

The End

trouble. Unfortunately he had another, probably smaller than a pea, in his brain stem at the junction of the pons and medulla, and this was the cause of his death. Since the walls of the dilated capillary blood vessels are not supported by fibrous tissue in the nervous system, as they are in the skin, one of the small vessels can easily break and leak blood. This happened in my brother's case, and caused the symptoms from which he suffered. The lesion was so small that in any other part of the nervous system it probably would not have caused much trouble, but in the brain stem the motor tracts coming down from the cerebrum and the sensory tract ascending from the spinal cord are confined in a small space. The lesion which killed him was no larger than a sixpenny piece.

He was buried at Finchingfield, in the little churchyard cemetery of the village he had loved so well. Several of his friends attended the funeral, including Ian Black, Doris Langley Moore, Vyvyan Holland and André Simon; Doctor Propert came over from Colchester to attend it; at the church the lesson was read by Sir Ronald Storrs. My last recollection is of his appearance in the coffin, when it lay in his study at Brick House. His hair was quite untouched with grey; he looked peaceful, and remarkably young.

CHAPTER XIV

A VALEDICTION, FORBIDDING MOURNING

T HE death, in that anxious August nine years ago, of a dandy, a gourmet, a writer who had not completely fulfilled his talents, was not likely to receive great notice. Holbrook Jackson wrote of him in *The Times* that "Symons was the complete amateur. . . . His first editions of the books of the nineties, his Bristol glass, his hoard of mother-of-pearl knick-knacks, and his musical boxes were part of his inevitable environment". Percy Muir wrote an obituary in *The Times Literary Supplement*, memorial essays by Vyvyan Holland and myself appeared in *Horizon*, and other essays in *Wine and Food*.

None of these pieces caught more than a fragment of him: and the epitaphs chosen by their writers were fragmentary also, or at least incomplete in the sense that his own brilliant phrase about himself: "No one so poor has lived so well" is incomplete. Most of his friends could put down in their sketches no more than one or two of the many faces that he presented to the world; they hardly touched the problem of his personality, any more than did the sonnet written after his death:

> You pass out with an age, an older day
> When Man's heart drew to kindness and to cheer,
> When thought had leisure, there you held a sway,
> Elegant Judge, who charmed our eye and ear!

A Valediction, Forbidding Mourning

My brother's personality exerted itself in very varying ways on different people: and he presents, accordingly, a study for the social historian, the psychologist, and the merely literal-minded who do not disturb themselves with speculations about subconscious forces or the movement of society, but drop their tear with human failure or clap their hands at dramatic success.

Of many well-known people it is enough to tell the facts of their lives: he was born, his actions were such and such, he died. Any kind of interpretation imposes an unworkable strain, or lends a ludicrous importance, to the simple pattern of their lives and thought. As the American critic James Burnham has observed, writing ironically of the myth built by many commentators around the personality of Franz Kafka: "Difficulties with family, work and money—who has not had them?—led him to postpone and finally break off a project of marriage. The war, as wars always do, for everyone, 'shattered all his plans'." The commentators on Kafka, he observes, recall "Personal traits no more eccentric than required to constitute anyone an individual." If this were all that could be said of my brother, a record of his life need hardly have been attempted. But it is not all. His activities and his character were both exceptional, and as he remarked himself the biographer, to understand and explain any unusual character and its talents, must invoke the aid of neurological science, since "Just as there is 'no excellent beauty without some strangeness in the proportions', so there is no exceptional man without some strangeness in his physical constitution. . . . The growth of scientific knowledge is teaching even biographers that heavy drinking is usually a symptom of some hidden need, and that even the normal man is mentally unstable when fatigued". It is impossible to trace exactly the *causes* of my brother's chief psychological characteristics, but he certainly showed in a mild form what Freudian psychologists call a father fixation, combined with what is termed an anxiety-neurosis. His life, that is to say, was unconsciously an attempt to escape from the impulsive and generous, yet also narrow and severe, character of his father. This desire did not interfere with the good relations that existed between them, or with the admiration that (like Kafka) he felt for the father from whose ideas he revolted. For his father's impulsiveness he attempted to substitute a calm calculation, against his father's sexual puritanism he counterposed his own interest in such psychologically abnormal characters as Wilde, Poe and Corvo. His anxiety neurosis was linked with this primary psychological trait. The course of his father's life had led to very varied turns of fortune in our family, and these induced in him an anxiety about his own future. To this cause for anxiety was added another, which he revealed to none of his friends (although some suspected his secret): the fact that, on his father's side, he was of Jewish birth. It is possible, I think, to overestimate the feeling of inferiority that traditionally marks out the Jew; there are many indications that, in favourable conditions, like those that have existed in England during the past hundred years, he can be absorbed easily and naturally into the framework of the society in which he lives, without injury either to his own talents or to the shape of that society. But the traditional insecurity of the Jew was certainly felt by my brother. Since his character was a strong one, his neurosis took the form of an aggressive resolve to achieve social success, to "build his life as an architect builds a house". Acknowledgement of Jewish birth might, obviously, be an obstacle to such success: therefore he did not acknowledge it. A secret of this kind, however, places a strain upon psychological equilibrium, and my brother felt the strain of secrecy all his life.

When these unconscious motive forces are understood, they explain many of the external events in his career, although they cast little light upon the aesthetic aptitudes which (as he remarked in writing of Corvo) cannot be explained, but only assessed. His creative talent was at war always with his desire for social success, and although generally subordinate to that prime motive, it was never unimportant in his life.

He invented in childhood the elaborate family games into which he poured all the force of a thwarted and passionate nature. These games provided an obvious compensation for the things he lacked, and desired: and it is instructive to notice that they all symbolize *external* activities. He was, vicariously, a racehorse owner, a business magnate, a general: not a writer, a playwright, or the editor of a magazine. He continued to indulge these, or other, forms of make-believe throughout his life; and he seems never to have realized the dangers inherent in them, as the Brontës, for example, realized the dangers of their literary games with the Angrians and Gondals. When she was twenty-five Anne Brontë wrote: "The Gondals in general are not in first-rate playing condition. Will they improve?" The Angrians and Gondals of the Brontës merge imperceptibly into their finest literary creations: and, in a similar way, my brother's early games mingled with his attitude towards reality so that, by an act of mental sleight-of-hand, he was able to consider the fortunes of his life in much the same way that he considered the fortunes of a game.

He reacted violently to youthful experiences (his apprenticeship, and life away from home) which are not themselves remarkable; and he developed an extreme

A. J. A. Symons

sensitiveness to a Christian name which seemed to him ridiculous, and also to the section of society in which he moved. He placed a screen round his birth and childhood partly because he had a particular secret to hide, partly because he had nothing romantically strange to tell; and on the subjects of his birth and occupation he was reticent, even to the girl with whom he was in love. Eagerness for social success occupied him in youth more than anything else: and "social success", for him, meant not simply entry into upper-class society, but also his complete acceptance as part of that society. His presence at the same table with those of good birth and social position was much, but it was not enough. They must admire him, and respect him. "Though I came into contact with men and boys who were clever and learned, not one of them could dwarf my inner consciousness of myself as their equal—their superior." This need for admiration raised barriers for him which do not exist for those who wish simply to mingle with "society"—which, in modern English life, is accessible to men of talent who have not attended a public school.

One turning point of his life was the foundation of the First Edition Club, and through it his immersion in bibliography. It is plain that such a career was not fortuitous, but inevitable for him, and that he would have found no occupation satisfactory which did not fulfil his need for social recognition. He might have found with luck, nevertheless, a congenial and profitable activity less damaging to his creative ability than the bibliographical pursuits which made him like "a Hermes in the underworld of letters". But he was unlucky: he found bibliography. For bibliography attracts naturally the parasites of letters, the cranks and the antiquarians, those who cherish the escatological works of Swinburne and those who pore pedantically over problems of authorship among the Brontës: those, at the best, who possess artistic sensibility without ability to create, and, however amiably or unintentionally, batten on the artist's by-products and can feed for hours on a problem of original publication dates or variations in binding of a first edition. My brother did not belong in this company: but he made himself master of it. These bibliographical occupations changed him gradually: on one hand they sobered his youthful romanticism, and on another put him out of sympathy with the best art and writing of his time, so that he could draw no sustenance from them. If only, some will think, he had begun differently, if he had written a successful novel or play in his early twenties! But the pattern of personality is not to be evaded. Such achievements were not beyond his ability, but they offered inadequate rewards in terms of social success.

So he passed through his twenties, surprising new friends by the extraordinary touchiness which was a mark of his feeling of social insecurity. He adopted an extravagant dandyism as a badge of individuality, and diverted his need for artistic expression into such unsatisfactory courses as his great Nineties bibliography, and a collection of mother-of-pearl counters. He led a life of great external activity, which fulfilled as nearly as possible the dreams of his childhood: and it must have seemed to him in those halcyon days that nothing, for him, could ever go seriously wrong.

But things did go wrong. The collapse of the First Edition Club was a heavy blow to him, and when he tried to stave it off, unavailingly, by the kind of sophistical ingenuity which he applied to games, some of his friends suffered financially. Yet few were alienated from him permanently. His charm, his amiability, and his manifest

intention to act in everybody's best interests, were so
patent that it was difficult to be angry with him for long.
He became aware at Bedford Square of the ambiguities
in his own nature which were caused by the desire for
artistic expression; and when, under monetary pressure,
he began to write seriously, chose subjects related in some
way to the personal contradictions he was trying to
resolve. Emin used an assumed name, and so did Corvo;
Stanley suffered from an inferiority induced by the
mystery of his birth; Poe was deeply conscious of his
character as an adopted child; Hook hid darkly a not very
shameful secret. He was able, with little effort, to make
their fears and struggles his own. But more than this, the
subjects of his choice, with the exception of Emin and
Stanley, were markedly pathological cases. His choice of
them compensated for the restrictions of his youth, when
he had not been allowed to keep the works of Oscar
Wilde in the house, when my mother had given him
money to buy *Mademoiselle de Maupin*. He read Freud,
Jung and Adler to try to discover an explanation of the
difficulty he found in writing. (Adler's theory of organic
inferiority, which he refers to in a letter, suggests that "all
pathological changes are associated with an hereditary
inferiority of the organ and the nerve superstructures"
and that some "compensation is generally found for the
resulting deficiency"). It is probable that this difficulty
was part of his anxiety-neurosis—that he feared always,
subconsciously, a revelation of inferiority and ignorance
through his writing; and this fear was never fully assuaged
by the fact, which he noted, that "whatever I have written
has from the first been received with a flattering unanimity
of praise". He needed continual encouragement and
flattery if he was to write at all: there can be few men—
certainly few so little prepared to tolerate adverse criticism

who have been so eager to submit their work to other eyes for approval.

The act of writing (which was "accompanied by more pain than pleasure") pulled the pattern of his career, for a short time, out of place. It moved back, and moved back finally, with the foundation of the Wine and Food Society. After that there was, until his loss of income through war and illness, no more writing. There was an ever-increasing number of compensations in the forms of musical boxes and other Victoriana; and, with the loss of artistic activity, these compensations became increasingly important to him. There were lunches, dinners, weekends, and an ever securer social position. There were the psychologically suggestive collaborations with Desmond Flower and André Simon, and the many other schemes for collaborations on different projects which, for one reason or another, came to nothing. There were moments, in the late thirties, of misgiving and self-distrust, such as that in which he felt a need to hear from his oldest friend, Harold Fisher: but these moments were few. He was, by this time, a complete character. His conversational powers had reached their peak, and so had his dandyism, he was accepted (almost as he wished to be) in society, he had made a place for himself in the world. Literature could be no more than a by-product of such a career. The complete character he had created, a man of fashion and a man of affairs, was an extrovert almost pure, though not at all simple.

The war might have made another turning-point for him (as Mr. Burnham says, it operated as wars always do, for everyone; it "shattered all his plans"). It changed the stresses in his character: now that all was lost, he could set to work seriously on another book. But now it was too late, for illness struck him down.

A. J. A. Symons

In the years that have passed since his death, his personality has not been forgotten. Whenever (one of his friends remarked to me) two people discover that they both knew him, their conversation moves naturally to the charm and ambiguity of his character. They speculate about the extraordinary stories he told, and the clothes he wore; they talk of his wit, and his ability to keep a roomful of people entertained for an hour or more; they lose themselves in the rich and strange labyrinths of his personality. They speculate also, sometimes, on his future. He was still a young man, they say, his career broken abruptly. What would he have written, what would he have done, given another ten years of life? Such questions are idle. A life has no standard length and a character, fully formed, does not change. My brother, however long he had lived, would have continued to make his attempts to reconcile the contradictions which lend flavour to a recital of his career.

But it is not simply as a remarkable character that he is set down here, but as a man of remarkable talent. The work that he did in raising the standard of English book production deserves more recognition than it has received. The Fifty Books of the Year exhibitions were more than an ingenious idea: they exerted a positive, and beneficial, influence particularly in encouraging publishers to experiment with fresh materials and styles in bindings. The interests of the *Book-Collector's Quarterly* ranged a long way outside the narrow corridors of bibliography, and there has been no more important periodical, in its field, than this one during the past thirty years. And, although he wrote so little, the work he produced is remarkable: how remarkable is not, I think, sufficiently appreciated. His uncomfortable fastidiousness helped to ensure the strength, the balance, and the easy movement of his prose: and Doris Langley Moore's words are almost true,

A Valediction, Forbidding Mourning

that in his handful of books and essays, "not a paragraph is
dull, not a sentence contains less than the full vigour of his
splendid intelligence". A collection of his essays, and of
the completed chapters in his unfinished biography of
Oscar Wilde, would show that he produced other work
than *The Quest For Corvo* which is worthy of remembrance.

There are as many possible interpretations of the significance and value of a life as there are interpreters. My
brother's life, for me, has interest because it shows in
microcosm one form of the frustration of the artistic
temperament in our time, and is also a revelation in
microcosm of the gay, desperate, but in the last resort
always vain, assault that the adventurer makes upon
society.

Triumphantly the adventurer, or the speculator, asserts
the power of his individual will: firmly he rejects all but
the desired end. But the end is not achieved, or if achieved
still is not satisfactory; behind the impulse to conquest lies
always, uncontrollable and fascinating, the terror of
defeat. ("The gambler wishes always in his heart to lose.
He is only content when he is ruined.") Nor, if the
speculator has a strong aesthetic feeling, can he suppress it.
Sealed off in one place, it springs up in another, creating a
private and a public life which cannot ever be completely
reconciled. If, like my brother, the speculator is generous
and amiable, he acknowledges one day the certainty of his
defeat and writes, humorously, his epitaph, as my brother
wrote his one day for Vyvyan Holland:

AJAS
ALAS

But on the next morning his restless, optimistic, acquisi-
tive spirit is abroad again, and he helps to found a Wine

and Food Society, addresses a Sette of Odd Volumes, or makes careful preparations for a country weekend:

> Travelling by daylight on from house to house
> The longest way to the intrinsic peace,
> With love's fidelity and with love's weakness.

THE END

THIRTY YEARS ON

T HIRTY is a convenient number for the heading, but in fact it is nearly forty years ago that I submitted the opening chapter of this book for a prize competition run by Eyre & Spottiswoode in conjunction with the American publishers Houghton Mifflin. The chapter plus an outline of the book's later development did not win the competition but Graham Greene, then editorial director of Eyre & Spottiswoode, gave me a commission on the strength of it and paid what was for the time a handsome advance.

I was put in mind of those distant days when a friend asked me recently whether, if I embarked on the biography to-day, I would write it differently. Of course the answer must be a general *yes*. One's feelings, attitudes, perceptions, are not the same in one's mid-thirties as when more than twice that age. The tone would be the same, affectionate but detached and never fervent, because that seems to me the right tone for its subject—and the one that comes most naturally to its author. There are, however, passages that now seem to me unwarrantably censorious, distressingly orotund. And today I should name freely some who then remained anonymous, say that "X" on page 222 was Tom Driberg, and that AJ's partner in the love affair mentioned was Natalie Sieveking, later Natalie Bevan. I should have liked to excise a paragraph here, expand details there: but the economics of photographic reproduction, or rather the limitations it enforces, prevented any changes greater than the replacement of a few words here and there by other words containing exactly the same number of characters. Such minor and difficult changes did not seem worth making, hence this Afterword.

The thing that immediately impressed me on re-reading the book was how unlucky AJ had been to pass so much of his adult life in a period of deflation. In that world the price of newspapers and bus fares, three course meals and ready-to-wear clothing, never varied. It was always low, and cut-price shops worked hard to make it even lower, selling twopenny bars of chocolate for three ha'pence, and twenty cigarettes for elevenpence ha'penny instead of a shilling, the actual copper coin enclosed in the packet. On another level the Wine and Food Society could provide for two guineas the astonishing cele-bratory dinner at Brighton's Royal Pavilion de-scribed in this book, with its forty-two courses and sixteen wines and liqueurs. In that world of what would now, remarkably enough, be called sound money (although the notable thing for most of us was the lack of money, sound or otherwise), musical boxes, glass obelisks, conversation pictures, and other Victoriana—and of course not only Victoriana but anything unfashionable—could be bought cheaply, although it could not easily be sold again. AJ survived, and enjoyed himself, but how trium-phantly he would have ridden the bucking bronco Inflation in the Seventies and Eighties. His advice to Ian Black in 1940 rings prophetically down the years: "It is quite clear that we shall have inflation.

Afterword

Whatever you do, keep all you own. This is a time to buy and not to sell. I am a rich man. My books, my wine, my house, my mother-of-pearl counters, are each day rising in value." Such words sound now like obvious wisdom, but that was not so during the two decades when AJ struggled to turn his bright ideas into money.

Today the First Edition Club would count its members in hundreds rather than dozens, there would be great demand for its projected service giving advice on the market price of books, the Secretary would be buzzing to and fro across the Atlantic making arrangements for the sale of Club publications to American bibliophiles. Today also the Hampstead housewives who felt that the Wine and Food Society was too grand, and its magazine too erudite for them, talk knowledgeably of first growth clarets and *nouvelle cuisine*. Unseduced by Simon and Symons, they have long since succumbed to the *Good Food Guide* and Egon Ronay and become worshippers at the shrines of Elizabeth David and Jane Grigson. And today—who can doubt it?—AJ might be a frequent magisterial presence on the box, prepared to pronounce on the genuineness of a questioned manuscript, emerge successfully from the blind tasting of several wines, invent his own panel game and play it, perhaps even demonstrate his spellbinding skills as a conversationalist in sessions of table talk.

Many new paths to popularity and public notice, along with fresh sources of income, would have been open to him in our present inflationary media-struck world, but would he have been happier in it? That seems to me doubtful. AJ wanted to make money, not to accumulate it. He had a sort of fastidiousness, much rarer today than in the Twenties and Thirties, that would have shuddered away from the crasser ways of making money available now to those with the talent (which he certainly possessed) for talking readily and knowledgeably on almost any subject. The Wine and Food Society would never, even if circumstances had permitted it, have turned into anything resembling the *Good Food Guide*. AJ, and André Simon too, may have willed such an end, but they would never seriously have contemplated the means. They would never have given approval to establishments merely 'better than average' or offering 'good value for money'. It was a natural progression for them that Wine and Food Society meals should have become fewer and more expensive.

If I were rewriting this book I should stress more strongly not simply the fact that AJ was a player of games, but the spirit in which he played them. Most were played for victory but not for money, and he approached them rather like Auden, who spoke of poetry as being first of all a game with words. AJ treated the events of his life with the intense seriousness that Auden gave to poetry, but always in the spirit of *homo ludens*, the player of games. He loved the bazaar of life for its dangerous as much as its smiling chances, and truly believed that for him the spun coin would always come down on the right side, even though he knew that such a belief was absurd.

In the years since this book first appeared I have received many letters about AJ: some sent by readers

of *The Quest For Corvo* who assumed (incorrectly)
that he was Catholic, homosexual, or both, some
telling stories of his skill in forgery, his conversational ability, his intricate ways with money and
credit. A letter from the Bishop of Derry gave a
glimpse of AJ's brief career in the Artists' Rifles during World War I, something about which, as the
Bishop suggested, I knew little. 'One got to like him
a lot. He is a very vivid memory over the years since
we soldiered together at Hare Hall Camp, Rom-
ford.'

The most interesting letter came in the late Sixties
from Dr Purdon Martin, the specialist to whom he
wrote the eight page letter mentioned on page 244. I
had suggested, Dr Purdon Martin said, that the doctors had not been very clever in failing to diagnose
the nature of AJ's illness, but this was not the case.

> My original and only diagnosis from the time I first
> saw him in January 1940 was that he had had a
> haemorrhage into his brainstem and (from my pre-
> vious experience of haemorrhage in that situation) that
> it would be from a vascular abnormality—one or other
> variety of angioma. I wrote this to his doctor at
> Clapham at the time and later in the year to Horder
> when he asked my opinion, and later still to Propert in
> reply to his enquiry. All these people had it in black
> and white ... AJ always came to see me alone and
> obviously he had to be told, and it is quite clear from
> the letter you published (p 227) that he knew it only
> too well ... I told him too that he would improve as
> the haemorrhage absorbed and that duly happened,
> and no one could have told how far the improvement
> would go, and whether he would have another bleed-
> ing, or when.
>
> He died, not from the angioma *per se*, which he had
> had all his life, but from the haemorrhage.

A. J. A. Symons

This letter is a corrective to my account of his illness, but it does pose some problems. The letter
mentioned does not show that AJ knew 'only too
well' the nature of his illness. On the contrary he says
that he has been told he 'may not have had a hemorrhage'. The eight page letter written in March 1941 to
Dr Purdon Martin is designed to be 'an account, for
your case-book, of my present condition'. It mentions Horder's suggestion of encephalitis, records his
recovery and decline after 'visitors here, dinners in
London, successive late nights', and implicitly poses
questions about the patient's future, without men-
tioning Dr Purdon Martin's uncheering diagnosis.

Was AJ then deceived, with benevolent intention,
by the other doctors he consulted? It looks like it.
And did he put Dr Purdon Martin's diagnosis out of
his mind as something too gloomy to be accepted or
even considered? That is perfectly possible, even likely. In a letter to him I had commented sharply on a
phrase of his about 'reasonable self-deception', saying I was 'agin' it. He replied: 'You are "agin" self-
deception. Yes. So are we all. But is it not part of
that duality of mind, so essential to our well-being,
by which we accept, for current convenience, that
which we know not to be true?' Such self-deception
is not the invariable human trait he suggests, but it is
certainly essential to *homo ludens*, and it may have
helped AJ to play the game of his life cheerfully and
courageously to the end.

INDEX

INDEX OF PERSONS MENTIONED

Index

Index

OXFORD

MORE OXFORD PAPERBACKS

Details of a selection of other books follow. A complete list of Oxford Paperbacks, including The World's Classics, Twentieth-Century Classics, OPUS, Past Masters, Oxford Authors, Oxford Shakespeare, and Oxford Paperback Reference, is available in the UK from the General Publicity Department, Oxford University Press (JH), Walton Street, Oxford, OX2 6DP.

In the USA, complete lists are available from the Paperbacks Marketing Manager, Oxford University Press, 200 Madison Avenue, New York, NY 10016.

Oxford Paperbacks are available from all good bookshops. In case of difficulty, customers in the UK can order direct from Oxford University Press Bookshop, 116 High Street, Oxford, Freepost, OX1 4BR, enclosing full payment. Please add 10% of published price for postage and packing.

H. H. ASQUITH:
LETTERS TO VENETIA STANLEY

Edited by Michael and Eleanor Brock

The passionate love letters of Prime Minister H. H. Asquith to beautiful socialite Venetia Stanley, who was less than half his age. This Oxford Paperback edition contains recently discovered letters that throw new light on the couple's relationship.

'absolutely packed with amusing material' Anthony Powell

'a document of matchless historical value. Reading (the letters) seems to be peering through a key-hole into a brilliantly lighted room in which great events are being enacted' *Financial Times*

A YORKSHIRE BOYHOOD

Roy Hattersley, MP

Roy Hattersley's engaging account of his boyhood has already been acclaimed as a classic of its kind. Born in Sheffield in 1933, he was a somewhat precocious only child. His memoir takes us through the hardships of the Thirties and the Blitz, and into the 1940s when he passed the eleven-plus examination and entered Grammar School. All the pleasures and pangs of a northern working-class childhood are evoked with wit, elegance, and candour.

'moving, funny, charming and enormously readable' *Listener*

'impressively candid and agreeably revealing' *New Statesman*

'A narrator who has the common touch . . . this gift for re-creating his childhood makes Mr Hattersley the Beryl Bainbridge of English politics.' Blake Morrison, *Observer*